JULIUS AND ETHEL ROSENBERG – SPIES OR SCAPEGOATS? YOU MAKE THE CALL

By - JOE BRUNO

Edited by - LAWRENCE VENTURATO

I0481146

Cover by - ALCHEMY COVERS

Published by - KNICKERBOCKER PUBLISHING COMPANY

*****

She was ostensibly a doting housewife and the loving mother of two. Considering what we now know, it's mind-boggling Ethel Rosenberg deliberately chose to die in the electric chair with her husband, Julius, a creep if there ever was one, to protect the names of other Russian spies. Ethel's callous decision left her two children without either blood parent for the rest of their lives.

Ethel Greenglass Rosenberg was born on September 25, 1915 to Barnet and Tessie Greenglass, in a dilapidated, unheated tenement on Sheriff Street on the Lower East Side of Manhattan. Ethel's father made a meager living repairing sewing machines, and the Greenglass family struggled to make ends meet.

Ethel was the only Greenglass daughter, and she was quite precocious at an early age. Ethel attended the Downtown Talmud Torah and then Seward Park High School. Plain and only slightly pretty, Ethel dreamed of becoming an actress and an opera singer. She did neighborhood performances with the Alfred Corning Clark Neighborhood House troupe, and she won a second-place singing prize at the Lowes Delancey Amateur Night. Ethel also sang on the Major Bowles Amateur Hour on nationwide radio, which was a springboard to success for many celebrated singers, including Frank Sinatra.

When she graduated from Seward Park at the age of 15, her senior yearbook beamed, "Can she act? And how!!!"

However, Ethel was not the apple of her mother's eye. According to her Aunt Esther, Ethel's mother's sister, Tessie

Greenglass felt, "Ethel was a snob, worrying over Italian arias and Russian peasants instead of her own family."

After graduation, to help support her family, Ethel took a job as a clerk for a shipping company. At work, Ethel was a progressive agitator; doggedly fighting for woman's rights.

All too often, after her workday was complete, instead of having dinner with her family, Ethel would traipse over to Greenwich Village where she got involved with the local Bohemian crowd. There Ethel met an artist whom she eagerly dated for a while, but the relationship ended after just a few months.

Years later, her brother, David, would remark, to his own chagrin, "If Ethel had married that other guy, everything would have been alright."

And after four years working at the shipping company, Ethel was fired for organizing a strike of 150 fellow women workers. Now out of a job, Ethel joined the Young Communist League, and she soon became a member of the American Communist Party.

Although she was a fierce communist activist, Ethel still craved a career in the theater. In late 1936, while she was waiting to go on stage to sing at a New Year's Eve celebration, Ethel Greenglass met Julius Rosenberg, and the world would never be quite the same.

*****

Julius Rosenberg, the son of Polish immigrants, was born on May 12, 1918, in East Harlem. His father, Harry, owned his own dry cleaning store, and his mother, Sophie, was a stay-at-home mom who took care of the five Rosenberg children. After his dry cleaning business went under, Harry took a job in the Garment Center, and he moved his family to the Lavenburg Homes, a Jewish philanthropic housing project on Goerck Street (later named Baruch Place), in Lower Manhattan near the East River.

As did Ethel, Julius Rosenberg attended the Downtown Talmud Torah and then Seward Park High School. Despite his father's expectations that his son, Julius, become a rabbi, Rosenberg attended the City College of New York to study engineering. This was after Rosenberg had failed the entrance exam for the prestigious Copper Union.

At City College, Rosenberg joined the Steinmetz Club - the City College campus branch of the Young Communist League. There he met Morton Sobell, with whom he would later engage in anti-American activities. In college, Rosenberg also joined the Federation of Architects, Engineers, Chemists, and Technicians, a group known for its radical activities. In addition, Rosenberg joined the American Communist Party.

After Ethel and Julius Rosenberg started "keeping company," Rosenberg did not endear himself to the Greenglass family. Right off the bat, Barnet Greenglass didn't like Julius Rosenberg. Mr. Greenglass was especially disgusted with Rosenberg's uncouth table manners. Rosenberg had the bad habit of speaking with his mouth full of food, which would cause the chow to splatter, sometimes on the table and sometimes on the person to whom he was speaking, which all too often was Barnet Greenglass.

The final insult was when Barnet Greenglass arrived for a fine dinner his wife had prepared, only to find Rosenberg sitting in Barnet's customary seat at the head of the table. From that point on, Ethel was told by her parents that Rosenberg was no longer invited to the nightly family dinner.

Nevertheless, the headstrong Ethel soon informed her parents, whether they liked it or not, she was going to marry Julius Rosenberg. The Greenglasses had no choice but to accept Ethel's wishes. However, they insisted Rosenberg graduate from college before their marriage took place.

This was fine with Ethel, but Rosenberg was not exactly a high-quality student. It was Ethel who helped Rosenberg do his homework, and it was Ethel who personally typed out Rosenberg's class papers after she helped him with the project itself (her facility at typing would come into play later). And when it was obvious Rosenberg was fonder of communist activities in college than he was of studying, it was Ethel who insisted Rosenberg finish college, or else find someone else to spend the rest of his life with.

In the summer of 1939, Julius Rosenberg graduated from City College in the bottom ten percent of his class (79 out of 85 students); one semester later than the rest of his graduating class. Weeks later, Rosenberg married Ethel Greenglass. They immediately took up residence in Ethel's room in the Greenglass residence on Sheriff Street. This did not please Barnet Greenglass too much.

The die was cast, when in the fall of 1940, Rosenberg took a position as a civilian employee for the U.S. Army Signal Corp. for $2000 a year. This position also gave Rosenberg a full draft deferment, which precluded him from being drafted into the United States military service.

Earlier that year, Ethel was hired at the U.S. Census Bureau; her pay: $1440 a year. With the money now rolling in, the Rosenbergs departed the Greenglass apartment on Sheriff Street and moved into an apartment in the Williamsburg section of Brooklyn, right across the Williamsburg Bridge.

While she worked at the Census Bureau, a neighbor in Brooklyn informed the Census Bureau that Ethel had signed a petition nominating Peter V. Cacchione as the Communist Party candidate for city council. To add to her leftist reputation, an anonymous person tipped the FBI that Ethel was "an extremely communistic person" and should not be employed in a government job. This caused Julius Rosenberg serious angst, since his job was now in jeopardy with the U.S. Army Signal Corp, as well as his draft deferment.

Rosenberg was ordered before the brass at the U.S. Army Signal Corp, and they demanded an explanation for Ethel's actions.

Rosenberg hemmed and hawed, and he begged his bosses to be considerate of his situation.

"I was not aware of my wife signing that petition," Rosenberg told the presiding officer. "And even if she did sign the petition, I don't see how that would affect me. After all, she is a different person and has rights."

After admitting that a "relationship between a husband and wife is generally a close one," Rosenberg pleaded with the presiding officer to accept his explanation that Ethel had either been "careless," or had lacked "sales resistance," when she was "pressured" into signing the petition.

For inexplicable reasons, the presiding officer accepted Rosenberg's version of his wife's actions, and in 1942 Rosenberg was promoted to inspector at the U.S. Army Signal Corp.

That was like the United States government giving the keys to the blood bank to a vampire.

Also in 1942, Rosenberg began secretly working as a spy for the Russian K.G.B. Eventually, his Russian handler became Alexander Feklisov, who gave Rosenberg the codename "Liberal," or "Libbi," for short.

In his book *The Man Behind the Rosenbergs*, Feklisov said he was put onto Rosenberg by fellow Russian spy Semyon Semyonov, who had cozied up to Rosenberg and found him a willing subject for the Russian communist movement.

In a dossier to Feklisov, Semyonov wrote, "Rosenberg is a man of left-wing ideas. He's pro-Soviet and completely committed to the fight against Fascism. He will no doubt be offended if you take him to a fancy restaurant and order expensive wine. He feels we have no right to celebrate, since our country (Russia) is at war."

Semyonov told Feklisov he had recruited Rosenberg on September 7, 1942 at a Labor Day rally in Central Park. Rosenberg had attended the rally with a pal, Bernard Schuster, who had already been drafted by the Russians and working under the codename "Echo."

Semyonov told Feklisov, "A podium was set up in Central Park with a few rows of chairs for labor leaders, public figures, cultural personalities, and Soviet representatives, surrounded by a dense crowd of 50,000 people. There, Schuster introduced Rosenberg to me. Rosenberg was delighted; he had never met a Soviet national before, while wholeheartedly supporting their struggle against Nazism."

Semyonov and Rosenberg exchanged contact information, and soon Rosenberg initiated a further exchange by inviting Semyonov to a restaurant to have lunch. At this meeting, according to Semyonov, Rosenberg "Fired away questions about life in the USSR, the attitude towards Jews, their extermination by the Nazis, and the harshness of the fighting on a front that was several thousand miles long."

Semyonov could see Rosenberg almost hyperventilating with his eagerness to help the Russian cause. However, Semyonov did not want to push the envelope on Rosenberg's cooperation too quickly. It wasn't until their second lunch meeting that Semyonov made his pitch.

While nibbling on cheese blintzes with sour cream, Semyonov casually told Rosenberg that, "America, despite of its commitment towards Russia, was hiding its latest technological innovations from its ally, who needs them very badly."

Rosenberg leaned forward; beads of sweat dripping down his forehead. He told Semyonov in a low but passionate voice, "I find it unfair that you should be fighting the common enemy alone. If I can do anything to help, you can count on me."

The line was baited, and the big fish swallowed it whole. Julius Rosenberg was now a full-fledged Russian spy, with the safely of his own country - the United States of America - the furthest thing from his mind.

*****

At their next meeting, Rosenberg gave Semyonov several hundred pages of classified documents, which Rosenberg, along with two more communist pals he had enlisted, had stolen from the U.S. Army Signal Corp. Delighted, Semyonov brought this information to Feklisov.

Feklisov wrote, "Since contacts between Americans were less risky, he (Rosenberg) collected the information they produced and handed it to us for a few hours. Rosenberg was not just a very valuable source himself, he was also the linchpin of a network growing in importance from month to month."

In 1942, Semyonov flew across the radar of the FBI. When the Russians discovered Semyonov was hot, they withdrew him from handling any more agents, and they immediately sent Semyonov back to the motherland: Russia. This presented a dilemma to Feklisov since he needed Rosenberg's continued information, but he had never met Rosenberg himself. And with Semyonov back in Russia, it was impossible for a personal introduction.

At first, Feklisov's bosses thought the best way to reestablish contact with Rosenberg was to simply phone him at home. However, they rejected this idea, knowing that since Rosenberg was handling sensitive information, his phones could be tapped. They finally decided that a visit to Rosenberg at his home at 10 Monroe Street, in downtown Manhattan's Knickerbocker Village, would be the best course of action.

"I began by exploring the location," Feklisov said. "I discovered that to gain entrance into Knickerbocker Village you needed a code, or had to use the intercom at the front door of Rosenberg's building."

Feklisov decided the best time to visit the Rosenbergs was on a Sunday afternoon, around 2 p.m.; a time Julius Rosenberg would most likely be at home.

Knowing he could be followed by American secret agents, Feklisov took a circuitous route to Knickerbocker Village. He set off by strolling along Central Park "like someone who doesn't know how to kill time on his day off."

Suddenly, Feklisov darted across the street, looking both ways to detect if he was being followed.

He saw nothing amiss.

Feklisov then went to Columbus Circle, where he took the subway to the Canal Street station near Little Italy, which is a 10-minute stroll from Knickerbocker Village. Feklisov hesitated before making the trek to Knickerbocker Village. Then, not completely satisfied he had not been followed, Feklisov did an about-face, and he jumped on a bus that took him uptown to Grand Central Station.

"I had a hot dog in the midst of a busy crowd, where idle individuals stand out conspicuously," Feklisov said. "I had no further doubts: I could go! I took the bus downtown once again."

Finally, Feklisov stood at the front door to Rosenberg's Knickerbocker Village apartment building. He pressed the intercom button to the Rosenberg apartment.

"Yes," a man's voice answered.

"Hello, I'm looking for Julius Rosenberg," Feklisov said.

"That's me," Rosenberg said.

"I am a friend of Henry's (Semyonov's code name)," Feklisov said. "May I come up for a minute?"

Rosenberg hesitated. "Okay, come in."

*****

The electric lock buzzed, and Feklisov entered the building. He took the elevator to the 11th floor, and when the elevator door opened, Feklisov came face-to-face with Julius Rosenberg.

Feklisov told Rosenberg why Semyonov had disappeared. "I'm the one who will come to see you from now on," Feklisov said.

Rosenberg told Feklisov they could not go back to Rosenberg's apartment. He said, "We're entertaining friends."

Feklisov told Rosenberg that he was only there to set up an appointment. However, Rosenberg became so excited at being back in the game, he told Feklisov he'd come with him immediately.

"Let's take the stairway down," Rosenberg said. "I'll explain things to my wife later."

Outside in the fresh air, Feklisov told Rosenberg it would be wiser if they took the subway uptown, separately.

Rosenberg suddenly seemed nervous at the thought of being followed. He began to perspire profusely, and his hands shook like he had Parkinson's.

Feklisov calmed Rosenberg down, and he told him to meet him at Childs Restaurant on East 30th Street, a dive where Rosenberg used to meet Semyonov. However, Feklisov was wary about Rosenberg being followed; Rosenberg did not know how to detect, or shake a tail like Feklisov did.

"I stood on the sidewalk across the street from Childs, and I pretended to look in the window of a bookstore." Feklisov said. "When Rosenberg arrived, I watched him enter the restaurant. And after making sure no one was following him, I pushed open the lacquered wooden door. A little bell announced my arrival."

They sat facing each other at a small table at the end of the dining room; tension cutting through the air like a hot Russian saber. Feklisov thought Rosenberg looked like he wanted to be anyplace else but in a restaurant talking to a Russian spy.

An aged, stooped waiter took their order. Feklisov was careful not to say anything in the presence of the waiter, knowing full well that waiters and bartenders were working undercover for either the local police, or the FBI.

As soon as the waiter took their order and departed to the kitchen, Feklisov put Rosenberg at ease. He started talking about his life in Russia; painting a rosy picture of his homeland.

Rosenberg listened, and then he shook his head.

Rosenberg clenched his fist, and said, "Why do the Germans hate us so much? What harm did we do to them?"

The drinks arrived; both men had ordered red wine. A few sips, and Rosenberg seemed to calm a bit. Before long, he became entranced with Feklisov's patter.

"I spoke to Rosenberg of my childhood in Moscow, my family, my two brothers at the front, and my two sisters, who had the hardest time reaching Moscow after digging trenches near Bryansk, which was encircled by the German offensive," Feklisov said. "Rosenberg listened to me with great interest, showing he was clearly amused, worried, relieved, and sympathetic as I spoke. Rosenberg then began speaking about his wife Ethel, whom he obviously adored."

Rosenberg became so emotional speaking of Ethel, he blew a kiss into this hand to show Feklisov how much he loved his wife

Feklisov sipped a bit of cold borsch, which was not quite as chilled as he desired. He pushed the dish aside and leaned forward.

"Tell me about Barr and Perl," Feklisov said. "I know nothing about them, and Semyonov could not vouch for them either. Are you sure they can be trusted?"

Rosenberg had previously recruited Joel Barr and William Perl as Russian spies. And although Feklisov needed Rosenberg as a spy recruit as much as he needed him as a spy, he wanted to be sure Rosenberg's two American pals were loyal to the Soviet cause.

Rosenberg was clearly flustered. He leaned across the table; his voice a whisper and his eyes tearing under his spectacles.

Rosenberg whined, "No, there is nothing suspicious! My friends are in place. Since I had no further contact from Henry (Semyonov) I asked them to stop bringing me anything. But they are ready to start again!"

Feklisov pursed his lips, and he imperceptibly shook his head. Feklisov was worried Rosenberg was too eager to help, and this type of man sometimes makes mistakes.

Still, Feklisov understood Rosenberg, and the men Rosenberg had recruited to the cause, could be of monumental importance to the Russians. Feklisov knew that America was spending tens of millions of dollars to produce more advanced military equipment. Feklisov also knew that Rosenberg and his friends were working on the production of new planes, artillery pieces, shells, radar, and electronic calculators. At this first meeting, Feklisov didn't realize how involved Rosenberg would eventually become in helping him, and how impatient Rosenberg was to do more. Furthermore, if Rosenberg was sincere about his intentions,

Feklisov knew the good things Rosenberg could do for Russia was immeasurable.

Later, as he reflected on his first meeting with Rosenberg, and how nervous and unsure of himself Rosenberg had been, Feklisov marveled that Rosenberg would become Russia's most valuable American spy. In the ensuing months, the problem wasn't motivating Rosenberg to do more; the problem was holding Rosenberg back, so that he could continue to be of value to the Russians and not get caught in the trap of over-zealousness.

*****

For the next several months, Feklisov met "Libbi (Rosenberg)" almost every week. Rosenberg and his cronies stole classified materials, and then, through Rosenberg, passed them on to Feklisov. The transactions between Feklisov and Rosenberg usually occurred in the next to the last row of a movie theatre (the last row was reserved for lovers). Back at his office at the Russian Embassy, Feklisov would microfilm the information, and then return the originals to Rosenberg the following day. With this quick turnaround, Rosenberg's employers never realized anything inappropriate had taken place.

Soon, Feklisov taught Rosenberg how to microfilm the documents himself; with a small Leica camera, so they could eliminate the second meeting and reduce of chances of being discovered. Feklisov was concerned, that if it were up to Rosenberg, "Libbi" would have stolen classified documents every day and delivered them to Feklisov. Feklisov was amazed Rosenberg was intent on helping Russia and was unconcerned about the possible adverse effects on the United States - Rosenberg's country of birth.

Rosenberg told Feklisov, "Listen Alexander (he enjoyed calling Feklisov by his first name). Your country has achieved such great things, and now everything is in ruins. You have to rebuild all that. I want to help you. But you must help me help you."

Feklisov tried to explain to Rosenberg that he (Feklisov) was being watched closely by the FBI. But Rosenberg seemed disinterested.

"When I told him this, he just shrugged his shoulders," Feklisov said. "He felt he was doing nothing wrong!"

Feklisov recalled the time Rosenberg was crossing the street to meet Feklisov. Rosenberg was smoking a large cigar, he obviously couldn't afford, and he was smiling like a loon. When he reached where Feklisov was standing, Rosenberg blurted out, "Hello, Comrade!"

Feklisov almost had a heart attack.

A few minutes later, while they were sitting in a small cafeteria near the East River, Feklisov told Rosenberg he had made a huge mistake addressing a Russian spy in public as "Comrade."

Feklisov put down his bagel, reached across the table, and he grabbed Rosenberg's wrist for emphasis. He told Rosenberg, that to avoid detection, it was best for "Libbi" to tone down his overt communist activities. Feklisov urged Rosenberg to stop subscribing to left-wing magazines and not to attend Red Army rallies. Feklisov made it clear to Rosenberg that for Rosenberg to be valuable to the Russian cause, he must maintain a low profile.

Rosenberg was crushed. He sipped his tea, took off his the eyeglasses, and he cleaned them with a napkin.

Rosenberg told Feklisov, "I know you may not be aware of this, but our meetings are among the happiest moments of my life. I have a wonderful wife and a son whom I adore. But you are the only person who knows all my secrets, and it is important to be able to confide in someone."

In the spring of 1943, to placate Feklisov and his Russian NKVD (communist secret police) superiors, Rosenberg abruptly quit the American Communist Party. However, in February of 1944, Rosenberg's previous communist activities were exposed, and even though he was no longer a member of the American Communist Party, Rosenberg was fired from his job at the U.S. Army Signal Corp.

Undaunted, four months later, Rosenberg took a position with the Emerson Radio Company, and through his position at this private sector company, Rosenberg continued to give the Russians valuable technical information.

*****

In mid-1944, Rosenberg stole sensitive documents from the Emerson Radio Company, which laid out the complete details of the United States production of a "proximity fuse." This fuse was a revolutionary device which changed the way a bomb shell exploded. Until the invention of the proximity fuse, bombs only exploded when they made actual contact with their target. However, the proximity fuse was designed to make the bomb explode at a short distance from its target. The fragments then scattered into balls, and at least some of these fragments were "guaranteed to cause irreparable dame to its target." The proximity fuse also automatically corrected the path of the explosive charges towards the location of the target itself, making it a precursor of future missile homing devices.

In 1960, an upgraded model of the proximity fuse was used by the Russians to shoot down an American spy plane piloted by Francis Gary Powers. So, in effect, even though he had been dead for several years, Rosenberg's treachery in aiding the Russians still caused direct damage to American property as well as to American military personnel.

*****

What surprised and sometimes irked Feklisov, was that Rosenberg, true to socialist ideals, put very little value on material things. When Feklisov offered Rosenberg monetary compensation, Rosenberg absolutely refused. No matter how hard Feklisov pushed, Rosenberg would not take any money from Feklisov, except for travel expenses and for restaurant bills for Rosenberg's colleagues, who had become spies for the Soviets.

"Even though I barely gave Rosenberg $25 a month for expenses," Feklisov said, "Rosenberg's contribution was such that even millions would not have compensated him for his true value to us."

Feklisov got an even bigger surprise when he cajoled Rosenberg into the idea of them exchanging Christmas presents (Rosenberg was Jewish, but he still celebrated the winter holidays). Feklisov insisted that he must buy two presents; one for Rosenberg and one for his wife, Ethel. Feklisov decided to give Rosenberg an expensive wristwatch - an Omega stainless steel watch with a stainless steel bracelet (for some reason, Rosenberg hated gold). However, Feklisov was unsure what to give to Ethel. So he asked Rosenberg.

Rosenberg replied, "You know what she'd really like? She's been dreaming for some time about a new handbag. The one she has now is old and out of fashion."

Feklisov asked his wife, Zina, to help him pick out Ethel's present. They went to the woman's department in Gimbels, and purchased a large brown crocodile handbag for Ethel; one Feklisov's wife said she would purchase for herself. They placed Rosenberg's watch into the handbag, along with a fluffy teddy bear they had bought for Rosenberg's infant son, Michael, who had been born in 1943. They put the bag into a large box decorated with wrapping paper and ribbons.

The exchange of Christmas presents took place on December 24, 1944, at the Horn & Hardart cafeteria on West 38th Street near Broadway. Feklisov felt Horn and Hardart was the perfect place to conduct secret meetings and to make document transfers.

And most importantly, there were no waiters on the premises.

Horn & Hardart was dotted with automatic food distributors. You put in the proper amount of coins, pressed a button, and a small glass door opened, giving you access to the plate of food or beverage you selected. Also, this particular Horn and Hardart had two exits: one on 38th Street and the other on Broadway. Consequently, Feklisov had two options in case a quick getaway was required.

Feklisov arrived fifteen minutes early for their meeting. Rather than enter Horn and Hardart right away, Feklisov stood on the sidewalk across the street and waited. Soon, Feklisov spotted Rosenberg entering the restaurant. Through the large glass window of the restaurant (which Feklisov said was like looking through an aquarium), he watched as Rosenberg put his hat and coat on a rack, and set down his package on a low window sill. Rosenberg poured himself a cup of coffee, sat alone at a table and started reading the *New York Times*.

A few minutes later, Feklisov entered Horn & Hardart. He took off his coat and placed his package on the window sill next to Rosenberg's. Feklisov served himself what he felt was a cup of bad American coffee, and to kill the taste, he bought himself a ham sandwich on rye. Feklisov sat at the same table, across from

Rosenberg, and he began reading his own copy of the *New York Times*.

Without looking up from his newspaper, Feklisov said, "Don't forget to take the box I brought you. Those are your Christmas presents."

Their eyes met for a moment, and Rosenberg smiled. "Thank you. Your present is in the big carton. Be careful; it's pretty heavy."

That said, Rosenberg chugged down the rest of his coffee, and he donned on his coat and hat. Rosenberg laid his newspaper on top of the box Feklisov had brought for him, picked up the box, and exited the restaurant.

Not to draw attention, Feklisov calmly read his newspaper, while finishing his coffee and sandwich.

Fifteen minutes later, Feklisov stood up from the table, put on his coat and hat, and after waiting for the two ladies talking near the window to leave, he picked up Rosenberg's package by the string wrapped around it and exited the restaurant.

While trudging down Broadway, Feklisov was struck by the immense weight of the package. It had to weigh at least 15 pounds, and Feklisov was afraid the string would break while he walked to the subway a few blocks away.

Suddenly, Feklisov spotted a cab. He hailed it and directed the cabby to drive him to his office in the Russian consulate.

Inside the Russian consulate, Feklisov took the package to a common meeting room, which was now empty because of the impending Christmas holiday. Feklisov tore open the package, and he came face-to-face with a fully-assembled proximity fuse.

Feklisov said, "I was totally flabbergasted! This was the short-range fuse, the one that exploded when it got close to a plane, guaranteeing its total destruction. It was the very item the Center had designated as being a priority in intelligence gathering. What I had now was not drawings or descriptions, but the complete metal device. It was in working order, brand new, smelling of metal and oil, with an additional supply of miniaturized replacement metal tubes fastened to the top."

Feklisov knew Rosenberg was foolhardy to take such a risk. But incredibly, Rosenberg had apparently pulled off the heist without a snag.

A few minutes later, Feklisov's NKVD boss, Kvasnikov, appeared in the conference room. When Feklisov told him the source of the object on the table, Kvasnikov's eyes narrowed.

"How could Rosenberg walk out with such a large object?" Kvasnikov said. "In his secret factory, the smallest part, even if defective, is under control. Can you give me an explanation?"

Feklisov said he could not.

Feklisov's face felt hot while Kvasnikov read him the riot act for not having complete control over his agent - Julius Rosenberg. Kvasnikov told Feklisov an agent acting by himself without Soviet direction was not what the Russians wanted or needed; too many things could go wrong.

At their next meeting, which took place outdoors on the top level of the Staten Island Ferry, Feklisov pressed Rosenberg for an explanation concerning Rosenberg's stealing of the proximity fuse.

With the winter wind whistling through the night air and no one within hearing distance, Rosenberg told Feklisov that months before Rosenberg had assembled the proximity fuse at his job, but it had been rejected as defective by his Emerson superiors. Instead of discarding the rejected fuse, Rosenberg had hid the fuse in a corner. Little by little he replaced the defective parts until the fuse was in perfect working order. Rosenberg then hid the fuse behind a box on a shelf where spare parts were kept.

The problem now was how to smuggle the fuse out of Emerson without being detected.

On December 23, Rosenberg was selected to ride in the van which was designated to get rid of all defective parts accumulated in the past month. With the driver humming along with a holiday tune playing on the van's radio, Rosenberg sat quietly in the passenger seat. He had hidden the proximity fuse in a box in the back of the van; a box identical to all the other boxes in the van. He was waiting for an opportunity to smuggle the fuse out of the van to a safe place - his apartment in Knickerbocker Village.

While the van bounced on the cobblestones on Essex Street near Grand Street, Rosenberg asked the driver to stop at a grocery store so that Rosenberg could purchase food for the holidays. The driver shrugged and did what Rosenberg had requested. Rosenberg jumped out of the van and into the grocery store.

Minutes later, Rosenberg emerged from the grocery store carrying a box of food, identical to the box that contained the proximity fuse in the back of the van. Rosenberg opened the rear door of the van, and he placed the two boxes next to each other.

"Can you make a stop at my apartment so that I can give my wife the groceries?" Rosenberg asked the driver.

Five minutes later, the driver stopped the van on Monroe Street in front of the West Court of Knickerbocker Village. Rosenberg went around to the back of the van and opened the rear door. He picked up both boxes - one filled with food and the other with the fuse - and headed toward the entrance of Knickerbocker Village

As Rosenberg tottered away, the driver asked, "Can I help you take them upstairs?"

Rosenberg, both boxes pressed against his chest, turned to the driver and smiled weakly. "No thanks," he said. "It's not that heavy."

Five minutes later, Rosenberg, whistling a holiday tune, returned to the van.

"Thanks. Now we can go," he told the driver.

After Rosenberg finished his incredible tale, Feklisov shook his head. His emotions flipped back and forth between anger and disappointment. Leaning forward against the chest-high railing on the top deck of the Staten Island Ferry, Feklisov stared at the Statue of Liberty in the distance; its bright torch illuminating New York Harbor. The sight of Lady Liberty increased Feklisov angst. He turned toward Rosenberg, who was also glaring out over the frigid water banging against the bottom of the ferry, causing whitecaps to tickle the sides of the boat.

Feklisov yelled at Rosenberg, "Julius, you should have never gone into this crazy scheme! It could have gone very wrong! Next time you feel like jumping head first, let me know in advance! We'll think about limiting the risks!"

Rosenberg's anger matched Feklisov's.

"It was not a crazy scheme at all!" Rosenberg said. "I planned my moves step by step, and I brought them to fruition at the moment of least risk. The day before Christmas people are only thinking about the holidays. One week before or after, and it never would have worked."

Rosenberg then smiled, and he lowered his voice. He put his hand on Feklisov's shoulder, and said, "Honestly, I wanted to set up my own operation that would be, well, not so heroic, but at least daring. Millions of Russians take even bigger risks every day, and I don't want to live off their sacrifices."

Feklisov tried to convince Rosenberg that acting in such a frivolous manner without confirmation of his superiors was not acceptable. But Rosenberg stood firm in his beliefs. When the ferry returned to the South Ferry Terminal in Lower Manhattan, the men disembarked separately and set out in different directions.

Feklisov turned, and he watched as Rosenberg dissipated into the night. Feklisov had the firm impression his lecture to Rosenberg had been a waste of time. Rosenberg was a militant Russian spy, and short of cutting him loose, there was nothing Feklisov could do to control "Libbi."

Years later, Feklisov discovered that of all the technical innovations created by the Americans during the Second World War, the proximity fuse was second in cost only to the atom bomb. In order to create and enhance the proximity fuse, America had spent over a billion dollars. And in a wink, Julius Rosenberg had stolen this very device from under the Emerson scientist's noses, at no cost to the Russians.

*****

By late 1944, Julius Rosenberg was recruiting heavily for the Russians. He now oversaw several spies, working in sensitive positions, who stole top-secret documents and handed them over to Rosenberg, who in turn handed them over to Feklisov. One of Rosenberg's recruits was Joel Barr, an old chum who had attended the same grammar and high schools as Rosenberg. Barr also attended City College with Rosenberg. (It's ironic that City College is free from tuition, and that neither man had to pay for an education that gave them the knowledge they later used to impede America's progress against the Russians.)

After graduating from City College, Barr assumed a position at a Western Electric plant in New York. His job was to design improvements on radar devices, which were used on B-type bombers. Barr was highly esteemed by his bosses, and he had access to the most secret documents concerning devices Western Electric had been working on.

Also in Rosenberg's inner circle was Alfred Sarant, who worked at Bell Research Laboratories, "developing electrical devices for military applications." Other men under Rosenberg's supervision included William Perl and Morton Sobel.

Through Rosenberg, Perl supplied Feklisov with thousands of secret documents from the National Advisory Committee for Aeronautics, including a complete set of design and production drawings for the Lockheed's P-80 Shooting Star, which in 1944, was the first "jet fighter" used operationally by the United States Army Air Force.

Sobel, who worked at the Navy Bureau of Ordinance in Washington D. C. and later at the General Electric Company in Schenectady, NY, handed over to Feklisov, through Rosenberg, the plans for the SCR 584 Radar System, which was used to shoot down United States aircraft both in the Korean and Vietnam Wars.

*****

The beginning of the end for Julius and Ethel Rosenberg was when Julius convinced Feklisov they should recruit Ethel Rosenberg's younger brother, David Greenglass, who worked as an Army machinist at the Los Alamos National Laboratory located in the desert of New Mexico.

Before Greenglass joined the United States Army, he and his wife, Ruth, were both members of the Young Communist League, and both were only 20-years-old when they were married. While at Los Alamos, Greenglass was promoted to sergeant and assigned to work on the top secret "Manhattan Project," which was developing the "Atomic Bomb" that effectively ended World War II against Japan.

Rosenberg made his pitch to Feklisov concerning the recruitment of Greenglass. However, although Greenglass was an extreme progressive, and decidedly anti-fascist and pro-communist, Feklisov was concerned about Greenglass's age. Greenglass was only 21-years-old when Rosenberg wanted to recruit him as a spy, and Feklisov, along with his NKVD superiors, reasoned a man of

Greenglass's age had not yet developed the strong convictions needed for such dangerous work.

At their next meeting, Feklisov told Rosenberg about his and his boss' concerns about Greenglass. This meeting took place in a tiny Chinese restaurant/coffee shop on Mott Street, where the chalkboard menus on the wall were written in Chinese scrawl. There was only a handful of patrons in the place, and everyone, including the waiters, were conversing loudly in bastardized versions of the Chinese language.

The two Russian spies sat facing each other at a tiny table in the back, near the kitchen. They pecked at pork fried rice and munched on egg rolls, and they sipped green tea from tiny white cups. Waiters continuously passed their table, transporting food and plates back and forth from the kitchen. However, being the only "Lo Fon" (non-Chinese) in the joint, except to order their food and pay their bill, neither Rosenberg nor Feklisov were paid any attention by the Chinese staff. Since Chinese people tend to mind their own business, Feklisov felt dives like this were perfect for spy meetings.

After Feklisov conveyed his feelings about Greenglass, Rosenberg leaned forward, specs of fried rice squirting from his mouth.

"Greenglass is part of my own family!" Rosenberg cried. "He's the same blood as my wife Ethel! He's devoted to our cause, and he's one hundred percent reliable!"

Rosenberg banged his fist against his own puffed chest, and said, "I'll give my right hand to be chopped off if he lets us down!"

Moved by Rosenberg's passion, Feklisov, after he wiped the spitted fried rice from his face and chest, told Rosenberg he would tell his superiors that he felt Greenglass would fit the bill as a Russian spy.

In November 1944, after getting the go-ahead from his NKVD superiors, Rosenberg asked Ruth Greenglass to meet him in his Knickerbocker Village apartment to have dinner with him and his wife, Ethel.

While they were sipping after-dinner coffee, Julius Rosenberg made his pitch.

"We both know you and your husband are both true communist sympathizers," Rosenberg told Ruth. "But are you willing to take risks to further the communist cause?"

"What kind of risks?" Ruth said.

Rosenberg told Ruth that David's job on the Manhattan Project, in the deserts of New Mexico, afforded David the opportunity to give the Russians information as to what the Americans were undertaking at Los Alamos. If they agreed to cooperate, Rosenberg said Ruth and her husband, David, would become very vital to the communist cause.

Ruth Greenglass beamed. Only in their early 20's, she and David had a chance to make a difference in a world, in which they felt the rich had an unfair advantage over the common working man. And, more importantly to Ruth, maybe there was some money to be made by helping the Russians.

"Yes, this is something I think my husband would be interested in," Ruth said. "I swear to you we will do whatever is necessary to further the communist cause."

It was obvious to both Rosenbergs that Ruth Greenglass meant what she had said. And, at that time, both Julius and Ethel felt Ruth was more enthusiastic than Ruth's husband, David, about helping the Russians.

Ruth also told the Rosenbergs she was planning to visit David for two weeks in Albuquerque in early December to celebrate their first anniversary. At that time, Ruth would confirm with her husband that they indeed would work for the Russians.

In late December, after meeting with his wife in New Mexico, David Greenglass returned to New York City, and he and his wife, Ruth, spent considerable time with the Rosenbergs. David was Ethel's youngest brother (David was seven years younger than Ethel), and she absolutely adored him.

While celebrating the holidays at Knickerbocker Village, David, at Julius Rosenberg's request, penned drawings of one of the lenses he was working on at Los Alamos, along with written explanations of the drawings.

Rosenberg passed on these drawings to Feklisov, saying, "It's very important that David be able to talk to one of your specialists on this matter. Is that possible?"

Feklisov hooked up Greenglass with Anatoly Yatskov, a top Russian engineer, and after grilling Greenglass on his work, Yatskov confirmed that Greenglass was indeed working on the Manhattan Project - the making of the first atomic bomb. From that point on,

David Greenglass knew exactly what was expected of him and what information he must uncover in his job at Los Alamos.

The atomic bomb information needed to be transported from Greenglass to the Russians. However, the Russians felt Rosenberg was too hot to be the middleman. The Russians decided to employ for the task a shadowy figure named Harry Gold. Gold, a Philadelphia research chemist, was, according to a July 1950 article in the *New York Times*, "A man who had found in the communists an outlet for the frustrations of a lonely poverty-stricken youth."

Gold had already proved himself valuable to the Russians when he stole, and turned over to the Russians, samples and production data of a high-powered explosive called RXD, which was being produced at the Holston Ordinance Works at Kingsport, Tennessee. This explosive, which has twice the blasting force of TNT, had been known for half a century, but no practical way to manufacture it had been discovered until the United States Armed Forces adapted it for use in Navy torpedoes and Army bazooka rockets.

In June of 1945, in his Knickerbocker Village apartment, Rosenberg gave Greenglass, who was on furlough in New York City, a half-torn Jell-O box. Rosenberg told Greenglass he (Greenglass) was to meet an unidentified man (Gold) in Albuquerque, New Mexico. As a means of identification, this man would have the other half of the torn Jell-O box, so Greenglass could confirm this was indeed the spy Greenglass was to do business with.

When Gold and Greenglass first met in New Mexico, Gold produced the other half of the Jell-O box, along with a payment of $500. In return, Greenglass gave Gold classified information concerning a lens mold and other secret projects, including the production of the atom bomb.

Greenglass and Gold met numerous times during the next two years. At these covert tête-à-têtes, Greenglass handed over to Gold classified documents. However, in later years, Gold maintained the information Greenglass had given to Gold, which Gold, in turn, had passed on to the Russians, was of little importance except to corroborate information the Russians had already collected from other spies.

"What we gave them was junk," Gold said years later, after he had been released from prison.

In December 1946, David Greenglass was discharged from the military, and he was no longer of any use to the Russians.

*****

In the fall of 1945, the NKVD, without giving Rosenberg any reason, removed Rosenberg's recruits from his supervision. The war was nearing an end, and it was clear, although the United States and Russia were Allies in the war against Germany, they would now, due to their severe differences in ideology, maintain an adversarial relationship. As the result, the FBI was increasing its surveillance of Soviet citizens living in the United States (Feklisov), and left-leaning American citizens like Rosenberg, who, in 1943, had been fired from the U.S. Army Signal Corp. for lying about his membership in the American Communist Party.

In the fall of 1945, at one of their last meetings, a distraught Rosenberg told Feklisov, "Alexander, I understand why you removed all my comrades from my supervision, and I accept that. I don't see them often, and I even avoid calling them up. I don't see you that much anymore. I understand everything, but it makes me sad. I'm bored. I was used to being involved, seeing people, convincing them, and making plans. That was my life. And now I have nothing."

Feklisov liked Rosenberg, but he knew, with Rosenberg under intense FBI surveillance, it would be risky to have Rosenberg doing any more covert work for the Russians; at least for the time being. Besides, Feklisov's NKVD superiors felt if Rosenberg was arrested, he would crack under duress and spill everything he knew about the Russian spy net in America (In light of future events, the Soviets were dead wrong about Rosenberg's toughness).

Feklisov tried to pacify Rosenberg by saying that with all his free time (Rosenberg was now without a military or civilian job), he should take Ethel and their young son, Michael, on a sight-seeing tour around the country. Rosenberg face turned sour, so Feklisov added, "You could take advantage of the time by meeting new people who could be useful to us in the future."

In August of 1946, Feklisov's NKVD superiors made arrangements for Feklisov to leave America. They reasoned, since the FBI was turning up the heat on Feklisov, it was only a matter of time before the feds put the cuffs on the Russian spymaster. One week before his scheduled departure, Feklisov contacted Rosenberg. They had not spoken for six months, and Rosenberg was despondent over no longer being a cog in the Soviet machine.

The meeting, which Feklisov called their "Farewell Dinner," took place at The Golden Fiddle, a Hungarian restaurant on the Upper West Side. Feklisov selected the upscale restaurant because he wanted his last meeting with Rosenberg to stand in stark contrast to their usual covert meetings in assorted New York City dives.

The two old pals dined on the house specialty – sautéed veal with spicy sauce – and drowned their sorrows in a bottle of Portuguese red wine. While they were eating, a violinist, accompanied by a small Hungarian band, circulated from table to table playing sad gypsy music. One of the songs they played was *The Storks Fly Away.* Rosenberg was so moved by the melancholy melody of this tune, after the violinist finished playing at the two Russian spies' table, he asked the violinist the name of the song.

After the busboys cleared the dishes from their table, Feklisov asked the waiter for two cognacs and the check. The drinks arrived, and Feklisov raised his glass in a toast.

"To old friendships," he said. "May they never be forgotten."

The two men clinked glasses and took sips of their drinks. Feklisov said Rosenberg looked like he was ready to cry.

Feklisov said, "Listen Julius, I have to give you some news. I'm about to leave New York in a very short time. I'm going back home."

"What do you mean?" Rosenberg said. "You're leaving me? Why?"

Feklisov took another sip of his cognac.

"You know the normal stay abroad is three to four years," he told Rosenberg. "I have been here for five and a half years."

"So?"

"So if I stay too much longer *you-know-who* might start getting suspicious. Even for your sake, it will be best to lay low for a while."

"You sure you can't stay any longer?"

"No Julius. It's not my call."

Rosenberg excused himself from the table, and he approached the violinist. Minutes later, the violinist, accompanied by his tiny band, circled the Russian spies' table, playing *The Storks Fly Away.*

Their final dinner a thing of the past, Feklisov and Rosenberg took a long stroll by Riverside Drive. The hot air was heavy with Rosenberg's angst, and the two men sat on a park bench and watched several luxury liners float up the Hudson.

Minutes of silence passed.

Then, the two men stood and engaged in a two-handed handshake. Feklisov wished Rosenberg "every success, happiness, and prosperity for himself, and his family."

While a vessel in the Hudson River blasted a mournful whistle, the two men embraced.

As he was ordered by his NKVD bosses, Feklisov gave Rosenberg one thousand dollars, which, since Rosenberg was still out of work and no prospects of landing another job, the Rosenberg family needed badly to survive. Feklisov also gave Rosenberg the date, time, and location of a meeting where Rosenberg would meet his new Russian contact, along with the password Rosenberg must use to use to identify himself (the password was "Libbi," Feklisov's codename for Rosenberg).

It was the last time the two men ever saw each other.

*****

With the money given to him by Feklisov, and more money borrowed from friends, Rosenberg and his brother-in-law, David Greenglass, opened a small machinist shop on the Lower East Side - Pitts Engine Product Inc. at 370 East Houston Street. However, business was slow, and in 1948, Greenglass quit and took a better-paying job at Arma Engineering at Bush Terminal in South Brooklyn (While they were partners, Greenglass and Rosenberg constantly argued about the other not pulling his weight). Rosenberg muddled along at Pitt Engine, but business never improved substantially and money was always hard to come by for the Rosenbergs.

In 1947, Ethel bore Julius a second son, Robert, dropping the Rosenbergs further into debt. Ethel, although she had a strong personality, was not physically able to work. As a result, the money Rosenberg now received from the Russians, no matter how sporadically, helped the Rosenbergs pay their bills.

For the next several years, Julius Rosenberg laid low, trying to keep under the FBI's radar. However, he occasionally met with his Russian contact, doing whatever he could to further the Soviet cause without exposing himself as a spy. Since Rosenberg's old crew was no longer under his supervision, Rosenberg was reduced to acting as a go-between for the transfer of American top-secret documents to the Russians. By this time, Rosenberg was in the habit of accepting whatever remunerations offered him by his Soviet bosses.

Plainly, Rosenberg needed the cash to survive.

In June of 1948, Rosenberg met with fellow spies, Max Elitcher and Morton Sobell, on Catherine Slip, behind Knickerbocker Village and 20 yards from the East River. The reason for this meeting was to exchange microfilm important to the Russians. The microfilm had been originally given to Rosenberg by his Russian contact. Rosenberg had taken the microfilm to his Knickerbocker Village apartment, where he had made photographic copies of the microfilm, using a living room coffee table/film developing unit given to him by the Russians.

In February 1950, following the arrest of German-born British scientist Klaus Fuchs, the Russian spy-ring dominos began tumbling. To reduce his sentence, Fuchs immediately gave up Harry Gold, who was arrested on May 23, 1950.

*****

When Julius Rosenberg heard about Gold's arrest, he told David Greenglass to leave America immediately and to hide in Mexico until he could arrange Greenglass's escape to Switzerland, which did not have an extradition agreement with the United States. Rosenberg told Greenglass he had made arrangements with the Soviets for Greenglass to report to the Czechoslovakian Embassy in Switzerland, where he would receive diplomatic immunity and then passage to Russia. Greenglass balked at doing so because his wife, Ruth, was six months pregnant.

According to the July 23, 1950 *New York Times*, "Greenglass vacillated between fleeing and killing himself, until the federal agents put an end to his indecision by arresting him."

On June 15, 1950, in his first interview with the FBI, Greenglass easily, and some say gladly, caved under FBI interrogation. Greenglass not only admitted, that in 1945 as a U.S. Army soldier stationed in Los Alamos, he had passed secret government information to Harry Gold, but that his wife, Ruth, and his brother-in-law, Julius Rosenberg, were also Soviet spies; Julius Rosenberg being the ringleader. Greenglass insisted it was Julius Rosenberg who had recruited him to do espionage work for the Russians at Los Alamos. Greenglass did not say his sister, Ethel, was also involved in the spying, but he would later change his tune.

Greenglass told the feds when he finally decided to accede to his brother-in-law's request to be a spy, "It was like jumping into a cold lake."

When asked by the feds why he had decided to betray his home country, Greenglass said he considered it "gross negligence on the part of the United States to withhold atomic data from its ally, Russia."

The noose closed on Julius Rosenberg's neck, when on July 1, 1950, the feds raided his Knickerbocker Village apartment. In front of his wife and two sons, they slapped the cuffs on Rosenberg, charging him with "conspiracy to commit espionage." Rosenberg told the feds he was a merely a hard-working, self-employed electrical engineer and that he had no idea what they were talking about.

J. Edgar Hoover, the headline-grabbing director of the FBI, announced Rosenberg's arrest; describing Rosenberg as "another important link in the Soviet espionage apparatus which includes atomic scientist Dr. Klaus Fuchs, Philadelphia biochemist Harry Gold, and David Greenglass, former United States Army sergeant."

Rosenberg was hauled before Judge John F.X. McGohey in the Federal District Court for the Southern District of New York City. Rosenberg was represented by top New York City criminal attorney, Emanuel H. Bloch, of 270 Broadway. Judge McGohey set Rosenberg's bail at $100,000, and he remanded Rosenberg to the Federal House of Detention, located on the corner of 11th and West Streets.

Bloch, who had contacts in the mostly-liberal press, soon released a statement contradicting Greenglass's claims about Rosenberg's Soviet spy involvements. Bloch especially blasted

Greenglass's assertion that it was Julius Rosenberg who tore off the top of a Jell-O box, and gave half to Greenglass and half to Harry Gold, as a means of them identifying each other in New Mexico.

According to the July, 20, 1950 *New York Times*, "Bloch quoted his client as saying the government's version of the Jell-O box-top episode was 'fantastic,' – something like the kids heard over the television on the Lone Ranger program."

Bloch also said that Rosenberg claimed his "brother-in-law must be crazy"; there was no truth to the charges, and that Rosenberg wanted to meet his accuser "face to face."

On August 11, 1950, 34-year-old Ethel Rosenberg was arrested on the steps outside the Federal Court Building in New York City, minutes after she had testified under oath that she knew nothing about her husband, Julius, or her brother, David Greenglass, being involved in a Soviet espionage ring. The newspapers described her as a "dark-haired housewife with Russian ancestry."

Ethel seemed disinterested during her 15-minute court appearance after her arrest. While being led from the courtroom in handcuffs, she curtly told reporters, "I have nothing to say."

Like her husband, Ethel was held under $100,000 bond. She wasn't even afforded the opportunity to arrange for the care of her two children who had spent the afternoon with neighbors.

Chief Assistant U.S. Attorney Miles J. Lane told the press the Rosenbergs had made arrangements to leave the country after the arrest of Harry Gold. In fact, Lane said they had already succeeded in "obtaining passport photos from a private Lower East Side photographer."

The primary evidence against Ethel Rosenberg were statements by her brother, David Greenglass, who said Ethel was present every time he met Julius Rosenberg at their Knickerbocker Village apartment to discuss their espionage activities. Greenglass also said that on several occasions Ethel had typed notes concerning classified government information.

The truth was, the feds had very little on Ethel Rosenberg. However, by arresting her they figured it might force her husband to crack and start naming names.

In fact, J. Edgar Hoover urged his federal agents to build a "triable case" against Ethel, saying, "There is no question, if Julius Rosenberg would furnish details of his extensive espionage activities, it would be possible to proceed against other individuals. Proceeding against his wife might be a lever in this matter."

While the FBI closed their net around Greenglass, Gold, and the Rosenbergs, several other Rosenberg's comrades went into the wind.

Joel Barr, who was a college classmate of Rosenberg and just as much a lefty, disappeared in Paris, leaving most of his worldly possessions behind. He soon resurfaced in Czechoslovakia, where the Soviets gave him a new identity: Joseph Berg.

After Greenglass was arrested, Morton Sobell fled to Mexico, where he lived under an assumed name, until the feds caught up with him in August of 1950.

The day after Rosenberg was arrested, a third Rosenberg crony, Alfred Sarant, was interrogated by federal agents in Ithaca, N.Y., where Sarant ostensibly lived. The agents claimed Sarant was keeping an apartment to conduct espionage activities at 65 Morton Street in New York City. Sarant adamantly denied the fed's allegations, and before he could be arrested, Sarant absconded with Carol Dayton, the wife of an Ithaca neighbor. They fled to Mexico, and as far as the FBI was concerned, Alfred Sarant and Carol Dayton had disappeared into thin air, never to be seen again.

Finally, in the summer of 1950, William Perl, another one of Rosenberg's spy recruits, was called before the Rosenberg Grand Jury. Perl denied he had any relationship with Rosenberg. He was immediately arrested and charged with perjury. At his 1953 trial, Perl was found guilty of two counts of perjury and sentenced to two consecutive five-year terms; which he served at the New York House of Detention, claiming his innocence to the end.

Ethel Rosenberg adapted to jail life quite well. She did whatever chores were asked of her, and more importantly, to the consternation of the feds, she kept her mouth shut. The government's hope to scare her into naming names didn't work. Her husband, Julius, was just as much a rock; refusing to say anything at all, even to save his own wife from the electric chair.

The key to the government expanding its net to catch more spies was Ethel. However, she acted "the innocent woman" part to the hilt, making the feds, and especially J. Edgar Hoover, look foolish, inadequate, and most importantly – downright mean.

William P. Rogers, who was the Deputy Attorney General at the time, later said, "She called our bluff."

There was heavy scheming within the Greenglass family to get Ethel to come clean; for the sake of her children. If Julius and Ethel were imprisoned for a long time, Tessie Greenglass told her family there was no way she could continue caring for Robert and Michael Rosenberg. There was no doubt, since no other relative was willing to care for the two Rosenberg boys, if Ethel and Julius both received long prison terms, their two kids would have to be put up for adoption.

Despite the fact Ethel was known in the family as being Julius Rosenberg's boss, the entire Greenglass clan blamed Rosenberg for Ethel's predicament, which was certainly possible, but not probable. Quite frankly, none of the Greenglasses ever liked Julius Rosenberg, who was, by all accounts, an utterly odious man.

However, Julius Rosenberg was Ethel's panting puppy dog, and the espionage Rosenberg perpetrated against the United States of America was mostly done to impress Ethel with his compassion for communism and the Soviet Union, and also with his mental toughness. Julius Rosenberg was considered a mealy-mouthed wimp on the streets of the Lower East Side, but to Ethel, Julius Rosenberg was Superman and the Lone Ranger all wrapped up into one.

Years later, the assistant prosecutor at the Rosenberg trial, Roy Cohn, told a confidant, "She was (Ethel) worse than Julius. She was the older one; she was the one with the brains, she recruited her younger brother into the Young Communist League and into the spy ring. She was the one who typed the atom bomb documents; she engineered the whole thing; she was the mastermind of the conspiracy."

In September of 1950, Sam Greenglass, Ethel's older half-brother, visited Ethel in prison. Sam Greenglass beseeched Ethel to tell all she knew about her husband's Soviet involvement, for the sake of her children. Ethel stonewalled Sam Greenglass; insisting she had absolutely no information to give the government.

After Sam Greenglass's failure to get Ethel to come clean, Tessie Greenglass, Ethel's old and frail mother, visited Ethel in prison. Her mission was to convince Ethel to divorce Julius Rosenberg, and then for Ethel to tell the feds all she knew about her husband's contact with the Soviets. Ethel was incensed at her mother's suggestions. She gave her mother the proverbial backhand to the face, and she told Tessie never to visit her in prison again.

After Ethel's rebuke of Tessie Greenglass, Sam Greenglass told family friends that the death penalty would be too good for Ethel and Julius Rosenberg. There was that much animosity in the family.

*****

On March 6, 1951, it was a cold and rainy day when the case of the United States versus Julius Rosenberg, Ethel Rosenberg, and Morton Sobell was called for trial. All three defendants were charged with "conspiracy to commit espionage," a crime that could lead to the death penalty.

The presiding judge was Justice Irving Kaufman, a man of brilliance, who had graduated from Fordham Law School at the age of 21. The lead prosecutor in the case was Irving Saypol, riding a high wave of popularity for his successful prosecution of Alger Hiss, a United States government official, who was found guilty of perjury in 1950 for lying under oath in 1948 that he was a not a Russian spy.

The first order of business was picking a jury. More than 300 people had been summoned to jury duty that day, but most wanted nothing to do with such a high-profile event. Some potential jurors said their employers could not spare them for the six weeks the prosecutors told the press it would take for the trial to reach a conclusion. Other jurors were eliminated because they said they opposed the death penalty. Still others said they were war veterans and could not be unbiased in judging people accused of having betrayed the United States of America. When Judge Kaufman asked potential jurors if they were against the use of atomic weapons, not one said yes.

Judge Kaufman read a list a of publications, that Kaufman said, if a potential juror read frequently, might influence them in deciding the guilt of the defendants. One such periodical was *American Legion Magazine*, which was decidedly pro-American, as was *Time Magazine*. Left-wing periodicals, bordering on socialistic, included *The Daily Worker* and *National Guardian*.
Several prospective jurors were eliminated by the government and the prosecution because of their reading habits. Potential jurors were

also asked if they knew anyone associated with either the prosecution, or the defense, and if they had any relatives who were connected to law enforcement.

Prosecutors later admitted they were opposed to having housewives on the jury. One reason was that housewives might sympathize with Ethel Rosenberg. Another reason was that housewives had family members to care for, and they might balk at being absent from their home, if jurors were ordered to be sequestered overnight or for several consecutive days and nights.

Defense lawyers admitted they wanted as many women and African-Americans on the jury as possible. However, neither the prosecution nor the defense were certain having Jewish jurors would be beneficial or detrimental to the defendants.

In the course of a day-and-a-half of jury selection, numerous jurors were disqualified for one reason or another; some genuine and some contrived.

Judge Kaufman remarked dryly, "I hope all these statements are being made in good faith, and not in an effort to avoid what might seem to the jurors to be an unpleasant task."

When the tedium of jury selection ended, the jury was comprised of eleven men and one woman; none of whom were, like the judge, the chief prosecutor, and all three defendants - Jewish.

The jury foreman was 30-year-old Vincent Labonitte, an assistant sales manager at Macy's in White Plains. While in the army, Labonitte had served as a member of the Military Police (MP) in Germany. The other jurors included a housewife, two bookkeepers, a company estimator, an accountant for a caterer, a bank examiner, the secretary of the State Board of Pilots, and an auditor for an oil company. Five of the jurors resided in the Bronx. Five came from Westchester County, one from Brooklyn, and one lived in Manhattan. The male Manhattanite was also the lone African-American on the jury, and he worked for Con Edison.

*****

The chief prosecutor, Irving Saypol, chest puffed and dressed like he was going nightclub hopping, addressed the jury first. He said that the defendants "have committed the most serious crime which can be committed against the people of this country. The Rosenbergs conspired to deliver to the Soviet Union the weapons the Soviet Union could use to destroy us."

The Rosenbergs' attorney, Emanuel Bloch, was notorious for defending those associated with communist causes. His court rants always adhered to the same story line: the mean and vicious United States government was out to get the poor working man.

Tears in his eyes and fury on his face, Bloch implored the jury, "Give the defendants a fair shake! Do not be influenced by bias, or prejudice, or hysteria!"

The first prosecution witness was Max Elitcher, whose principal purpose for the prosecution was to implicate Morton Sobell in numerous spying activities for the Russians. "Mad Max," as he was called by his buddies, was an old pal of Sobell and Rosenberg from their City College days. Elitcher had also worked closely with Sobell at the Navy Bureau of Ordinance in Washington, D.C., and in addition, Sobell and Elitcher had shared an apartment in Washington D.C.

On the stand, Elitcher recalled for the jury the night he and Sobell met Rosenberg on Catherine Slip, behind Rosenberg's Knickerbocker Village apartment, to exchange microfilm of secret government documents. On the stand, Elitcher also admitted that he had been afraid he would be indicted for perjury because he had "falsely denied membership in the Communist Party on a Federal Loyalty Oath form." Elitcher said that his fear of being arrested caused him to flip on Rosenberg and Sobell. Because of Elitcher's testimony, the feds gave Elitcher a "get-out-of-jail-free" card; Elitcher was never prosecuted, and he was never heard from again.

To the fed's delight, Elitcher's testimony was so damaging to Sobell and his closeness to Sobell so apparent, Sobell refused to take the stand in his own defense.

The second government witness was Ethel Rosenberg's former-favorite brother - David Greenglass.

The 29-year-old canary was questioned by Saypol's 24-year-old chief assistant, Roy Cohn, who would later go on to a successful career as a "mob lawyer." Cohn's future clients would include "Fat Tony" Salerno, Carmine "The Cigar" Gigante, and John "The Teflon Don" Gotti. As a defense attorney, Cohn's tactics bordered on the illegal, and in fact, he lost his license to practice law in July 1986, weeks before he died from AIDS at the age of 59. As he lay on his deathbed, the much-maligned Cohn was called "an ice-cold sleaze," by *National Review* senior editor Jeffrey Hart.

However, it was the Rosenberg trial, and especially his grilling of David Greenglass, which propelled Cohn to national prominence.

While Greenglass answered the questions Cohn was peppering him with, Greenglass's face transformed into a saintly smile, as if he were telling a tale which gave him much pleasure.

The back and forth between Cohn and Greenglass is paraphrased below:

> *COHN: Tell us about the first time you and your wife, Ruth, met with the Rosenbergs to discuss spying activities for the Russians.*
> *GREENGLASS: It was in early 1945 when I was back in New York City on leave. My wife had already met with them earlier.*
> *COHN: Was there anyone else present this meeting?*
> *GREENGLASS: Yes, there was a woman named Ann Sidorovich. Julius told me that I would probably meet this woman in Denver in a movie theater, and that I should give her the information I was able to get in Los Alamos.*

However, according to Greenglass's testimony, Julius Rosenberg was not absolutely sure Ann Sidorovich would be Greenglass next contact.

> *COHN: So what did Julius Rosenberg do next?*
> *GREENGLASS: He went into the kitchen and returned with a Jell-O box. He cut it in half with scissors and gave my wife one half. He kept the other. He said that in case I met someone else, that person would have the other half of the Jell-O-box.*

It turned out that not only would Greenglass's next spy contact not be Ann Sidorovich, but it would be Harry Gold instead. Moreover, the location of the meeting was changed from a movie theater in Denver to Greenglass's apartment in Albuquerque.

COHN: *Would you tell us exactly what happened from the first minute you saw Gold?*

GREENGLASS: *There was a knock on the door and I opened it. We had just completed eating breakfast, and there was a man standing in the hallway who asked if I was Mr. Greenglass, and I said, yes. He stepped through the door and said, "Julius sent me," and I said, "Oh" and walked to my wife's purse, took out the wallet, and took out the matched part of the Jell-O box. He produced his piece, and we checked them and they fitted, and the identification was made. I offered him something to eat, and he said he had already eaten. He just wanted to know if I had any information, and I said, "I have some but I will have to write it up. If you come back in the afternoon, I will give it to you." I started to tell him about one of the people who would be good material for recruiting into espionage work. He cut me short, and he left, and I got to work on the report.*

Greenglass said he spent several hours drawing and explaining in writing lens molds and how they related to the Manhattan Project's creation of the atomic bomb. Greenglass also said he drew up a list of potential recruits for the Russian spy ring. The next exchange shows that while the Rosenbergs were in the Soviet spy ring because of their communistic principles, Greenglass was mainly involved for the cash, as was his wife, Ruth.

COHN: *Did Harry Gold come back in the afternoon?*
GREENGLASS: *Yes, at 2:30 p.m. I gave him my report in an envelope, and he gave me an envelope, which I felt and realized there was money in it, and I put it in my pocket.*
COHN: *Did you examine the money at that point?*
GREENGLASS: *No, I didn't. Gold said, "Will it be enough?" And I said, "Well, it will be plenty for the present." And he said "You need it," and we went into a side discussion about the fact that my wife had a miscarriage earlier in the spring, and he said, "Well, I will see what I can do about getting some more money for you."*
COHN: *How much was in the envelope?*

GREENGLASS: My wife and I counted it later. There was $500, and I gave it to her.

Cohn then asked Greenglass about a surprise visit Julius Rosenberg paid to Greenglass in Greenglass's Lower East Side apartment while Greenglass was on an Army furlough.

GREENGLASS: He came up to the apartment, and he got me out of bed, and we went into another room so my wife could dress.
COHN: What did he say to you?
GREENGLASS: He said to me that he wanted to know what I had for him. I told him "I think I have a pretty good description of the atom bomb."
COHN: The atom bomb itself?
GREENGLASS: That's right.

Greenglass then testified Rosenberg had requested that Greenglass prepare a written description of all the experiments taking place at Los Alamos. Greenglass told Rosenberg he was short of money at the time and a little contribution to his cause would gladly be accepted.

Greenglass said Rosenberg's mouth curled into a snarl and then a smirk.

"It's always money with you isn't it?" Rosenberg said.

"I'm not as idealistic as you are, Julius," Greenberg said. "I want to get paid for what I do."

Greenglass said Rosenberg pulled out a white sealed envelope from his inner jacket pocket. Instead of handing the envelope to Greenglass, Rosenberg smacked the envelope hard against Greenglass's chest.

"Open it and count the money," Rosenberg said. "I want to make sure you're satisfied with the amount."

Greenglass opened the envelope, and he counted out $200.

"This is fine, for now," Greenglass told Rosenberg.

COHN: Did you then draw up a sketch of the atomic bomb itself?
GREENGLASS: I did.

COHN: Did you prepare descriptive material to explain the sketch of the atom bomb?

GREENGLASS: I did.

COHN: Was there any other material that you wrote up on that occasion?

GREENGLASS: I gave some scientists' names, and I also gave some possible recruits for espionage.

COHN: Now, about how many pages would you say it took to write down all these matters?

GREENGLASS: I would say about twelve pages or so.

Greenglass then testified when his writing was complete, he and his wife, Ruth, traveled to the Rosenbergs' apartment in Knickerbocker Village. There, he gave Julius, in the presence of Ethel, the requested hand-written material. In addition, Greenglass said while he and his wife were present, Ethel typed on a portable typewriter what Greenglass had written out in long hand, occasionally pausing to clarify with Greenglass and Rosenberg confusing, or grammatically incorrect comments Greenglass had written.

While Ethel was typing, Julius bragged to Greenglass that he had personally stolen the proximity fuse while he was working at Emerson Radio. Upon hearing this, Greenberg said he saw a smile crawl across Ethel's thin lips. Greenglass said he thought Ethel seemed extremely pleased Rosenberg had stolen the proximity fuse from under the Emerson Radio scientists' noses.

After the meeting between David and Ruth Greenglass, and the Rosenbergs in the Rosenbergs' Knickerbocker Village apartment, David Greenglass said he had no doubt his sister, Ethel, was as much a part of the Soviet spy ring as was her husband. Greenglass didn't know of any instances where Ethel was involved in the transfer of government documents, but Greenglass was sure Ethel knew what Julius Rosenberg was doing, and she supported her husband's actions every step of the way.

After Cohn excused David Greenglass, Ruth Greenglass took the stand. Her lips tight with indignation (unlike her husband's silly smile), Ruth confirmed what her husband, David, had said about Ethel typing up the secret documents. In addition, Ruth claimed that it was Julius and Ethel Rosenberg, in concert, who had urged her to convince her husband to work for the Soviets.

In 2001, decades after serving 10 years of the 15-year sentence he had received for espionage, Greenglass was interviewed by Sam Roberts for Roberts' book, *The Brother*.

Concerning Ethel's typing of the classified documents, which turned out to be the most damaging evidence against Ethel, Greenglass told Roberts, "I don't know who typed it, frankly, and to this day I can't remember that the typing took place. I had no memory of that at all—none whatsoever."

Greenglass also told Roberts that he willingly gave false testimony to protect himself and his wife, Ruth. And furthermore, he was encouraged by the government (Cohn) to do so. In return, Greenglass received a lighter prison sentence than he would have otherwise received, and his wife got total immunity from prosecution.

Greenglass told Roberts, "Look, I had a wife and two children. I didn't care so much what happened to me, but I cared what happened to them."

Greenglass also told Roberts that while he was being interrogated by the FBI, he told them, "If you indict my wife you can forget it. I'll never say a word about anybody."

When Roberts asked Greenglass if he would have done anything differently, Greenglass replied, "Never. I would not sacrifice my wife and my children for my sister."

Furthermore, Greenglass told Roberts he had no remorse for what he had done. But that he did not think his sister, Ethel, based on his testimony, would have received the death penalty.

*****

David Greenglass's cross examination by the Rosenbergs' lawyer, Bloch, did little more than confirm the fact that Greenglass was testifying against the Rosenbergs to save his wife from going to jail, which would have left his two children without both parents, a fate now suffered by the Rosenbergs' two young boys.

Try as he may, Bloch could not shake Greenglass from his contention that both Julius and Ethel Rosenberg were Russian spies. To add to Bloch's frustration of not being able to crack Greenglass's testimony, Greenglass's ever-present smile was beginning to annoy Bloch.

> BLOCH: *You knew at that time, did you not, that you were engaging in the commission of a very serious crime?*
> GREENGLASS: *I did.*
> BLOCH: *Did it occur to you at the time that you finally said to your wife, "I will do this" and then transmitted to her certain information that there was a possible penalty of death for espionage?*
> GREENGLASS: *Yes.*
> BLOCH (exasperated): *Are you aware that you are smiling?*
> GREENGLASS: *Not very.*

Bloch turned his attention to Greenglass's relationship with his wife, Ruth. Bloch wanted to cement into the jury's mind that Greenglass was lying about the Rosenbergs in order to save Ruth from prosecution.

> BLOCH: *You have known your wife Ruth since childhood days?*
> GREENGLASS: *Yes.*
> BLOCH: *Did you love her when you married her?*
> GREENGLASS: *I did.*
> BLOCH: *Do you love her today?*
> GREENGLASS: *I do.*
> BLOCH: *Do you love her more than you love yourself?*
> GREENGLASS: *I do.*
> BLOCH: *Do you love your children?*
> GREENGLASS: *I do.*
> BLOCH: *Did you at any time think of your wife while you were down here telling your story to the FBI?*
> GREENGLASS: *Of course, I thought of her.*
> BLOCH: *Did you think of your wife with respect to the fact that she may be a defendant in a criminal proceeding?*
> GREENGLASS: *I did.*
> BLOCH: *Now, Mr. Greenglass, your wife has never been arrested, has she?*
> GREENGLASS: *She has not.*

BLOCH: And she has never been indicted, has she?
GREENGLASS: She has not.
BLOCH: And your wife is at the present time home, taking care of your children, isn't that right?
GREENGLASS: That's right.
BLOCH: All right. Do you believe that by testifying here that you will help your wife?
GREENGLASS: I don't know what the Government has in mind with my wife, and I can't answer for them.

Unfortunately for the Rosenbergs, that was all Bloch could squeeze out of David Greenglass.

After Sobell decided not to testify on his own behalf, the only witnesses called by Bloch were Julius and Ethel Rosenberg. Both were stone-faced while being questioned. Maybe if they had expressed some emotion, the jury would have considered more strongly that David and Ruth Greenglass were possibly lying to save their own butts.

It was also damaging to the Rosenbergs that every time the government directed its questions to their involvement in the Communist Party, both Rosenbergs quickly asserted their Fifth Amendment right against self-incrimination. This was a tactic fashioned by Bloch to thwart any questions from the prosecution concerning fellow communists who may have been members of the Rosenbergs' spy ring (Bloch was a lefty himself and didn't want any more communists exposed).

On the witness stand, Julius Rosenberg issued a long string of denials; repudiating everything David and Ruth Greenglass had said on the stand. In fact, trying to turn the tables on Greenglass, Rosenberg said Greenglass has begged him for money in 1950 so that Greenglass could flee the country before he was arrested. Rosenberg's comments implied that Ruth and David Greenglass were the Soviet spies and not Julius and Ethel Rosenberg, which in light of the facts, was patently absurd.

Members of the press covering the trial were astounded Julius Rosenberg seemed so unconcerned about the severity of the proceedings; he was almost flippant. They wondered if Rosenberg fully understood the dire circumstances he and his wife were facing if they were convicted of espionage against the United States government. Nothing in Rosenberg's demeanor, or in the way he phased his answers, showed that Rosenberg knew he was on trial for his (and his wife's) life.

Immediately after her husband had struck out on the witness stand, Ethel Rosenberg was called up to bat next. While Julius seemed indifferent on the stand, Ethel was flat-out feisty, and some thought her demeanor showed contempt for the entire court proceedings.

On several occasions, when even her own lawyer, Bloch, thought it was not necessary, Ethel, her nose up in the air, cited the Fifth Amendment against self-incrimination. At times, Bloch advised her to answer the question (not cite the Fifth). And on other occasions, Ethel refused to answer the questions even before she got the nod from her lawyer.

One such exchange went like this:

SAYPOL: Did you help him (Greenglass) join the Communist Party?
ETHEL ROSENBERG: I refuse to answer.
SAYPOL: She knows the answer.
BLOCH: She is a better lawyer than I am, no doubt.
SAYPOL: Go ahead.
ETHEL ROSENBERG: I am going to refuse to answer on the ground of self-incrimination.
SAYPOL: Now that your lawyer has interrupted, do you so refuse?
ETHEL ROSENBERG: That is right.

Bloch tried to elicit sympathy from the jury for Ethel's two children, now living in a homeless shelter. However, even when she answered questions about the plight of her two young boys, court observers said Ethel showed not one iota of motherly concern.

One court observer described her as "robotic" on the stand. Another said "Her disposition was not conducive to eliciting sympathy from a jury, who knew the death penalty was in play."

On March 28, 1951, the prosecution and the defense presented their final arguments.

The prosecutor, Saypol, fire in his eyes, was up first. He spoke, not in complete sentences, but in short blasts, raising his voice on the last syllable of each declaration.

Saypol said, in part:

This description of the atom bomb, destined for delivery to the Soviet Union, was typed up by the defendant Ethel Rosenberg that afternoon at her apartment at 10 Monroe Street. Just so had she on countless other occasions sat at that typewriter and struck the keys, blow by blow, against her own country in the interests of the Soviets.

We know what Julius Rosenberg told Ruth Greenglass on that occasion, and what he and his wife told Ruth and David on every occasion when they were together. The Rosenbergs told them to go and commit espionage in the interests of communism in the Soviet Union, just as Rosenberg and Sobell told that to Elitcher and countless others, and that is what happened.

I am a firm believer in the American jury system. I have confidence in the perception of the jury of twelve intelligent American citizens. I am confident that you will render the only verdict possible on the evidence presented before you in this courtroom; that of guilty as charged by the grand jury as to each of these three defendants.

The Rosenbergs' attorney, Emanuel Bloch, matched Saypol in intensity.

Block said, in part:

The fear that an impartial jury could not be secured was particularly important in this type of case. Now, all of you are New Yorkers, or you come from the environs of New York. We are a pretty sophisticated people. People can't put things over on us very easily. We are fairly wise in the ways of the world and the ways of people, and we all know that there is not a person in this world who hasn't some prejudice, and you would be inhuman if you didn't have some prejudice. But we ask you now as we asked you before, please don't decide this case because you may have some bias or some prejudice against some political philosophy.

If you want to convict these defendants because you think that they are communists, and you don't like communism, and you don't like any member of the Communist Party, then, ladies and gentlemen, I can sit down now, and there is absolutely no use to me talking. There was no use in going through this whole rigmarole of a three-week trial. That is not the crime.

Now, I want to conclude very simply. I told you at the beginning and I tell you now that we don't come to you in this kind of charge looking for sympathy. Believe me, ladies and gentlemen, there is plenty of room here for a lawyer to try to harp on your emotions, especially so far as Ethel Rosenberg is concerned; a mother, she has two children, her husband is under arrest. No, because if these people are guilty of that crime they deserve no sympathy. No, we want you to decide this case with your minds, not with your hearts, with your minds. I say that if you do that, you can come to no other conclusion than that these defendants are innocent, and you are going to show to the world that in America a man can get a fair trial.

On March 29, 1951, at 4:43 p.m., the jurors were led out of the courtroom. After a quick dinner at an Italian restaurant near the courthouse, they started their deliberations. The first vote was 11-1 for the conviction of Ethel Rosenberg, but unanimous on the guilt of Julius Rosenberg and Martin Sobell.

The jury foreman, Lebonitte, later told the press, "One juror was squeamish about the possibility of a woman being put to death. He was under the impression that it was almost a foregone conclusion that she would suffer the loss of her life. He also brought out the mother angle. The idea that a mother with two children could be put to death was revolting to him."

In order to try to convince the dissenting juror to go along with the program, the other jurors insisted that it was Ethel's own fault for her children's present predicament. Their message to the unbeliever was: "Feel sorry for the Rosenberg children, but not for their mother. She's the one who's putting her two kids through this nightmare."

The dissenting juror was James Gibbons. He later said, "I believed they were guilty then, and I believe now that they are still guilty. But there were two children involved, and I have two children of my own."

At 10:44 p.m. Lebonitte sent a message to Judge Kaufman, which said, "One of the jurors has some doubt in his mind as to whether he can recommend leniency for one of the defendants. He is interested in knowing your mind on this matter."

Judge Kaufman told the jury they surely could make a recommendation, but he could either agree or disagree with that recommendation.

At 12:22 a.m., the jury decided to pack it in for the night. They told the judge they still hadn't convinced the dissenting juror about Ethel Rosenberg's guilt, and it was futile to continue tonight.

This sent the U. S. Marshalls assigned to the jury room scrambling to find a hotel which had 12 vacant rooms for the 12 jurors. Luckily, the Knickerbocker Hotel on West Forty-Fifth Street fit the bill, and at 2 a.m., the jurors retired for the night (The Knickerbocker Hotel had no connection with Knickerbocker Village, where the Rosenbergs resided when they were arrested).

At 10 a.m. the following morning, after a hearty breakfast at Schrafft's, the jurors resumed deliberations. With 11 jurors already firm in their convictions, foreman Lebonitte went to work on Gibbons.

Lebonitte later told the press, "I told him (Gibbons) this woman (Ethel Rosenberg) that you want to save, could possibly, in the future, be part of a conspiracy to transmit secret information to a foreign power that could result in your own doom, and the destruction of your wife and children. That changed his way of thinking."

Gibbons later said, "I felt like Pontius Pilate washing his hands."

When the jurors reentered the courtroom, one member of the press remarked, "It was like the air was sucked out of the room."

After the jurors were seated, and each was identified by name, the Clerk of the Court said, "Mr. Foreman, have you reached a verdict?"

Foreman Labonitte replied, "Yes we have, your honor."

"How say you?"

"We, the jury, find Julius Rosenberg guilty as charged. We, the jury, find Ethel Rosenberg guilty as charged. We, the jury, find Morton Sobell guilty as charged."

All eyes in the courtroom were glued to the defendants' table. Both Rosenbergs appeared unaffected, while Martin Sobell looked like he was about to faint.

Judge Kaufman immediately concurred with the verdict. He told the court, "I must say as an individual, I can't be happy, because it is a sad day for America when citizens lend themselves to the destruction of our country by the most destructive weapon the world has ever known. I can't find the words to describe this loathsome offense."

Judge Kaufmann also praised the FBI for "doing such a wonderful job in this case."

While the judge addressed the court, Julius Rosenberg rocked slightly in his chair. For the first time in court, Julius Rosenberg looked slightly nervous.

However, his wife, Ethel, dressed in a navy blue shirt, pink blouse, and red waistcoat, was the Iron Maiden. Her face was set in stone; her chin held up high.

Outside the courtroom, Rosenberg's attorney, Emanuel Bloch, was all fire and brimstone. He raised his right fist over his head, and he punctuated each sentence with a forward blow.

"Despite the jury's verdict, Ethel and Julius Rosenberg maintain they are innocent of the crime of which they have been convicted!" Bloch said. "They intend to appeal to the highest court in the land!"

The guilty verdicts prompted the FBI, and especially its boss, J. Edgar Hoover, to almost wrench their shoulders out of their sockets patting themselves on their backs.

Hoover gushed to the press, "This case is truly a sterling example of our democratic process in action, and a distinctive achievement to be enrolled in the annals of our American courts' history."

Unfortunately for the Rosenbergs and Sobell, Judge Kaufman did not have much latitude in the sentencing guidelines. The statute they had been convicted under afforded two sentences only; either thirty years in jail, or death.

*****

On April 5, 1951 the Rosenbergs and Sobell stood before Judge Kaufman awaiting their sentences.

Prosecutor Irving Saypol was the first to speak to the Court.

He said, "In terms of human life, these defendants have affected the lives, and perhaps the freedom of whole generations of mankind. Leniency would be merely an invitation to increased activity by those dedicated to the concept that compassion is decadent and mercy and indication of weakness."

The Rosenbergs' attorney, Emanuel Block, then told the Court, "They (the Rosenbergs) have informed me that they are innocent, and no matter what, they will always maintain their innocence."

Block then dropped a bombshell when he said that despite what the Rosenbergs had done, the Russians would have been able to get the secrets to the atom bomb anyway.

Block said, "Let's not believe, as seems to be the current American thinking, that our entire security depends upon the atom bomb, a thought expressed by Mr. Saypol, when he said our boys are drying in Korea because of the Rosenbergs."

Judge Kaufman spoke next.

He said, "Because of the seriousness of this case and the lack of precedence, I have refrained from asking the Government for recommendations. The responsibility is so great that I believe that the Court alone should assume this responsibility."

But in fact, Judge Kaufman had already solicited the advice of prosecutor Saypol himself, and also that of Peyton Ford and James McInerny, both Assistant Attorney Generals of the United States of America. Even J. Edgar Hoover pitched in with advice for the judge; suggesting the death penalty for Julius Rosenberg and for Martin Sobell, but only 30 years in jail for Ethel Rosenberg. Hoover figured with her husband dead, Ethel, while still languishing in jail, might spill the names of several Soviet operatives who were still working undercover in the United States.

In addition, Hoover had asked Judge Kaufman for leniency for David Greenglass. Hoover reasoned that without Greenglass's testimony, the government would have had very little evidence with which to convict Greenglass's sister, Ethel.

(Editor's note: Greenglass was scheduled to be sentenced the same day as the Rosenbergs and Sobell, but not be seen in the same

courtroom with his now-hated brother-in-law and an angry sister, Greenglass asked that his sentence be put back one day. That request was granted by the Court).

Hoover recommended, since Greenglass had pleaded guilty and was not under the same strict sentencing guidelines as the Rosenbergs, Greenglass should be given only 15 years in prison. This opinion was also echoed by the assistant prosecutor, Roy Cohn.

Hoover told Judge Kaufman, "Greenglass was a very important witness for the prosecution, and he furnished information to the special agents of the Bureau, which led to the securing of corroborative information of great value."

As if the weight of the world was on his back, Judge Kaufman glared directly at the Rosenbergs, who were standing defiantly before him. Standing next to the Rosenbergs was Morton Sobell.

Judge Kaufman said in a ponderous voice:

Citizens of this country who betray their fellow-countrymen can be under none of the delusions about the benignity of Soviet power that they might have been prior to World War II. The nature of Russian terrorism is now self-evident. Idealism as a rational dissolves.

I consider your crime worse than murder. Plain deliberate contemplated murder is dwarfed in magnitude by comparison with the crime you have committed. In committing the act of murder, the criminal kills only his victim. The immediate family is brought to grief and when justice is meted out, the chapter is closed. But in your case, I believe your conduct in putting into the hands of the Russians the A-bomb, years before our best scientists predicted Russia would perfect the bomb, has already caused, in my opinion, the communist aggression in Korea, with the resultant casualties exceeding 50,000, and who knows but that millions more of innocent people may pay the price of your treason. Indeed, by your betrayal you undoubtedly have altered the course of history to the disadvantage of our country.

The evidence indicated quite clearly that Julius Rosenberg was the prime mover in this conspiracy. However, let no mistake be made about the role which his wife, Ethel Rosenberg, played in this conspiracy. Instead of deterring him from pursuing his ignoble cause, she encouraged and assisted the cause. She was a mature woman - almost three years older than her husband and almost seven years older than her younger brother. She was a full-fledged partner in this crime.

The defendants, Julius and Ethel Rosenberg, placed their devotion to their cause above their own personal safety, and were conscious that they were sacrificing their own children, should their misdeeds be detected - all of which did not deter them from pursuing their course. Love for their cause dominated their lives. It was even greater than their love for their children.

While Judge Kaufman ripped the Rosenbergs a new one, the bell of nearby St. Andrew's Catholic Church ominously tolled the noon hour. As the judge droned on drowning out the bells, Julius Rosenberg rolled forward and backward on the balls of his feet.

Ethel, her thin lips set in defiance, clamped her right hand on the chair in front of her, so tightly; court observers saw her knuckles turn white.

Martin Sobell, standing next to Ethel, stared blankly out the window.

Judge Kaufman continued his soliloquy concerning the Rosenbergs' fate.

"I have deliberated for hours, days, and nights. I have carefully weighed the evidence. Every nerve, every fiber of my body has been taxed. I have searched the records; I have searched my conscience to find some reason for mercy, for it is only human to be merciful, and it's natural to try to spare lives. I am convinced, however, that I would violate the solemn and sacred trust that the people of this land have placed in my hands were I to show leniency to the defendants Rosenberg.

You are hereby sentenced to the punishment of death, and it is ordered upon someday within the week beginning with Monday, May 21, you shall be executed according to law."

Their fates sealed, Julius Rosenberg turned to his wife, Ethel, and gave her a curt nod; his signal for them to leave the courtroom. The Rosenbergs shuffled stiffly through the side door of the courtroom, accompanied by four burly marshals.

After most of the press had busted out of the courtroom to file their Rosenberg reports, Judge Kaufman turned his attention to Martin Sobel - the forgotten man.

It was precisely 12:30 p.m. when Judge Kaufman said, "I cannot be moved by hysteria, or motivated by a desire to do the popular thing."

Judge Kaufman thereby sentenced Sobell to thirty years in prison, which is the best sentence Sobell could have hoped for; the other one being fried in the Sing Sing electric chair like the Rosenbergs. His shoulders slumped, Sobell, escorted by two marshals, trudged out of the courtroom.

After the Rosenbergs had exited the courtroom, they were placed in adjacent holding cells in the basement of the courthouse. To the repulsion of the nearby guards, Ethel caroled to her husband a moving rendition of *One Fine Day* from Madame Butterfly; during which Ethel clearly envisioned herself as *Madame Butterfly*, and Julius Rosenberg as the husband referred to in the song.

Ethel sang:

Weeping? And why? And why?
Ah, 'tis faith you are lacking
Hear me
One fine day we'll notice
A thread of smoke arising on the sea
In the far horizon
And then the ship appearing
Then the trim white vessel
Glides into the harbor
Thunders forth her cannon
See you? Now he is coming
I do not go to meet him
Not I
I stay upon the brow of the hillock
And wait there
And wait for a long time
But never weary of the long waiting
From out the crowded city
There is coming a man
A little speck in the distance

Climbing the hillock
Can you guess who it is?
And when he's reached the summit
Can you guess what he'll say?
He will call, "Butterfly" from the distance
I, without answering
Hold myself quietly concealed
A bit to tease him and a bit
So as not to die at our first meeting
And then, a little troubled
He will call, he will call
"Dear baby wife of mine,
Dear little orange blossom"
The names he used to call me when he came here
This will all come to pass as I tell you
Banish your idle fears
For he will return
Return

Julius Rosenberg, not as talented a songster as his wife, nor as imaginative, blasted back with a gruff rendition of The *Battle Hymn of the Republic*, which began with: *Mine eyes have seen the glory of the coming of the Lord.* And ended with: *Glory, glory, hallelujah. Our God is marching on.*

*****

The following day it was David Greenglass's turn to face Judge Kaufman.

In a short statement, prosecutor Irving Saypol told the judge that he had agreed with the Rosenberg and Sobell sentences, and that he was recommending that David Greenglass be sentenced to only 15 years.

However, Greenglass's lawyer, O. John Rogge (rhymes with foggy), saw things differently.

In a 36-minute soliloquy, Rogge defended Greenglass, and he said amongst other things, that Greenglass "deserved a pat on the back" for his actions instead of "a stiff sentence for informing on his relatives."

"Let David Greenglass have a fair deal," Rogge said. "If we do, it will encourage others to come forward and tell the whole story on espionage. Fanatics with rebellion in their hearts are going to betray their country no matter what the sentence is. They may even laugh at it. But if the government wants help, it must give help. Any sentence of over five years would be so severe as to discourage anyone else from coming forward with information."

Rogge then went on to recommend the ridiculously light sentence of a-year-and-a-day for David Greenglass.

Rogge also told the court that Greenglass should be forgiven for his actions because, "David's fuzzy thinking occurred at a time when Russia was a wartime ally, and many were engaged in a fuzzy thinking about the Soviet Union at that time."

This line of reasoning did not please Judge Kaufman one bit.

Judge Kaufmann roared at Rogge. "Let's get one thing clear! Russia did not come to our aid! We came to Russia's aid! Your argument is confusing to me, and I hope you are not trying to condone the actions of Greenglass. No American has a right to decide for himself how much aid should be given to Russia.

"You have stressed a light sentence, but I like to think that I never impose either a light sentence, or a heavy sentence, but rather a sentence within the framework of the facts in this case."

Judge Kaufman then turned to David Greenglass. The judge's flaming eyes bored a hole in Greenglass's forehead.

Wagging his forefinger, Judge Kaufman told Greenglass, "The fact that I am going to show you some consideration does not mean I condone your acts, or minimize them in any way. They were loathsome. I must recognize, however, the help given by you in apprehending and bringing to justice the arch-criminals in this nefarious scheme: Julius Rosenberg and his wife, Ethel Rosenberg."

Then instead of a nice pat on the back, Judge Kaufman gave the 29-year-old David Greenglass a proverbial swift kick in the butt.

Judge Kaufman said, "I shall therefore follow the Government recommendation and sentence you to fifteen years in jail."

According to the April 7th 1951, *New York Times*, "As the last words fell, Ruth Greenglass almost toppled from her front row seat on the left side of the courtroom. After a massive shudder,

Greenglass's 27-year-old wife dropped her bare head forward to the rail and gripped hard with her right hand to steady herself."

As for David Greenglass, the *New York Times* said, "Aside from a sharp forward jutting of his head, he showed no emotion at the sentence."

Greenglass was removed from court and transported to the city prison to begin his sentence. His wife, who was sitting only twenty feet away from Greenglass during sentencing, returned to her cold water flat at 265 Rivington Street on the Lower East Side of Manhattan to care for her two children, 4 ½ years old, and ten months old. Neither child had been born when Greenglass was doing all his spying for the Russians.

Almost immediately, Julius Rosenberg began a smear campaign against his brother-in-law and former business partner, David Greenglass.

Rosenberg released a statement through the press, which said: "History records will show that David Greenglass stands without parallel ahead of Judas Iscariot in infamy."

Outside the courtroom after Greenglass had been sentenced, Prosecutor Saypol told the press that, "With good behavior, Greenglass could be a free man in about ten years."

That statement turned out to be prescient, since, on November 12, 1960, David "Judas" Greenglass was released from Lewisburg Federal Prison in Pennsylvania after serving a little more than 9 ½ years of his 15-year sentence. He was sent to the Federal House of Detention on the West Side of Manhattan to be processed.

On November 17th, Greenglass emerged from the prison walls into the cool, fresh, and now-free air. Outside to greet Greenglass was his lawyer, Rogge, but not his wife, Ruth. David had told Ruth to stay home to avoid the nasty circus that was sure to await him.

As soon as David Greenglass trudged no more than ten feet into freedom, Greenglass and Rogge were surrounded by scores of reporters and photographers. One scribe asked Greenglass if he had anything to say. Greenglass pulled his collar up over his neck and face, and then he pushed his head downward into his coat, like a turtle skulking into his shell.

As they headed toward a waiting cab, Rogge told the press, "David Greenglass is out on mandatory release. He does not now have a statement, nor will he ever."

That said, Rogge pushed Greenglass into the back seat of the cab and then followed him inside.

A group of longshoremen, who had wondered what the fuss was all about, finally found out the truth. They surrounded the cab, in which Greenglass was crunched down in the back seat, trying to make himself invisible. The longshoremen, traditionally a patriotic bunch of violent hooligans, screamed at Greenglass.

"You lousy communist! You ought to kiss the ground!"

"You lousy bum you ought to commit suicide!"

The longshoremen then yelled at the cab driver, "Drive him off the pier into the river, that dirty rat!"

They also said other things not printable in a family publication.

The cab disappeared into the New York City traffic, but the intuitive press, not to be denied, sped away to Rogge's law office, located downtown at 401 Broadway.

The scribes beat the cab to Rogge's office, but Rogge emerged from the cab alone, with a shit-eating grin on his face.

The press then realized they had been hoodwinked.

Rogge told them, "I lost him (Greenglass), and I hope he stays lost. I hope he is back in the current of life as we speak."

Rogge called a press conference later that afternoon, in which he issued the statement, "We would like the Greenglasses to live like a normal American family now. It has been very carefully arranged so that they will have a maximum of privacy. All David Greenglass wants is to be forgotten."

David Greenglass and his wife, Ruth, immediately disappeared from the public consciousness. They changed their last names, and they lived in various parts of New York City's five boroughs, before finally settling down at a home in the Laurelton section of Queens. Neither Greenglass has ever shown any remorse for their actions that led to the death of Julius and Ethel Rosenberg.

In 2001, David Greenglass told reporter Sam Roberts in Roberts's book *The Brother*, "As a spy who turned my family in, I don't care. I sleep very well."

When Roberts asked Greenglass how he felt about the fact his testimony led to his sister, Ethel Rosenberg, being executed, Greenglass flashed his habitual inane smile, and said, "You know, I seldom use the word sister anymore; I've wiped it out of my mind. My wife put her (Ethel) in it (the conspiracy). What am I going to do, call my wife a liar? My wife is my wife. My wife says 'Look, we are still alive.'"

Ruth Greenglass lived a long, if not especially prosperous or illustrious life. She died on April, 7, 2008, at the age of 83. No reason was given in the newspapers for the cause of her death.

As of the writing of this book, there have been no report of David Greenglass's demise.

*****

On April 11th, 1951, Ethel Rosenberg was transferred from the Women's House of Detention in Manhattan to Sing Sing Prison in upstate Ossining, New York. At first, she was isolated from her husband, Julius, who was still in the New York City prison system.

Ethel was not a happy camper. Things were so bad for Ethel, she told the warden that she "dreaded each day because it brought her that much closer to her punishment." Ethel also said she, "would rather kill herself rather than face the electric chair."

That all changed on May 16, when Julius Rosenberg was transferred to the same prison as Ethel. Before long, they were granted the right to see each other once a week, which they did, separated by a wire-mesh fence. It was a regular event for the prison guards to watch the two lovebirds attempting to kiss each other with the taut fence wire impeding their lips.

For the next two years, the Rosenbergs, through their attorney, Emanuel Bloch, tried every possible avenue to avoid execution. Besides attempting to use the United States courts to save the Rosenbergs, Bloch showed no shame in also using the court of public opinion. Spurred on by outbursts from the Soviet regime in Russia, thousands of people marched on two continents in protest of the Rosenbergs' execution. Even the Pope made an impassioned speech asking for mercy for the Rosenbergs.

Famed leftist trial lawyer, Louis Nizer, backed Bloch's outlandish actions to the hilt. Nizer issued a statement to the press, saying Bloch was "an advocate in the classic sense, whose hands were charged with electricity and his face ablaze with concern for his quivering clients."

In January of 1953, Tessie Greenglass made a final attempt to convince her daughter, Ethel, to give up her husband, Julius, and save her own life. In letters Ethel sent to her lawyer, Bloch, Ethel said she was shocked by her mother's intervention. Ethel said Tessie implored her to contradict her sworn testimony in court and to back up David's version of the events, even if they weren't true. Bloch asked Ethel if her mother was suggesting that Ethel commit perjury. Ethel said she asked her mother that exact question, and in reply Tessie Greenglass just shrugged her shoulders, and said, "Well, you wouldn't be here."

Still, Tessie Greenglass wouldn't give up trying to convince her daughter to save her own skin.

By the spring of 1953, it was clear the government did not want to execute Ethel Rosenberg, and they only wanted her to start naming names of Russian spies in America in order to have her death sentence commuted. Besides, killing a mother of two was becoming a public relations nightmare for the feds.

On March 14th, 1953, Tessie Greenglass took one last shot. Tessie, accompanied by Ethel's older brother, Bernie, implored Ethel to reconsider her fate; if not for herself, then for her two children, Michael and Robert. Ethel, again the Iron Maiden with a heart of stone, told her mother and brother, "Don't mention the children. Children are born every day of the week."

On Mother's Day, May 20th, 1953, communist sympathizers handed out pamphlets on the street corners of New York City and throughout America in protest of the Rosenbergs' approaching execution. Lee Harvey Oswald, then a 14-year-old boy, received one of these pamphlets. He would later tell a Moscow reporter that, "this marked the beginning of his interest in socialist literature." Oswald said he read the pamphlet and soon became a self-described "lifelong Marxist."

The low point in Bloch's crusade to save the Rosenbergs was when the two Rosenberg sons, Robert and Michael, were seen picketing outside Sing Sing Prison, carrying signs that read, "Don't kill my mommy and daddy."

On May 26th, 1953, the Supreme Court of the United States refused for the third time to grant a hearing to the Rosenbergs. Likewise, the Supreme Court directed the New York Court of Appeals to vacate its stay of execution for the Rosenbergs, which it had granted in February. The Rosenbergs had been previously scheduled to die on March 9th. Seven justices favored denying the appeal, while two justices, Hugo L. Black and William O. Douglas, held the opposing view. The Supreme Court also left it to Judge Kaufman to set a new execution date.

In a separate action, the Supreme Court also refused, for the second time, a hearing for Morton Sobell.

However, the Justice Department let it be known to Bloch and the Rosenbergs that any information the Rosenbergs could give the government about other Russian spies and their activities would be "more important to the government than their (the Rosenbergs') execution."

On February 11th, 1953, the Rosenbergs were denied clemency by President Dwight D. Eisenhower. The President's formal statement said, "The betrayal of the Rosenbergs in giving atomic secrets to Russia could bring death to many American citizens."

However, in a letter to his son, John, who was serving in the military in Korea, Eisenhower expounded on his feelings.

The president wrote, "It goes against the grain to avoid interfering in a case where a woman is to receive capital punishment. But Ethel Rosenberg has obviously been the leader in everything they did in that spy ring. And if there would be any commuting a woman's sentence without the man's, then from here on, the Soviets would simply recruit their spies from among women."

Nevertheless, even after clemency had been shot down by the President of the United States, the Justice Department again told Bloch that any information the Rosenbergs would give the government concerning Soviet activities in America would be considered in another request of clemency to President Eisenhower.

Still, Bloch would not give in to any of the United States government's demands. He told the press, "We still have a lot of water to swim before we're through in the courts."

On May 30th, Judge Kaufman, for the fourth time, set a date for the execution of the Rosenbergs - the week of June 15th, 1953.

On June 17th, the Polish Embassy in New York City told the United States government that Poland would accept the Rosenbergs as citizens if "the United States would lift the death sentence and permit the Rosenbergs to go to that country."

The United States' silence on that matter spoke volumes.

On July 17th, Supreme Court Justice William O. Douglas unilaterally granted the Rosenbergs a stay of execution (they were set to be executed on July 18th).

However, his fellow Supreme Court members would have none of that.

The Supreme Court was called back into session, and at noon on July 19th, they vacated the Douglas stay for execution. The Supreme Court set the time of execution for 8 p.m. that very night.

Julius Rosenberg was the first to take the long walk from his cell to the electric chair. He was selected to go first, since, if his wife went first, she would have to pass Julius's cell, and that could cause a scene.

The execution room was small and square, with four rows of seats, like pews in a church, which were placed in front the electric chair itself, which was set on wheels.

A few minutes before 7 p.m., the party of official witnesses entered the "death chamber." All were somber, and some looked like they would rather be anyplace else in the world than in this stifling room.

At exactly 7:02 p.m., a voice was heard in the corridor outside. In seconds, Rabbi Irving Koslowe entered the execution room; his head down. He was reading a black religious book. Rabbi Koslowe wore black robes with a white shawl, and a rabbinical hat sat straight on his head.

The rabbi droned the worlds for the 23rd Psalm: "The Lord is my shepherd. I shall not want…"

Julius Rosenberg entered right behind the rabbi, accompanied by two guards. He wore brown pants, a white shirt, and low slippers without heels. Rosenberg's face was blank. His mustache had been shaved off and his eyeglasses removed. Without being asked, Rosenberg sat down in the hot seat. Rabbi Koslowe moved to the left, next to the spectator benches. The rabbi kept praying softly, and when he was finished, he kissed the black book, twice.

While black straps were fastened around his chest, a black helmet was placed over Rosenberg's head with an electrode attached to it. Another electrode was placed against his right leg (Rosenberg's pants had been slit, leaving his right leg bare from the knee down).

The guards stepped away from the chair, and the warden motioned to the executioner, Joseph Francelli. Francelli pulled down a large black lever, and a metallic rumble, like marbles running down a washboard, permeated the room.

Rosenberg's chest bulged; straining against the straps. His fists were clenched in tight knots, and his neck and shoulders turned bright red. Rosenberg was hit with three massive surges of electricity. The first lasted only three seconds, but the second and the third jolt each lasted 57 seconds.

Francelli flipped the lever up, and the rumbling suddenly stopped.

Two guards rushed to the electric chair and unbuckled the straps. Dr. H.W. Kipp and Dr. George McCracken, both holding stethoscopes, bent over Rosenberg's limp body and listened for a heartbeat.

It was Dr. Kipp who told the warden, "I pronounce this man dead."

Julius Rosenberg's execution had lasted less than three minutes.

As Rosenberg's body was lifted onto a white table and wheeled from the room, Rabbi Koslowe exited the death chamber, and he went to Ethel Rosenberg's jail cell. Rabbi Koslowe told Ethel that her husband was gone, but that she could still save herself if she would give the government information about Soviet spies and Soviet espionage in America.

"I have nothing to say," Ethel told the rabbi.

At 7:10 p.m., Rabbi Koslowe entered the death chamber again, followed by Ethel Rosenberg; her hair cropped short brown.

According to reports in the local press, "She wore a green shapeless dress, with a small white pattern. It had no belt. The sleeves were short, and the neckline was high and round. She also wore slipper-type shoes."

Two women had followed Ethel Rosenberg into the death chamber. One was identified as Mrs. Helen Evan, a prison matron;

the other, Mrs. Lucy Many, a former prison matron and now a telephone operator.

Before she could be seated, Ethel Rosenberg spun away from the electric chair and outstretched both hands to Mrs. Evans. Mrs. Evan took Ethel's hands, and the women embraced. They exchanged words, but no one in the room could hear what they had said to each other. Later, when asked by the press, Mrs. Evans could only remember saying goodbye.

Ethel sat down in the electric chair, and like her husband, the black helmet was placed over her head and electrodes run down her right leg. Ethel closed her eyes, and she winced slightly as the electrode was set onto the helmet on her head.

After she was fully secured to the chair, and as the rabbi continued his prayers, the executioner threw the lever again.

Ethel Rosenberg had stretched out her arms along the arms of the chair; palms up, and as the hot juice jolted her body, her upward palms transformed into tight fists. Ethel received the same jolts of electricity as had her husband: one three-second jolt and two 57-second jolts. When the same two doctors checked her body, unlike her husband; Ethel Rosenberg was still alive.

The warden ordered the executioner to give the dying woman two more jolts; each 57 seconds long. When Dr. Kipp was finished with his second examination of Ethel Rosenberg, he turned to the warden, and said, "I pronounce this woman dead."

Ethel Rosenberg's execution had lasted five minutes; two minutes longer than her husband's. She was the first woman executed by the United States Government since 1865, when Mary Surratt was hanged for her role in the assassination of President Abraham Lincoln. Ethel and Julius Rosenberg were buried at Wellwood Cemetery in Pinelawn, New York.

One of the reporters present at the execution was noted newsman Bob Considine, feature writer for the Hearst-owned International News Service, the precursor to the United Press International (UPI).

After the Rosenbergs' execution, Considine wrote, "They gave off different grotesque mannerisms. When he entered the execution chamber, Julius Rosenberg didn't seem to have too much life left in him. She died a lot harder. And when she meets her maker, she'll have a lot of explaining to do."

While his sister and brother-in-law were being executed, David Greenglass was still serving his time at the Lewisburg Federal Prison in Pennsylvania. Although most of the country, if not the world, considered Greenglass a despicable rat for informing on his sister, Ethel, Greenglass's mother, Tessie, and his brother, Bernie, felt quite different.

Five days after the Rosenbergs' execution, Greenglass received a letter written by Bernie, who had done so at the urging of their mother, Tessie.

The letter read, in part:

It's been a long time since you've heard directly from me, but at the present time I feel a few lines representing the views of the family, and mom in particular, will straighten out any doubts you may have.

To begin with, we feel you did the proper thing; whereas Eth and Julie did not. They not only did a disservice to the country, but from a more personal viewpoint, they put their children in a most horrible situation.

Then too, they were willing to trade yours and your family's lives for their stinking principles, but only succeeded in forfeiting their own, by insisting they were absolutely blameless; the victims of a government frame-up, spearheaded by you and Ruthie.

Don't lose any sleep over them. For although I don't think they deserved what they got, nevertheless, they were the masters of their own fate, and could have saved themselves, to say nothing of the heartaches they could have spared all their families and friends through the last 2 ½ years."

*****

While their parents were being executed, the two Rosenberg sons, Michael and Robert, were being cared for by family friends at a farm in Toms River, New Jersey. The older son, Michael, spent the day watching the Yankees-Tigers baseball game on television. After the game, he played catch until sunset. Then Michael went indoors with the older people, who were sitting mesmerized by the radio, listening to updates concerning the Rosenbergs' execution.

After his parents' fate was sealed, Michael, only 10, issued a statement to reporters waiting outside the New Jersey home.

The statement said, "You can quote me. The judges of the future will look upon this case with great shame."

For the next several decades, the Rosenberg sons, now Michael and Robert Meeropol (they were adopted by the writer and songwriter, Abel Meeropol and his wife Anne, and took their last name) were adamant their parents had been wrongly executed by the government. They insisted their mother had not been a spy, but had been framed by her brother, David Greenglass, and that she should have never been prosecuted, let alone executed.

However, Russian communist leader, Nikita Khrushchev, said in his 1990 posthumously published autobiography, that he, "cannot specifically say what kind of help the Rosenbergs provided us," but that he learned from Russian dictator Joseph Stalin and Old Bolshevik leader Vyacheslav Molotov that the Rosenbergs "had provided very significant help in accelerating the production of our atomic bomb."

In Khrushchev's third and final volume of *Khrushchev Remembers*, Khrushchev said of the Rosenbergs, "Let this be a worthy tribute to the memory of those people. Let my words serve as an expression of gratitude to those who sacrificed their lives to the great cause of the Soviet state at a time when the United States was using its advantage over our state to blackmail our state and to undermine its proletarian cause."

On September 12, 2008, Morton Sobell finally broke his silence about his involvement with the Rosenbergs.

In answer to the question "Were you a Russian spy?" Sobell told the *New York Times*, "Yeah, yeah, yeah, call it that. I never thought of it in those terms. Now, I know it was an illusion. I was taken in (by the Soviets)."

Sobell still hedged in admitting he had done the United States any harm.

"What I did was simply defensive: an aircraft gun," Sobell said. "You cannot plead that what you did was only defensive stuff, but there's a big difference between giving that and stuff that could be used to attack our country."

When asked if Julius Rosenberg had also been a spy, Sobell said, "His intentions might have been to be a spy."

However, it was Sobell's contention that Ethel Rosenberg had been much less culpable than her husband.

"She (Ethel) knew what he (Julius) was doing," Sobell said, "But what was she guilty of; of being Julius's wife?"

After Sobell's admissions in the *New York Times*, the Rosenbergs' youngest son, Robert Meeropol, told that same newspaper that Sobell's confession was "powerful," and that he "didn't have any reason to doubt Morty."

As far as his father being guilty as charged, Robert Meeropol said, "I've always said that was a possibility. This is certainly evidence that would corroborate that possibility as a reality."

Still, Robert Meeropol said he understood his parents' silence after they were arrested.

"What Julius was asked to do was send his best friends to jail, and he could not do that," Meeropol said. "My parents would have to have made a bigger betrayal to avoid betraying me, and frankly I don't consider myself that important."

*****

Knickerbocker Village (KV), a state-subsidized housing development with over 1500 apartments, has gone through several transformations since the time of the Rosenbergs. In 1951, when the Rosenbergs were arrested, KV residents were mostly Jewish. After the Jews moved out of KV (the 1950s-1960s), Italians-Americans and Irish-Americans, both heavily Catholic, moved into KV. Starting in the early 1980s Chinese from nearby Chinatown moved in whenever anyone else moved out. Now, KV residents are mostly Chinese.

A longtime KV resident (we'll call him Pete) is angry the way the history of KV has been and is now being portrayed by the press.

"Whenever you see or hear about Knickerbocker, in the newspapers, or on television, all you get are stories about all the mob guys who lived in KV throughout the years," Pete said. "It's always 'Mafia this' and 'Mafia that.' But you never hear about the Rosenbergs. Why? Mob guys only kill each other, but what the Rosenbergs did affected the lives of every American; whether they served in future wars, or members of their families served in future wars, or even if they only knew somebody who served in future wars.

"Still, the media is obsessed with the so-called 'Mafia,' and that's what they shove down our throats. The real 'dirty little secret' of Knickerbocker Village is the Rosenbergs. But you'll never hear that from the media, which is mostly far-left anyway."

Another longtime KV resident (we'll call her Andrea) recalled when the Rosenbergs were arrested and when they were executed.

"I was only a kid at the time, maybe 10-11 years old, but I clearly remember what happened, even after the Rosenbergs were executed," Andrea said. "Knickerbocker was sharply divided as to the Rosenbergs' guilt. Most of the Jews thought they were not guilty and were being framed by the government. Most of the non-Jews thought the Rosenbergs were guilty as sin, and they got what they deserved."

It is also clear that after the Rosenbergs had been arrested, Jews began moving out of Knickerbocker Village in droves.

The question is why.

"I think the reason is pretty simple," Pete said. "It was no secret that from the time Knickerbocker was built in the mid-1930s, it was mainly comprised of people, mostly Jewish, who were either members of American communist groups, or communist sympathizers. When the Rosenbergs were arrested and exposed, several left-leaning KV residents, some of them card-carrying members of the American Communist Party, were afraid they would be arrested too; so they flew the coop. Other Jews were ashamed one of their own kind could do so much damage to the United States. So, those people left too; moving to places like Brighton Beach and Manhattan Beach in Brooklyn. Some moved all the way out to Long Island and some to New Jersey; anything to get away from Knickerbocker Village, which had so many bad memories for them."

Pete and Angela feel basically the same about the Rosenbergs' punishment.

"Julius Rosenberg was a crumb of a man; the worst kind of human being," Pete said. "I knew people who knew him, and they all said he was a jerk with an attitude and not very bright.

"But make no mistake about it, Julius Rosenberg got what he deserved. And, knowing what we know now; how much more he was involved in Russian espionage than we originally thought he was in the early 1950s, if it were possible, I'd dig up Julius Rosenberg right now and execute him again. As for Ethel, they (the government) went overboard. She should have gotten some jail time, but not the electric chair."

Angela also knew people who were acquainted with both Rosenbergs.

"From what I heard, Ethel was much different than Julius, who was a real bum," Angela said. "He was a traitor to his country, and I'm glad he got executed. But most people I spoke to actually liked Ethel. She was a little shrill and bossy, but so were a lot of women in Knickerbocker; Jewish, Irish, and Italians. So she fit right in with the crowd.

"But there's one thing everyone agreed on; Ethel was the boss of that family. There was no way Julius did what he did without Ethel's knowledge, and most importantly - her approval. Ethel knew what her husband was doing, and maybe, considering her past with the American Communist Party, she even helped her husband in dealing with the Russians. But truthfully, there is no hard proof I have ever heard about that would confirm her involvement (with the Russians). It was just common sense; putting two and two together. It sounded bad for her, but still, I don't think she should have been executed. Prison – yes. But the chair - absolutely not."

*****

Author's note:

As Naval Air Vietnam veteran (1966-72), and a 33-year resident of Knickerbocker Village (1963-1996), it pains me more than most people to contemplate the damage Julius Rosenberg did to the United States of America and to people close to me (uncles and cousins of mine served in both the Korean War and the Vietnam War). The thought that Julius Rosenberg could have been, in any way responsible for the North Koreans and the North Vietnamese improving their weaponry, plainly pisses me off.

So yes, Julius Rosenberg got what he deserved; in spades.

However, I agree with Angela and Pete regarding Ethel Rosenberg, who should not have been executed based on the best evidence we now have (not speculation).

If David Greenglass, who admitted to stealing atom bomb specs and then cooperated with the government, got a 15-year jail sentence, and Martin Sobell received a 30-year jail sentence, Ethel Rosenberg should have gotten something in line with what Greenglass received; maybe even less. With good behavior, Ethel could have gotten out in 5-10 years, and she would have been able to see her young sons grow into men.

Ethel Rosenberg may not have been an active Russian spy. And maybe she was, or was not, the puppeteer behind the scenes pulling Julius Rosenberg's strings. But that is all speculation; with the majority of the concrete evidence suggesting she was not.

However, Ethel Rosenberg was, without a doubt, no matter how much the Meeropol sons rhapsodize about her virtues, a despicable mother for willfully abandoning her sons.

Most people I know would consider the latter offense a much more serious offense than the former.

THE END

*****

I hope you enjoyed reading this book as much as I enjoyed writing it. If you want to be added to my email list, email me at jbruno999@aol.com.

*****

Bonus Book!

MOBSTERS, GANGS, CROOKS, AND OTHER CREEPS – VOLUME 1 – NEW YORK CITY

By Joe Bruno
PUBLISHED BY:

Knickerbocker Literary Services

EDITED BY:
Marc A. Maturo and Lawrence Venturato

*****

What people are saying about "Mobsters, Gangs, Crooks, and Other Creeps – Volume 1 – New York City."

Great Books for a true crime fix!!! - RJ Parker- Best Selling Author/Publicist

If you're a mobster fan, this is the book for you! - Desmond Gill

Great Read!!!!! Short and informed information about early NY. Criminals and history -- Efrain Perez

I absolutely loved this book. In fact I could not put it down. As the title describes, when I finished it I really felt as if I just took an introductory course on this subject - Eponym

A very interesting book with even more colorful characters - Mrs. Brady

If you liked "Gangs of New York, if you liked "The Godfather," you must read all three books - Rony Barbery.

*****

Product Information

I have been a criminal defense lawyer for 34 years, specializing in organized crime cases. Like Joe Bruno, I was born in New York City's Little Italy. My first residence was 146 Mulberry Street on top of Angelo's Restaurant. At the age of six, I moved a mile south to the Lower East Side to a place called Knickerbocker Village, which borders the East River, and is located between the historic Manhattan Bridge and the majestic world-famous Brooklyn Bridge.

Like Joe Bruno, I lived in Knickerbocker Village for more than three decades. Our neighborhood was filled with unforgettable characters, most of whom were criminals, and many of whom were in the Mafia. Joe got to meet and see many famous criminals during his years in Little Italy, and in Knickerbocker Village. It is no surprise to me that he was fascinated not only with the mafia characters, but with the entire history of Lower Manhattan, and New York City in general.

His book, " Mobsters, Gangs, Crooks and Other Creeps-Volume 1- New York City" is a composite of characters and events, that weaves the denizens of the underworld with the rich history of New York City, from the early 1800's, through the early 1900's. Although Italian-American criminals are covered, this is not just another mafia book. The book covers the Jewish gangsters as well (who truly were the pioneers of organized crime) and the Irish gangs, who were one of the first ethnic groups to run the New York City rackets. Joe even presents a few "lady gangsters" too.

Most of all, " Mobsters, Gangs, Crooks and Other Creeps-Volume 1- New York City" is easy to read. The short-chapter format is a stroke of genius. It is interesting, informative, entertaining, and to the point. You won't be bored reading it.

Joe Bruno has hit the mark in presenting Old New York the way it really was. Rough and bloody!

######

Ah Hoon - The Murder of Chinese Comedian Ah Hoon

Sometimes a comedian can be dead funny, but after one of his onstage performances, Chinese comedian Ah Hoon turned up quite dead instead.

The Tong Wars started in Chinatown in 1899, with the powerful On Leong Tong dominating the gambling and drug interests in downtown Manhattan. The smaller Hip Sing and the Four Brothers Tongs joined forces and engaged in violent confrontations with the On Leong Tong, over the rights to control Chinatown's illegal activities. Almost daily, dead bodies littered the streets of Chinatown, which at the time only consisted of Mott Street, Pell Street, Chatham Square, and Doyers Street.

Ah Hoon was a famous Chinese comedian, who was featured often at the Chinese Theater at 5-7 Doyers Street, right in the middle of the Tong War Zone. The Chinese Theater was a venue, not only for the Chinese, but for English speaking audiences who were brave enough to venture into an area where gunpowder permeated the air. Ah Hoon was an associate of the On Leong Tong, and the content of his jokes, in which he constantly disparaged the Hip Sing and Four Brothers Tongs, made it seem like he thought he was bullet-proof.

Things started to get hairy for Ah Hoon, when the Reverend Huie Kim, the pastor of the Christian Morning Star Mission on Doyers Street, warned Ah Hoon that his jokes were not too funny with certain people. The good reverend also told Ah Hoon that Ah Hoon could get badly hurt if he kept telling his jokes on stage, where hundreds of people could hear the many indignities he spewed disparaging the Hip Sing and Four Brothers Tongs.

Ah Hoon thumbed his nose at the Reverend Huie Kim, and as a result, the Hip Sing and Four Brothers Tongs formally declared war on the On Leong Tong. Instead of holding back, Ah Hoon stepped up the frequency and the ferocity of his jokes on stage. This thoroughly annoyed the Hip Sing and Four Brothers Tongs, so they announced publicly that they were going to kill Ah Hoon. To make sure Ah Hoon got the message, they sent an emissary to Ah Hoon, giving him the exact time and date he was going to be murdered.

Ah Hoon took the threat with a shrug. But it was Hoochy-Coochy Mary, who lived on the floor below Ah Hoon, in a boarding house on Chatham Square, who ran to the police and begged them to protect the comedian. On December 30, 1909, Police Sergeant John D. Coughlin and two patrolmen accompanied Ah Hoon to his performance at the Chinese Theater. Word had spread quickly on the streets of Chinatown that Ah Hoon was scheduled to be murdered, and as a result, the theater was packed with people hoping to see a live execution for the price of a simple theater admission. Standing-room-only tickets were also sold out, and there was a huge crowd outside, not too happy at being turned away from witnessing Ah Hoon's dramatic demise.

Seeing the police presence, inside and outside the theater, the Hip Sing Tong decided to back away from their word, and at the end of the show, Ah Hoon, to the chagrin of the crowd, was still alive and joking. Sergeant Coughlin and his two underlings hustled Ah Hoon out of the theater, through a hidden underground tunnel, to his dwelling on Chatham Square. Ah Hoon climbed the stairs of his building, entered his room and locked the door. A group of heavily-armed On Leong bodyguards stood guard outside Ah Hoon's door, while dozens milled in the street outside his building looking for any impending attack. Ah Hoon went to sleep that night, but he did not wake up the following morning.

Hoochy-Coochy Mary heard a shot in the middle of the night, and she ran upstairs to alert the On Leong bodyguards. When they broke through the door, they found Ah Hoon dead on his bed with a bullet hole in his chest. What made the matter all the more vexing was that there was only one window in Ah Hoon's room and it faced a blank building wall five feet away.

The solution to Ah Hoon's death was quite simple and complicated at the same time.

So they wouldn't be seen by the On Leong bodyguards, the Hip Sing assassins had slipped into a tenement several buildings down from Ah Hoon's building. They climbed the stairs to the roof, then they jumped across three roofs to the roof of the building next to Ah Hoon's building. There they lowered the killer on a boatswain's chair tied to a rope, down the narrow alley, until he was parallel to Ah Hoon's window. The killer then quietly entered Ah Hoon's room and shot the Chinese comedian right through the heart. The deed being done, the killer exited the room in the same manner in which he had entered.

The Hip Sing Tong was so overjoyed at the success of their mission, they held a parade the next day in the streets of Chinatown, complete with fireworks, ancestral music, and the dancing of the mythical Chinese dragons.

On New Year's night 1910, two days after the murder of Ah Hoon, the Chinese Theater was packed to the rafters again. In the middle of the performance, someone threw several packs of lit firecrackers into the air. People panicked, and they fled the theater quickly; except for five On Leong Tong members who were shot dead during the distraction of the fireworks.

No one was arrested for their murders, and the Tong Wars continued for another generation.

Allen, John

He was a con artist, a drunk, a murderer, and a pimp, and he ran one of the most obscene dance halls in the history of New York City. For all his vast transgressions, John Allen was dubbed "The Wickedest Man in New York City."

John Allen, the youngest of eight sons, was born in 1823 in upstate New York. His father was a prominent Presbyterian minister, and two of Allen's brothers became Presbyterian ministers too, while a third became a Baptist minister. The rest of his brothers absconded to New York City and became burglars, crooks, and confidence men.

Allen's father sent him to the Union Theological Seminary, hoping young John would pick the righteous path rather than the wicked road his brothers had traveled in New York City. Allen studied religion for a few months. But wanting more out of life, he packed his bags and joined his evil siblings in downtown Manhattan.

Allen's brothers showed him the tricks of their trade, and in no time Allen became proficient at the crimes his brothers had taught him. One day, one of his brothers became suspicious of Allen, when he realized the police in the area seemed to know, in advance, what crime they were going to commit, and where and when they were going to commit it. His brothers accused Allen of being a stool-pigeon. Allen reluctantly admitted they were right, which induced his brothers to beat him to a pulp, then cast him out into the street, never again to return.

In 1855, after freelance thievery earned him a significant sum of cash, Allen met and married a known criminal named Little Suzie. Little Suzie's specialty was rolling drunks, after she seduced them with sex, and then put knockout drops in their drinks. While Little Suzie plied her trade in the waterfront district of the 4th Ward, which included Cherry, Water, Dover, and Catherine Streets, Allen got a job working for a waterfront crimp who ran a boarding house for sailors.

Allen's job was to entice sailors into the crimp's establishment, where they would get the sailor drunk, then drug his drink. When their mark was out cold, they robbed him of all his possessions. Then Allen and his boss would carry the unconscious sailor to an outgoing vessel, in which the sailor was shanghaied to faraway places, where he would spend several months, if not several years, in servitude.

One day, Allen was dumb enough to have a drink with his boss. And the next thing he knew, Allen was on a ship to South America, not to return to New York City for six months. After Allen's return, his former boss was soon found beaten to death, courtesy of an iron belaying-pin, which was a device used on ships to secure lines of rigging. Allen was the obvious suspect, but since the cops had no evidence, and also because the dead man was so intensely disliked by everyone on both sides of the law, no charges were ever brought against Allen.

Allen reconnected with Little Suzie, and they went to work for Hester Jane Haskins, called "Jane the Grabber," a monster-of-a-woman, who ran several houses of ill-repute in the area surrounding Sixth Avenue and 30th Street, in the middle of what was called Satan's Circus.

Allen's and Suzie's gig was to travel throughout the northeastern states and fetch young girls, with the promise of getting them well-paying jobs in New York City. Of course, when these poor girls were introduced to "Jane the Grabber," Jane immediately beat them and drugged them, then forced them to work as prostitutes in her brothels.

This all went fine for Allen and Little Suzy until "Jane the Grabber" got greedy and started abducting women from prominent families, including the daughter of the Lieutenant-Governor of a New England state. Knowing heat from the police was inevitable, Allen and Little Suzie quit their jobs for "Jane the Grabber," and headed back to the confines of the 4th Ward. That turned out to be good timing for them, since "Jane the Grabber" was soon arrested for her crimes and sent to prison for a very long time.

In 1858, the Allens opened John Allen's Dance Hall, at 304 Water Street, which became known as one of the most licentious establishments in New York City. Allen dressed his 20 or so "dance hall girls" in short skirts and red-topped boots, with sleigh-bells circling their ankles. All sorts of vices and sexual obscenities were performed in private rooms in the dive, and sometimes right out in the open. These actions were so visibly decadent, journalist Oliver Dyer wrote in *Packard's Monthly*, that John Allen was "The Wickedest Man in New York City."

Allen was so proud of his new moniker he made up business cards, saying:

John Allen's Dance Hall

304 Water Street

Wickedest Man in New York:

Proprietor

John Allen's Dance Hall was so prosperous, in just 10 years Allen banked more than $100,000, making him the richest pimp in New York City.

Soon, Allen came up with a new angle to make even more money. Falling back on his seminary background, Allen decided to turn his dance hall into a semi-religious experience. In spite of the sexual romps that were going on nightly inside his joint, Allen placed a Bible in every room, and on Saturday nights he gave away copies of the New Testament, as souvenirs to his guests. In time, Allen held religious sing-a-longs, in which his scantily-clad girls would croon spiritual songs, while Allen read passages of the Bible. Showing no shame, Allen placed on every bench and table in his joint the popular hymn book, *The Little Wanderer's Friend*.

Yet, Allen's intended monetary windfall never materialized. His usual guests fled his premises and headed for other joints like The Haymarket, McGuirk's Suicide Hall, and Paresis Hall. So Allen decided to go with another gimmick.

Allen turned his dance hall into a place for local clergymen to hold marathon prayer meetings. Religious men, like the Reverend A.C. Arnold, paid Allen $350 a month to hold such meetings in Allen's establishment. Allen even thickened the crowd by paying "newly reformed sinners" 25 cents a head to take part in the festivities. Allen was so certain he would hit the religious jackpot, he closed his dance hall and put a sign on the outside door saying, "This Dance Hall is Closed. No gentlemen admitted unless accompanied by their wives."

Unfortunately, Allen had overlooked the power of the press. In a shocking expose', the *New York Times* ran a series of stories exposing Allen in the worst possible light. Immediately, the duped reverends stopped holding their prayer meetings at Allen's joint, causing his cash flow to disintegrate.

Allen tried opening his bawdy dance hall again, but his previous customers chose to stay away. After a few months of bleeding money, Allen closed down his dance hall for good.

Allen disappeared from the public eye for a while. Then he resurfaced in late 1868, when Allen and Little Suzie were arraigned in the Tombs Police Court, for stealing $15 from a sailor. The Allens were released on $500 bail, which they promptly jumped, then fled to places unknown.

"The Wickedest Man In New York City" died from causes unknown in West Perth, Fulton County, New York, in October 1870.

After Allen's death, a *New York Times* reporter revealed for the first time Allen's true intentions when he appeared to go all pious. Years earlier, Allen had confessed to the reporter, "I duped them religious fellers because I thought I could make more money out of silly church folk, than I could out of bad sailors."

Anti-Abolition Riots of 1834

It started as a peaceful service given by a black minister at the Chatham Street Chapel, but it transformed into four days of riots that turned the streets of New York City into a cauldron of hate.

In the early 1800's, there was a vibrant movement in the United States to end slavery. Yet, there was no other place in the country that displayed more animosity towards blacks than the mean streets of Manhattan's Lower East Side. The Abolitionist Movement (to abolish slavery) was spearheaded by men like William Lloyd Garrison, and bothers Arthur and Lewis Tappan. Yet, the hatred for black slaves permeated throughout New York City and was incited by the ruling Irish faction of Tammany Hall. This malevolence was punctuated by a multitude of atrocities, perpetrated against the slaves by the Irish Five Points street gangs, which Tammany Hall overtly protected from prosecution for their heinous crimes.

In 1833, aided by the fiery speeches of William Lloyd Garrison, slavery was abolished throughout the British Empire. Many of the Brits living in America also spoke out vociferously against slavery. This did not go over too well with the powers that be at Tammany Hall, which had convinced the Irish street gangs that the Abolitionists were looking to transform America back into a British colony.

Anti-Abolitionist James Watson Webb provoked the Irish gangs even further, when he printed in his *Courier and Enquirer* that, "Abolitionists had told their daughters to marry blacks, black dandies in search of white wives were promenading Broadway on horseback, and Arthur Tappan had divorced his wife and married a negress."

All Webb's statements were lies, but they were believed by the rabble nevertheless.

On July 7, 1834, a group of black slaves gathered in the Chatham Street Chapel to hear a sermon by a black minister. In the audience, lending his support, was Arthur Tappan. The sermon had just begun, when members of the New York Sacred Music Society broke in, claiming they had rented the chapel for the evening. The slaves, who had already paid for the use of the chapel, refused to leave. The street gangs, with members of the Plug Uglies, Forty Thieves, and Roach Guards, banded together and attacked the slaves with leaded canes, seriously injuring several slaves.

An angry mob had formed outside the chapel, and as the police arrived to try to quell the disturbance, Tappan hurried from the scene to his house on Rose Street, which is now the site of the New York City Municipal Building. Knowing he was an avowed abolitionist, a crowd followed Tappan, and as he rushed inside, they pelted his home with rocks.

Webb's paper predictably lied again, when he described the event as a "Negro riot," owing to "Arthur Tappan's mad impertinence." *The Commercial Advertiser*, another pro-slavery rag, said, "Gangs of blacks were preparing to set the city ablaze."

This was just the beginning of a string of atrocities. The next night, a mob of gang members broke down the door of the Chatham Street Chapel. And while they held an impromptu meeting inside, W.W. Wilder yelled, "To the Bowery Theater!"

The reason for their attack on the Bowery Theater was because its manager, and British actor, George P. Farren, another avowed abolitionist, had recently said of the pro-slavery crowd, "Damn the Yankees; they are a damn set of jackasses, and fit to be gulled."

Farren had also just fired an American actor, and as a result, anti-abolitionists posted handbills, detailing Farren's actions, throughout New York City.

An estimated 4000 rioters broke down the doors of the Bowery Theater, interrupting the performance of beloved American actor Edwin Forrest, who was a favorite of the Five Point gangs. Forrest tried to quiet the angry mob, but they insisted on knowing the whereabouts of Farren, who was hiding somewhere on the premises. Before the mob could take the place apart looking for Farren, with the intention of hanging him, a large contingent of police officers arrived and drove the mob from the theater with billy clubs.

Still, the mob was not through. They yelled, "To Arthur Tappan's house!"

Tappan and his family had already escaped before the mob showed up. Yet, when the mob did arrive, they tore down Tappan's house, board by board. They also piled Tappan's furniture into the street, and set it on fire until there was nothing left but a painting of George Washington.

As one rioter tried to throw the Washington painting into the fire, another one ripped it from his hands saying, "It's George Washington! For God's sake, don't burn Washington!"

The mob rampaged through the city, torturing and raping black slaves and even gouging out the eyes of an Englishman, after they had ripped off his ears. The worst rioting was in the Five Points area, where dozens of houses, including St. Phillip's Church, were burned to the ground. Several English sailors and black slaves were captured and mutilated. Word soon spread in the streets that every house in the Five Points area that did not have a candle burning in its window would be burned down. In minutes, candles appeared in every window; saving the neighborhood from destruction at the hands of the out-of-control racist lunatics.

On the afternoon of July 11, Mayor Cornelius Lawrence issued a proclamation asking all good citizens to band together to stop the rioting. He also ordered Major General Shadford to call in the 27th Regiment of the National Guard Infantry. At 9 p.m., around 300 Five Point Gang members assembled before the Laight Street Church, which was run by vocal abolitionist Reverend Samuel Hanson Cox. The church was guarded by several New York City policemen, but the mob charged anyway, forcing the outmanned policemen to run for their lives.

As the mob destroyed the church, Mayor Lawrence ordered the infantry into action. Armed with clubs, bayonets, muskets, and pistols, the infantry drove the rioters from several downtown churches, and the surrounding streets, back into the Five Points area.

The next day, armed soldiers and policemen scoured the Five Points, looking for known mob members. They rounded up and arrested 150 Five Pointers, but then, inexplicably, Tammany Hall stepped in and released almost all of them.

Only 20 gang members, out of the thousands who pillaged the streets of New York City in July of 1834, were ever tried, convicted, and sent to jail.

Astor Place Theater Riots of 1849

One of the worst riots in New York City history took place on May 10, 1849. It started over an impassioned disagreement over who had the better Shakespearian Actor: the United States, or hated Mother England.

British actor William Macready was considered to be the most accomplished actor on both sides of the pond. Yet Macready, who called himself an aristocrat, was a snob, who looked down on America in general and their inferior actors in particular. One of those actors who caused Macready to sniff in superiority was the Philadelphia-born Edwin Forrest, a self-taught thespian, who was the darling of the rough and tumble New York City crowd. To make matters worse for Forrest and his followers, the New York City aristocracy much preferred the foreigner Macready instead of the homegrown Forrest.

In 1848, Forrest, on a mission to prove to the world that he was the equal of any actor alive, traveled to London, England, to play Hamlet. Even though Forrest dined with Macready the night before Forrest's performance, when Forrest took the stage he was brutally hissed by the audience. Forrest's performance was panned viciously in the London newspapers and repeated in the American press. Forrest blamed this on Macready, and by the time Forrest arrived back in the United States, there was a global feud ready to explode.

Two New Yorkers were instrumental in fanning the flames of discontent concerning the rude treatment of their homeboy Forrest in England. One was Captain Isaiah Rynders, who owned the notorious Empire Club on Park Row. Rynders was also the mob boss, who controlled all the vicious gangs in the Five Points area. The other instigator was E. Z. C. Judson, who wrote under the pen name - Ned Buntline. Both men hated the English, and in the weekly newspaper, *Ned Buntline's Own*, Buntline turned a mere heated actors' dispute into an international incident.

The tension mounted, when it was announced in the New York City press that Macready would make a four-week "farewell" appearance in America, commencing on May 7, 1849. His first show was scheduled to be at the new Astor Place Theater, on Astor Place in Manhattan. As soon as Macready graced the stage with his presence, Rynders rose from his seat, and in concert with hundreds of his gang thugs in attendance, they peppered Macready with rotten eggs, ripe tomatoes, and old shoes. Macready, incredulous at the blatant disrespect for his great talents, thundered off the stage. He canceled the rest of his four-week engagement and vowed never to appear in the United States again.

This caused great consternation among the blue-bloods in New York City's society crowd. Quickly, they assembled a petition with 47 signatures, which included those of Washington Irving and Herman Melville, begging

Macready to stay and continue his tour. Macready, against his better judgment, caved in and agreed to give it one more try.

The news hit the newspapers, that on May 10, just three days after he was rudely chased from the stage, Macready would appear as Macbeth in *Macbeth*; again at the Astor Place Theater. Coincidentally, Forrest also opened that same night, playing Spartacus in *The Gladiator*, in a playhouse a mile south of the Astor Place Theater. The newspapers played up the rivalry and the British crew of a docked Cunard liner said they would make their presence known at Macready's performance, lest an unruly American mob again tried to insult their countryman.

This incited Captain Rynders to plaster New York City with thousands of posters saying, *"Workingmen, shall Americans or English rule this city? The crew of the English steamer has threatened all Americans who shall dare to express their opinion this night at the English Aristocratic Opera House! We advocated no violence, but free expression of opinion is to all men!"*

New York City mayor Caleb C. Woodhull anticipated a riot, and he sent 350 policemen, under the command of Police Chief G.W. Matsell, to the Astor Place Theater to quell any possible disturbances. In addition, General Sanders, of the New York Militia, assembled eight companies of guardsmen and two troops of Calvary to patrol the area around the playhouse.

When the show started, all 1,800 seats had been sold, with the pro-Macready crowd vastly outnumbering the pro-Forrest crowd. It was estimated that more than 20,000 people stood outside the theater, making Astor Place, from Broadway to the Bowery, one large sea of discontent.

At 7:40 p.m., the play started, and the first two scenes played out without any interruption. However, when Macready majestically strode on stage for the third scene, all hell broke loose. Captain Rynders and his gangs hooted and hollered and hissed at Macready. Outside, the angry crowd, hearing the animosity inside, started to bum-rush the theater. They threw rocks and stones, breaking all the theater's windows. And just because they could, the mob smashed all the street lamps in the area too.

The police attacked the angry mob with clubs, but to no avail. The mob screamed "Burn the damned den of aristocracy."

The police were getting the worst of the riot, and at 9 p.m., the first of the militia arrived. They too were pelted by bricks and stones. Ned Buntline was at the head of the angry mob chanting, "Workingmen! Shall Americans or Englishmen rule? Shall the sons whose fathers drove the baseborn miscreants from these shores give up liberty?"

Chief Matsell, after being hit with a 20-pound rock in the chest, gave the order for the militia to shoot into the crowd. And they did just that, hitting men, women, and children, and even a lady who was sleeping in her bed 150 yards from the theater.

When the dust cleared hours later, 22 people were killed and 150 were injured. Five of those who were injured, died within five days. 86 rioters were arrested, including Ned Buntline, who received a year in jail and a $250 fine. Captain Rynders escaped without arrest, or injury, only to torment the city for many years to come.

The lawmen were not without their own injuries. More than a hundred policemen and militia were injured by rocks and stones, and another six were shot; but none died.

The next night, another mob tried to burn down the Astor Place Theater. But they were beaten back by a new battalion of militia, which had been brought into the city in case of further disturbances.

On the night of May 12, another crowd assembled at the New York Hotel, where Macready was staying, screaming for him to come out and be hanged like a man. However, Macready somehow slipped away. He boarded a train to New Rochelle, and then to Boston. From Boston, he sailed to England, never again to set foot in America.

Bow Kum -- The Vicious Killing of Bow Kum

In 1899, the Tong Wars began in New York City's Chinatown, when the smaller Hip Sing and Four Brothers Tongs joined forces against the powerful On Leong Tong, in a battle for the immense illegal profits generated in Chinatown from gambling and drug dealing. There were sporadic killings throughout the first decade of the 20th Century, but the blood started flowing more rapidly in 1909. It was sparked by the vicious murder of a Chinese slave girl named Bow Kum, known as "The Little Flower."

In the Canton Region of China, Kum was sold by her father for a few paltry yen. She was then brought to the United States where she was sold at the slave-trade market in San Francisco, for the huge sum (at the time) of three thousand dollars. The buyer was Low Hee Tong, a high-ranking member of the Hip Sing and Four Brothers Tongs.

Kum lived with Tong for four years, but then the San Francisco police discovered the illegal servitude. When Tong could not produce a marriage license, Kum was taken away from Tong and placed in a Christian mission run by Donaldina Cameron, a Scotswoman famous for helping young Chinese slave girls escape from the terrible Tongs. Soon, gardener Tchin Lee, a member of the On Leong Tong, married Kum and took her to New York City.

Tong was furious he had lost the services of his female slave, but more furious over the loss of his three thousand dollars. As a result, Tong demanded that Lee give him back the money he spent on purchasing Kum.

Lee refused.

Tong then listed his grievances in a letter to the Hip Sing and Four Brother Tongs in New York City. Tong's Tongs agreed with him, and they demanded that the On Leong Tong force Lee to return Tong's money. Their request was denied, and immediately the Hip Sing and Four Brothers Tongs flew the red flag from their building on Pell Street, indicating they were declaring war against the On Leong Tong.

On August 15, 1909, a Hip Sing assassin broke into Lee's apartment at 17 Mott Street. The assassin stabbed Kum three times in the chest, cut off several of her fingers, and then mutilated her torso. This started a bloody war that resulted in over fifty killings in just a few short months.

In late 1909, Captain William Hodgins, the Commander of the 5th Precinct on Elizabeth Street, interceded, and he tried to make peace between the factions. He approached the On Leong Tong first, and they agreed to end the war, but only if the other two tongs gave them, as reparations, a Chinese flag, a roasted pig, and ten thousand packs of fireworks. The two smaller tongs considered this a huge insult, and the killings intensified for another year.

In late 1910, the United States government became involved. The Chinese Minister, in Washington D.C., appointed a committee of 40 Chinese merchants, teachers, and students to mediate the Tong Wars. An agreement was forged between the On Leong Tong, and the Hip Sing Tongs. However, the Four Brothers Tong refused to participate in the peace. As a result, the killings continued but not at the same pace as before.

Kerosene was thrown on the fire in 1912, when a new Tong, the Kim Lan Wui Saw Tong, suddenly appeared in New York City. In a battle for the illegal buck, these upstarts inexplicably declared war on the other three established Tongs. This was a dumb move, since the three older Tongs, instead of fighting among themselves, turned all their venom on the outmanned Kim Lan Wui Saw Tong.

The bodies continued to pile up in Chinatown, bringing outside business into the area to a halt. Finally, the Chinese government on mainland China, in conjunction with the New York City Police Department, compelled the warring factions to formally agree to halt the hostilities. The treaty was signed on May 22, 1913, by the Chinese Merchant's Association.

Since tourists were no longer afraid to enter Chinatown (and get caught in the cross hairs of the daily gunfire), peace and prosperity returned to the area.

That is, until 1924, when the bloody Tong Wars resumed.

Bowery Boys Street Gang

The Bowery Boys street gang ruled the Bowery area, just north of the Five Points, from 1840 through 1860.

The Bowery Boys were an anti-Catholic, anti-Irish gang, who fought tooth and nail with the other Lower Manhattan gangs, most notably the Dead Rabbits from the Five Points area. Unlike the other gangs of its era, who were predominantly thugs, robbers, and murderers, the Bowery Boys were mostly butchers, mechanics, bar bouncers, or small businessmen. They wore a uniform of sorts, consisting of red shirts, and black trousers; the pants of which were shoved inside their calfskin boots. Most of the men had oil-slicked hair, covered by black stovepipe hats.

The Bowery Boys were ardent volunteer firemen, who aligned themselves with the Know-Nothing, or American Political Party (which lasted from 1849 to 1856) and later the Democratic Party. All of the big politicians of the time, including William "Boss" Tweed and future first United States President George Washington, were at one time volunteer firemen in Lower Manhattan. The Bowery Boys were attached to various firehouses, with names like the White Ghost, Black Joke, Dry Bones, and Red Rover. Each of the other downtown gangs, like the Dead Rabbits, Roach Guards, and the Plug Uglies, were also affiliated with various firehouses too, and the competition over who would arrive first at a fire was fierce and often bloody.

The Bowery Boys were said to love their fire engines almost as much as the loved their women. The worse thing that could happen was to arrive at a fire and find that all the fire hydrants had already been taken by other firehouses. The Bowery Boys often used a scheme to prevent this embarrassment.

As soon as a fire alarm sounded, the biggest Bowery Boy available would grab an empty barrel from a grocery store, and run to the fire plug closest to the burning building. He would turn the barrel over, cover the fire hydrant with the barrel, sit on it, and defend his position, battling men from other firehouses, who were trying to remove him, and the barrel, from the fire hydrant. It was said that the fights for the fire hydrants were so ferocious, the battling volunteer firemen sometimes didn't have enough time to actually extinguish the fires, which caused many buildings to burn to the ground.

The most famous Bowery Boy of his time was "Butcher" Bill Poole, a butcher by trade, and a volunteer at Red Rover Fire Engine Company No. 34, at Hudson and Christopher Streets. Poole was a bare-knuckle fighter of much renown. His arch enemy was John Morrissey, an Irish immigrant and strong-arm-man for Tammany Hall. Morrissey was a prodigious fighter too (he later became World Heavyweight Champion), and he challenged Poole to a bare-knuckles fight. Poole hated the Irish and Catholics with a passion (Morrissey was both), and he gladly accepted the challenge.

On July 26, 1854, the men squared off at the Amos Street Dock, near Christopher Street. After Morrissey extended his hand, in a symbolic gesture to start the fight, Poole feinted, and instead of fighting, he grabbed Morrissey is a frontal bear hug. Poole lifted Morrissey up into the air, and squeezed the breath out of him for a full five minutes. Before Poole could crush Morrissey to death, wiser heads prevailed, and they separated the men. Morrissey was hurt so badly, he couldn't walk the streets of New York City for six months. When he finally did, it was curtains for Poole.

On February 25, 1855, Lew Baker, a friend of Morrissey's, shot Poole at Stanwix Hall, a bar on Broadway, near Prince Street. Poole lingered for a little more than a week, but he finally died on March 8, 1855.

The downfall of the Bowery Boys started during the savage three-day New York City Draft Riots. On July 13, 1863, incensed at the imminent possibility of being drafted into the war down south they wanted nothing to do with, thousands of gang members took to the streets of New York City. These out-of-control maniacs looted and burned down stores, factories, and houses. Then they violently mutilated and killed Negroes, whom they blamed as the cause of their predicament.

The Bowery Boys, in actions normally adverse to their nature, were an integral part of these deadly riots, in which more than a thousand people were killed and thousands injured. The New York State Militia was called in to quell the riots, and when the dust settled three days later, the drafting of New York City men into the armed forces continued, but only for a short time.

Many Bowery Boys were drafted into the war. Some died, some returned badly injured, or missing arms and legs; others joined rival gangs. By the end of the 1860's, the Bowery Boys ceased to exist, but other gangs rose from their ashes, to take their place of ignominy in downtown Manhattan.

Bristol Bill The Burglar

He was a hardened criminal, who escaped from a British prison in Australia and made his way to New York City. In the 1840's, the New York City Police Gazette wrote that Bristol Bill the Burglar was, "the most celebrated bank robber and burglar of our time."

The London police knew his real name, but they never revealed it. However, we do know the following about Bristol Bill:

He was born in the early 1800's, to an aristocratic family, the son of a Bristol MP. When Bristol Bill was in his second year at Eton College, his family adopted a 16-year old orphaned daughter of a poor cleric. Bristol Bill was the handsomest of men; almost 6-feet tall, with piercing brown eyes and a broad forehead. In no time, he had seduced the young girl and got her pregnant. Bristol Bill's father was so outraged when he found out about the young girl's delicate condition, he beat Bristol Bill to a pulp, then banished the girl from his home. His father sent Bristol Bill back to Eton, but Bristol Bill soon located his love, and they both absconded to London.

A child was born, and to pay the bills, Bristol Bill got a job at a local locksmith. Soon, Bristol Bill was so adept at key, lock, and tool making, he started selling his wares to a London Gang called the Blue Boys. The Blue Boys were so successful at burglarizing and bank robbing, they soon made Bristol Bill their leader.

This went on for half a dozen years, until Bristol Bill had accumulated approximately $200,000 in American money. With his newfound riches, and with the police nipping at his heels, Bristol Bill abandoned his wife and child and headed to Liverpool, where he planned to board a ship to America. However, a certain London policeman was on his trail, and this policeman arrested Bristol Bill in Liverpool. This same policeman would eventually play a big part in Bristol Bill's life on the other side of the pond.

After his arrest, Bristol Bill's money was confiscated, and he was sentenced to 14 years in prison at a penal colony in Botany Bay, Australia. After serving 10 years, Bristol Bill escaped by swimming four miles to an American whaler. He first landed in Bedford, Mass., but soon Bristol Bill made his way to New York City, where, at the time, almost all the professional thieves were of British extraction.

Bristol Bill's mission was to hook up with a robbery gang, which was called "the most extensive association of burglars, counterfeiters, and swindlers the Western world has ever seen." The London contingent consisted of such noted "crossmen" (a London term for thieves) as Billy Fish, Billy Hoppy, "Cupid" Downer, Bill Parkinson, Bob Whelan, Jim Honeyman, and Dick Collard. They were joined by two New Yorkers: Joe Ashley, and "One-eye" Thompson.

The brains of the operation was a shady character named Samuel Drury, who was known as a banker and a financier, but was, in fact, a counterfeiter of great renown and a prodigious fence of stolen goods. Whatever his gang robbed, Drury would buy and sell, and keep the majority of the money for himself.

Bristol Bill met a girl named Catherine Davenport, who was an expert sneak-thief and pickpocket. Davenport also worked for Drury as a "koneyacker," or a passer of counterfeit cash. Davenport informed Drury that the famous Bristol Bill was in New York City, and that he wanted to join their operation. When Bristol Bill first met Drury, he thought he looked familiar.

"Were you ever a policeman in London?" Bristol Bill asked Drury.

Drury admitted he had been.

"I knew it!" Bristol Bill said. "You're the same hound that tracked me to Liverpool and had me pinched for 14 years."

Drury told Bristol Bill that he was caught stealing himself, and he had to leave London for New York City. Drury told Bristol Bill, "If you have any grudge against me, you must forget it. I can make you a fortune in this country."

Bristol Bill worked with Drury and his crew for a full four years, robbing banks, valuables, and jewelry, from various places as far away as New Orleans. He even traveled to Montreal, to steal a large quantity of silver plate from the home of the Governor-General of Canada.

Bristol Bill's specialty was making his own burglary tools, and he was the best lock-picker in the entire United States. He once escaped from jail with a key he had made from silver oak. Another time, Bristol Bill opened his cell door with a key he had fashioned from a piece of stove pipe.

Bristol Bill's biggest heist was the robbery of the barge "The Clinton." After opening the ship's safe with a key he had made from a wax impression, Bristol Bill walked away with $32,000 in cash. He kept $10,000 for himself, and sold the rest of the money to Drury for $7,000, which Drury disposed of, little by little, from a bank he owned in upstate New York.

By 1849, Bristol Bill had earned over $400,000 in America, which he spent mostly on his three "wives": one living in Manhattan, one in Brooklyn, and one in New Jersey. The three women were fast friends, and they usually accompanied Bristol Bill on his out-of-town robberies; one posing as his wife and the other two as his sisters.

Living the lush life, Bristol Bill thought it was finally time to exact his revenge on Drury. Bristol Bill knew that Drury had bombed the home of a lawyer with whom Drury had quarreled. Not needing Drury as a fence anymore, Bristol Bill, at the request of the *New York Police Gazette*, provided information to the police about Drury's involvement with the bombing. While Drury and his son, along with One-Eyed Thompson, were in jail awaiting arraignment, the police raided Drury's mansion in Astoria. They found counterfeit plates and thousands of dollars in counterfeit cash.

For his help in nailing Drury, the New York City police gave Bristol Bill a pass. Knowing New York City was not safe for him any longer, Bristol Bill traveled to Vermont with his current squeeze, a former opera singer known only as "Gookin' Peg." Bristol Bill was also accompanied by a counterfeiter named Christian Meadows and a London crook, English Jim.

They leased a cottage in Groton, near the Canadian border, and got ready to engage in what they did best: robbing banks. In the spring of 1850, acting on information supplied by the *New York Herald* and the *New York Police Gazette*, the Vermont police raided the cottage. They found Bristol Bill's home-made burglary tools, a counterfeit machine, and freshly made bills. In addition, there were several diagrams of the banks Bristol Bill had planned to rob.

Faced with insurmountable evidence, Bristol Bill and Meadows were arrested. English Jim was not at the cottage when the police arrived, and for some reason, "Gookin' Peg" was never charged. Bristol Bill and Meadows were sentenced to ten years at the Windsor State Prison. When Bristol Bill was released, he was almost 60 years old, and he disappeared from the American crime scene. Some said Bristol Bill went back to London. Others said, he died broke in America.

While he was in prison, Bristol Bill confided to fellow inmates that the biggest mistake he had ever made was inventing an unpickable lock in his early locksmith days in London. This lock was subsequently sold widely in the United States.

Bristol Bill said there were many times when he encountered his own invention on bank vaults and on the front doors of homes, which made his mission of breaking, entering, and stealing almost impossible.

Capone - Al "Scarface"

Most people associate Al Capone with Chicago, but in fact, Al Capone was born and bred, and got his start in the mob in the borough of Brooklyn, New York.

Alphonse Gabriel Capone was born the fourth of nine children, on January 17, 1899, on Navy Street, in the section of Brooklyn now known as DUMBO (Down Under the Manhattan Bridge Overpass). Capone stayed in school until the 6th grade, when in a fit of rage, he beat up one of his teachers. A resulting trip to the principal's office caused Capone to get beat up himself, and after licking his wounds, Capone left school for good.

Capone hooked up with a street mob called "The James Street Gang," which was an offshoot of the powerful Five Points Gang in Lower Manhattan. "The James Street Gang" was run by the rough and ruthless Johnny Torrio, who became the teenaged Capone's mentor for many years to come.

Torrio, along with his partner Frankie Yale, hired Capone to be their chief bouncer at their bar/brothel in Brooklyn. It was there that Capone got his nickname "Scarface," after his cheek was slashed by a hoodlum named Frank Galluccio, in a bar fight over a girl, whom Capone had insulted (apparently, the girl was Galluccio's sister, and Capone had made a tasteless remark about her shapely figure). Capone later told the press he had gotten his scar fighting for the "Lost Battalion" in France, during World War I. However, the truth was, Capone never served a day of military service in his entire life.

In 1919, Torrio moved to Chicago to run the rackets of his uncle-through-marriage: Big Jim Colosimo. Capone was suspected of a few murders in Brooklyn, so in order to avoid the heat, Capone headed west to Chicago to aid Torrio in his takeover of the town. Their first order of business was to take out Colosimo, who was a hindrance to Torrio and Capone getting into the illegal booze business. Brooklyn pal Frankie Yale traveled to Chicago, and he took care of Colosimo, personally and permanently, with bullets.

With Colosimo out of the way, the Torrio/Capone duo attempted to organize Chicago into separate but equal fiefdoms, each with protection and exclusivity in their own territories. Irish mobster Dion O'Banion, the head of Chicago's "North Side Gang," told Torrio he wanted nothing to do with Torrio's proposal, signing his death warrant in the process. Again, Frankie Yale was called into action, and O'Banion was shot to death by Yale and two associates in O'Banion's florist shop, in November of 1924.

After Torrio was seriously wounded in an assassination attempt by O'Banion's successor, Hymie Weiss, Torrio went into retirement at the age of 43, willing all his rackets to the 26-year-old Al Capone.

Capone took Chicago by the throat, and he had over 1,000 experienced gunmen under his control. Even the Chicago police turned a blank eye to Capone's murderous activities.

Capone once boasted, "I own Chicago, and I own the police."

Add aldermen, mayors, legislators, governors, newspapermen, and congressmen to the list of people on Capone's payroll. To deflect any possible heat from people not on his payroll, Capone widely limited his business endeavors to things that were popular with the people: booze, gambling, and prostitution.

Capone once boasted to his adoring press, "I'm just an honest businessman who's giving the public what they want."

Capone was so popular with the common man, he was wildly cheered at Chicago Major League baseball games.

Capone's downfall started on February 14, 1929, when he orchestrated the "Valentine's Day Massacre." While Capone was sunbathing in Miami, his shooters lined up seven men against a garage wall in Chicago. The killers machine-gunned the seven men to death, but they missed Capone's main intended target and owner of the garage: George "Bugs" Moran.

All of a sudden, Capone was no longer the people's choice. Even the jaded citizens of Chicago were aghast at the savagery of the vicious murders. Despite the fact the government had no proof of Capone's involvement in the "Valentine's Day Massacre," they plotted to put him in jail, any way they could.

As a result, Capone was hit with 11 counts of income tax evasion, and in 1931, he was tried, convicted, and sentenced to 11 years in prison.

In 1934, Capone was transferred to Alcatraz, a maximum security prison called "The Rock." There, the effects of syphilis Capone had acquired in his brothel days in Brooklyn took control of his mind. Capone was diagnosed with dementia, and when he was released in November 1939, Al Capone was a broken man, given to outbursts of rage, over anything: from the government, to the Communists, to his old foe "Bugs" Moran.

Capone spent his last years flowing in and out of lucidity, and on January, 21, 1947, he died of a heart attack at his home in Miami Beach, Fla.

Civil War Draft Riots of 1863

Never in the history of New York has there been a more brutal mass insurrection than the New York City Civil War Draft Riots of 1863.

In March of 1863, the seeds were planted for these riots when President Abraham Lincoln issued a proclamation, called The Conscription Act (or Enrollment Act), stating he needed 300,000 more men to be drafted into the Northern Army, to beat back the Southern Rebels in the Civil War. This act required every male citizen, between the ages of 20 and 40, to be drafted into the war. Each man who joined the army was given a bounty of up to $500, as an enlistment bonus. The gravest inequity, however, was that for the sum of $300 a man could buy himself out of being drafted. The rich could afford the $300, but the poor could not, which led to the Civil War being called "A rich man's war and a poor man's fight."

New York City (only Manhattan at the time) had more than 800,000 citizens, of which more than half were foreign. Of that half, half again were poor Irish, who had no desire to fight in a war to end the slavery of Negroes, whom they despised. These poor, low-class Irish people had settled in the Five Points and in the Mulberry Bend areas in downtown Manhattan (the 6th Ward), and also in the 4th Ward near the East River. In these slums, gangs like the Plug Uglies, the Bowery Boys, the Roach

Guards, and the Dead Rabbits, committed atrocious crimes. And this downtown area is where the draft rioters began their bloodthirsty march.

President Lincoln had announced that Draft Day in New York City would commence on Saturday, July 11. On that day, with only minor disturbances throughout the city, 1,236 men were drafted into the war. When the draft ended that day, it was announced that the draft would bypass Sunday and continue again on Monday morning.

However, the seeds of discontent grew during the rest of the weekend, spurred by an article in Saturday evening's *Leslie's Illustrated*, which stated, "It came like a thunderclap on the people, as men read their names in the fatal list, the feeling of indignation and resistance soon found vent in words, and a spirit of resistance spread fast and far. The number of poor men exceeded that of the rich, their number to draw from being that much greater, but this was viewed as proof of the dishonesty in the whole proceeding."

As Monday morning drew near, the poor slum-living Irish began planning how to voice their displeasure, and it wouldn't be pleasant. At 6 a.m. Monday, men and women started spilling out of the downtown slums, and they began their resolute march to the north. At every street corner, more discontents joined their forces, and the group became so huge it split into two groups. It was estimated that eventually 50,000 to 70,000 people took part in the four-day Draft Riots, and the New York City Metropolitan Police had only 3,000 men to combat the rioters.

As the rioters moved north along Fifth and Sixth Avenues, they turned east and made a beeline toward the main draft office, at 46th Street and Third Avenue. Police Superintendent John A. Kennedy, realizing trouble was brewing, dispatched 60 police officers to guard the Third Avenue Draft Office, and another 69 to guard the draft office at Broadway and 29th Street.

The rioters on Third Avenue were led by the volunteer firemen attached to Engine Company 33, known as The Black Joke. They consisted of members of the Plug Uglies street gang, who by now had stopped traffic completely and were pulling people out of their carts. Signs in the crowd were held saying "NO DRAFT!!", when suddenly someone in the crowd shot a pistol up into the air, and the riots commenced.

The mob threw bricks and stones at the draft office, breaking all the windows in the building. Then they surged forward, thousands of them, while 60 cops tried in vain to hold them back. The rioters stepped over the now-battered and unconscious policemen, and as draft officials jumped out the rear windows of the building, the mob set fire to the Third Avenue Draft Office.

Meanwhile, Superintendent Kennedy had left Police Headquarters at 300 Mulberry Street, wearing civilian clothes as a disguise. He took a horse carriage to 46th Street and Lexington Avenue, but when he saw the smoke, he jumped out of the carriage and proceeded on foot.

Kennedy was immediately recognized, and beaten to a bloody pulp, until he was unconscious. A Good Samaritan named John Egan saved Kennedy, when he announced to the mob that Kennedy was dead. Kennedy was covered with a gunny sack and put into a wagon, which drove him to Police Headquarters. When he was examined by doctors, Kennedy was found to have 72 bruises on his body and over two dozen cuts.

The rioters then attacked the Colored Orphans Asylum, on Fifth Avenue and 46th Street. As the rioters stormed the building, 50 matrons and attendants snuck 200 Negro children out a secret back exit. The mob rushed in, stole blankets, toys, and bedding, and then set fire to the building. One young Negro girl, who was accidentally left behind, was found hiding under a bed. She was dragged out and savagely beaten to death.

All throughout the streets of New York City, angry Irish mobs chased Negroes, whom they blamed for the drafts in the first place. The Negroes who were caught, were beaten to death and sometimes hanged. As their bodies hung from trees and rafters, mad Irish woman, glee in their eyes, stabbed the dead Negroes' bodies, while they danced under lit torches, and sang obscene songs.

Finally, Mayor George Updyke wired the War Department in Washington D.C. for help. During the next three days of unspeakable mayhem, hundreds of buildings were burned down, innumerable business looted, and Negroes were killed for no other reason than for the color of their skin. When the order was given, the United States Militia, armed, trained, and 10,000 strong, stormed New York City to quell the riots.

On Tuesday, July 14, New York Governor Horatio Seymour stood on the steps of City Hall, and said to the assembled crowd "I have received a dispatch from Washington that the draft is now suspended."

Governor Seymour was booed and jeered, and the riots continued for two more days.

It is impossible to estimate how many people were killed in the four-day riots. The New York Post reported that, under the blanket of darkness, the bodies of dead rioters were shipped across the East River, and quietly buried in Brooklyn. Police Superintendent Kennedy put the total dead at 1,155, but that did not include those buried secretly at night. Of the tens of thousands of rioters involved, and despite the brutal murders of scores of Negroes, only 19 people were tried and convicted of any crimes. The average prison sentence was a mere five years.

Diarist George Templeton Strong summed up the disgrace of the 1863 New York City Civil War Draft Riots, when he wrote "This is a nice town to call itself a center of civilization."

Coll - Vincent "Mad Dog"

He was known throughout the underworld as the "Mad Mick," but when he gunned down five children in Harlem, Vincent Coll forever became known as "Mad Dog" Coll.

Vincent Coll was born on July 20, 1908, in Gweedore, a small town in County Donegal, Ireland. When he was an infant, Coll's parents relocated to America; settling in a cold-water flat in the Bronx. After five of his siblings died, from either accidents or disease, his father left the family, never to be seen again.

Coll 's mother died from pneumonia when he was seven, and Coll and his older brother Peter were taken by the state of New York and put in the Mount Loretto Orphanage, in Staten Island. The Coll brothers stayed at the orphanage for three years, both being beaten repeatedly for insubordination. Finally, the Coll Brothers escaped, and insinuated themselves into New York's Hell's Kitchen, where they became members of the notorious street gang called The Gophers.

Soon, the Coll Brothers were working as go-fers for the infamous bootlegger Dutch Schultz. They were paid a hundred bucks a week to do Schultz's dirty work, which included a few killings when requested. Finally, fed up with Schultz's known cheapness as far as paying his crew, Coll approached Schultz, and demanded he become a full partner.

"I ain't your nigger shoeshine boy," Coll told Schultz. "I'll show you a thing or two."

Coll started up a small gang, which included his brother Peter, and his girlfriend and future wife, Lottie Kreisberger, who did little more than keep Coll company. Coll's first move on Schultz was a brazen daytime robbery of Schultz's Sheffield Dairy in the Bronx. Schultz was so angry at Coll's treachery, he thundered into the 42nd Precinct, and announced to a room full of cops, "I'll buy a house in Westchester for anyone in here who can kill that Mick (Coll)."

Coll then tried to lure Schultz's gang members into Coll's gang. Through an old school acquaintance named Mary Smith, the Coll brothers set up a meeting with one of Schultz's top boys, Vincent Barelli. At that meeting in a Bronx apartment, when Barelli rebuffed their advances, the Coll Brothers calmly shot him to death. Mary Smith, horrified at what she had just seen and unwittingly set up, tried to escape from the apartment. Coll chased her down, and shot her in the head, killing her in the middle of the street.

A few days later, members of Schultz's gang machine-gunned Peter Coll as he was driving in Harlem. The death of Peter Coll precipitated a large-scale war between Vincent Coll and Schultz, which resulted in at least 20 more killings.

Needing fast cash, Coll accepted an assignment from Italian Mob boss Salvatore Maranzano, to kill Lucky Luciano in Maranzano's midtown office. Maranzano paid Coll $25,000 up front, with another $25,000 due upon completion of his task.

Coll was in the lobby of Maranzano's office building, with a machine gun hidden under his coat and waiting for the elevator, when three men rushed out of the stairwell and plowed right into Coll. Knowing who Coll was, the men told Coll they had just killed Maranzano and for Coll to beat it before the cops arrived. Coll smiled, did an about-face, and he exited the building, whistling a happy tune, knowing he had just pocketed twenty-five grand for doing absolutely nothing.

To further inflate his bank account, Coll started kidnapping top aides of big-time gang leaders like Owney "The Killer" Madden, an Irishman himself. Madden paid Coll $35,000 for the return of his partner Big Frenchy DeMange, who was co-owner with Madden, in the Cotton Club in Harlem. Coll then kidnapped Madden's front man at the Stork Club, the very popular Sherman Billingsley. Again Madden paid the ransom, and Billingsley was soon back at the Stork Club, still in fine health.

Next on Coll's hit list was Joey Rao, Schultz's top numbers man in Harlem. Rao and a bunch of his boys were standing in front of their Helmar Social Club on East 107th Street, divvying out pennies to neighborhood kids, when Coll and his gang came barreling around the corner in a touring car. Coll let go with several blasts from a machine gun, missing Rao and his men completely, but instead striking five children. Little five-year old Michael Vengali took several bullets in the stomach, and he died before he could be rushed to the hospital.

Incensed at the killing of a child, the New York City newspapers ran frightening headlines about the "Baby Killer." They dubbed Coll -- Vincent "Mad Dog" Coll. And like any "mad dog," the public, and the underworld, demanded that Coll be put down. New York City Mayor James Walker offered a $10,000 reward for anyone who provided information that led to Coll's arrest. Madden and Schultz upped the ante, each offering $25,000 to any mug who could put the "Mad Dog" down with bullets.

Coll hid out in various parts of the Northeast, before finally returning to New York City with Lottie. They were holed up in the Cornish Arms Hotel on West 23rd Street, when the cops, acting on a tip, barged in and arrested Coll. Coll's trial was expected to be a slam-dunk for the prosecution, but the brilliant legal tactics of Coll's lawyer, Samuel Liebowitz, got Coll off the hook.

After his trial, Coll held court with the press outside the Criminal Courts Building.

He told the reporters, "I've been charged with all kinds of crimes, but baby-killing was the limit. I'd like nothing better than to lay my hands on the man who did this."

Coll was back on the streets, but still a marked man by the mob. He married Lottie at City Hall, but they were constantly on the run, moving quickly from hideout to hideout.

On February 1, 1932, four men busted into a home in the north Bronx, guns blazing. They shot a table full of people playing cards. Two Coll gang members were killed (Fiorio Basile and Patsy Del Greco), and another one wounded. Also killed was Mrs. Emily Torrizello, who just happened to be in the wrong place at the wrong time. Another unidentified woman was wounded. Miraculously, two babies lying in their cribs were found unharmed. Luckily for Coll, he showed up at the house a half hour later, just as the police arrived.

As a result, Coll went on the run again. After hiding separately for a while, Coll wound up back with Lottie at the Cornish Arms Hotel. Coll decided this was a good time to start kidnapping again, but this time with a twist. Coll phoned Madden, and told him he wanted $100,000, *not* to kidnap Madden.

"Imagine how the Dagos and Kikes is gonna feel when they have to shell out a hundred grand to save your sorry ass," Coll told Madden. "Pay me now, up front, and I'll save you the trouble."

Madden said he needed some time to think it over.

On March 8, 1932, Madden phoned Coll, and told Coll to call him from the phone booth at the drug store across the street from his hotel. At 12:30 am, Coll strode into the New London Pharmacy on West 23rd Street, and he headed for the phone booth in the back. While he was talking to Madden on the phone, a man with a machine gun hidden under his coat, calmly walked to the back of the drug store and opened fire. The gunman riddled Coll's body with 15 bullets.

Hearing the commotion, Lottie arrived a few minutes later, to see her husband's dead tattered body. Lottie Coll refused to speak with the police, but she cried to someone standing nearby, that their life savings, at the time, was a measly hundred dollar bill, she had stuffed inside her bra.

This proved, without a shadow of a doubt, that Vincent "Mad Dog" Coll, despite his dreadful bite, had died doggone broke.

Crowley - Francis "Two Gun"

They called him a "Half-Pint Moron," and "The Puny Killer." Yet for a short three-month span in 1931, Francis "Two Gun" Crowley was the most dangerous man in New York City.

Crowley was born in New York City, on October 13, 1912. His German mother was not married, and as soon as little Francis saw his first light of day his mother gave him up for adoption. It was rumored Crowley's father was a cop, which explained his hatred for anyone in a blue uniform. Crowley was brought up by a woman named Anna Crowley, and he took her name, calling her his only mother.

By the time Crowley was 18, despite the fact that he stood only 5-foot-3 inches and weighed 130 pounds, he was already a full-blown criminal and a murderer. Crowley teamed up with the hulking Rudolph "Fats" Duringer (who was said to be the largest man ever to sit in Sing Sing's electric chair). Soon, the Mutt and Jeff crime team started terrorizing New York City.

On February 21, 1931, Crowley, Fats, and another unidentified male, burst into an America Legion Dance Hall in the Bronx. They were uninvited, and when a slew of Legionnaires tried to toss them out, Crowley began firing with two guns, which gave him his nickname "Two Gun" Crowley. No one was killed, but two men were injured, and Crowley was now hunted by the police for attempted murder. Crowley was cornered in an office building on Lexington Avenue, but he shot his way out of the arrest, plugging Detective Ferdinand Schaedel in the process.

Crowley continued his crazed crime spree in rapid fashion. First, Crowley and his crew robbed a bank in New Rochelle. Then they staged a home invasion of the West 90th Street apartment of rich real estate investor Rudolph Adler. Crowley shot the feisty Adler five times, and just as he was ready to fire the final bullet into Adler's skull, Adler's dog Trixie went into attack mode and chased Crowley and his crew from the apartment.

Some tough guys.

In Crowley's first involvement in a murder, he wasn't even the shooter.

On April 27, 1931, Crowley was driving a stolen car, with his pal Fats in the back seat. Fats was busy trying to make the moves on a dance hall girl, Virginia Brannen, who had just come along for the ride. Brannen told Fats, in no uncertain terms, to keep his chubby hands to himself. This did not please the hulking gangster too much, so Fats shot Brannen dead. Crowley and Fats discarded Brannen's body outside the St. Joseph Cemetery in Yonkers.

After finding Brannen, the New York City and the Yonkers police departments, put out an all-points bulletin for the fat and skinny psychopaths. On April 29, a passing police car spotted Crowley as was driving a green Chrysler on 138th Street in the Bronx. The cops sped in hot pursuit after Crowley, firing shot after shot at the speeding Chrysler. Crowley returned fire, and somehow he managed to escape. The next day, the police found Crowley's abandoned car, riddled with bullets and smeared with blood.

The manhunt for Crowley continued.

On May 6, Crowley was smooching in a car with his 16-year old girlfriend Helen Walsh, in a secluded spot on Morris Lane in North Merrick, Long Island. Patrolmen Frederick Hirsch and Peter Yodice approached the car, and they asked for Crowley's identification. Instead of drawing his wallet, Crowley pulled out a pistol, firing. He shot Hirsch to death and wounded Yodice, before he fled the scene.

Now branded a cop-killer, the daily newspapers brought Crowley instant fame. The *New York Daily News* wrote: "Francis Crowley, who glories in the nickname 'Two Gun Frank,' and is described by the police as the most dangerous criminal at-large, was hunted throughout the city last night."

On May 7th, the police traced Crowley to a top-floor apartment on West 90th Street. Crowley was holed up there with Fats and Helen Walsh, and what transpired next will forever be known as "The Siege on West 90th Street": the most fierce gun battle in New York City's history.

First, two detectives tried to enter the apartment to arrest Crowley and his crew peacefully. But Crowley would have none of that. Crowley screamed through the door, firing lead, "Come and get me coppers!"

The detectives retreated down to the street, where they were joined by an estimated 100 police officers rushed in from all parts of the city. Crowley yelled down at the assembled cops, "I'm up here! Come and get me!"

Over the course of the next several hours, and while an estimated 15,000 onlookers gawked from the streets and open tenement windows, more than 700 bullets were fired into Crowley's apartment. Crowley had an arsenal himself, and he brazenly returned fire. Safely under the bed, Helen Walsh and Fats reloaded Crowley's guns for him.

At one point, the police cut a hole in the roof, and they dropped gas canisters into Crowley's apartment. Crowley calmly picked up the smoking canisters and threw them out the window, overcoming several police officers below. Finally, a dozen cops broke down Crowley's door, and with four slugs in Crowley's body, the police were finally able to subdue him. Fats and Helen gave up without a whimper.

The newspapers had a field day with this one. Crowley was described as "A Mad Irish Gunman" (even though he was actually German), with "the face of an altar boy." Crowley and Fats were convicted of the murder of Virginia Brannen and Crowley of the murder of patrolmen Frederick Hirsch. They were both sentenced to die in the Sing Sing electric chair.

In jail, Crowley kept up his tough-guy act. He made a club from a wrapped-up newspaper and some wire from under his bed. Then he tried to fight his way out of prison, by cracking a guard over the head with his handmade club. His escape attempt having failed, Crowley set fire to his cell. And when that didn't work, he took off all his clothes and stuffed them into his toilet, flooding his cell. For these disturbances, Warden Lewis E. Lawes forced Crowley to sit naked in his cell for several days until the young maniac quieted down.

During his last days on earth, Crowley mellowed a bit. A bird flew into his cell, and he nurtured it. Crowley also began drawing pictures, a skill for which he had more than a little talent.

On December 10, 1931, Fats got the juice first. After Fats and Crowley hugged a last goodbye, and Fats started his last lonely trek down the hall to the chair, Crowley told a guard, "There goes a great guy, a square-shooter, and my pal."

Crowley was not so charitable to Helen, whom he refused to see, even though she visited the prison almost every day.

"She's out!" he told the newspapers, "She's going around with a cop! I won't even look at her!"

On January 21, 1932, Crowley followed the same path to the electric chair which his old pal Fats had traveled. After the black leather mask was pulled over his face, Crowley's last words were, "Send my love to my mother."

The lever was thrown, and Francis "Two Gun" Crowley was executed at the tender age of 19.

Daybreak Boys

When the Daybreak Boys formed their treacherous little gang in the late 1840's, there were said to be three dozen members, none of whom was over the age of 20. Some of the Daybreak Boys were as young as 10 years old. However, lack of age never meant a paucity of violence.

The Daybreak Boys' first leaders were Nicholas Saul and William Howlett, who were 16 and 15 years-old, respectively, when they took control of the gang. Other noted members were murderers like Slobbery Jim, Sow Madden, Cow-legged Sam McCarthy, and Patsy the Barber.

It was rumored that every member of the gang had committed at least one murder and scores of robberies before they reached the age of 16. The police said The Daybreak Boys not only murdered in the course of a robbery, but also for the sheer ecstasy of doing so, even if there was no hope of cashing in on a score. The police estimated in the three years that Saul and Howlett were their leaders, the Daybreak Boys robbed over $100,000, and killed as many as 40 people.

The Daybreak Boys' base of operations was the Slaughter House Point, owned by Pete Williams, located at the intersection of James and Water Streets. On August 25, 1852, a passing policeman looked in at the Slaughter House Point, and he saw Saul and Howlett huddled in a corner with low-level gang member Bill Johnson, who was half-sloshed. The policeman suspected the three men were up to no good, and he decided to drop by later. When he did, the three men were gone.

In the darkness, Saul, Howlett, and Johnson had taken a row boat, and navigated the East River to a ship named the *William Watson*, intent on stealing valuables they had heard were on board. The three men were met by the night watchman, Charles Baxter, and they shot Baxter dead on the spot. Thinking the gunshot would attract attention, the three men jumped ship from the *William Watson*, empty-handed, and they rowed back to shore.

The policeman, who had spotted the three men earlier, saw the rowboat dock, and he watched as Saul and Howlett dragged Johnson, who was now totally drunk, from the boat and carry him into the Slaughter House Point. Soon after, the body of the night watchman on the *William Watson* was found, and a group of 20 policemen, armed to the hilt, bum-rushed the Slaughter House Point.

After a long and bloody battle, in which a score of Daybreak Boys tried to thwart the capture of their three cronies, Saul, Howlett, and Johnson were finally arrested. After a short trial, Johnson was sentenced to life imprisonment, but Saul and Howlett were smacked with the death sentence. On January 28, 1853, Saul and Howlett were hanged to death in the courtyard of the Tombs Prison. Saul was barely 20 years old and Howlett was one year younger.

After the deaths of Saul and Howlett, Slobbery Jim assumed the leadership of the Daybreak Boys. However, Jim soon had to take it on the lam, after he whacked his old pal Patsy the Barber.

In 1857, The Daybreak Boys continued their decline. The Slaughter House Point, which had been the base of their operations for a decade, closed its doors (with a little prompting from the New York City Police Department). In 1858, more than a dozen gang members were killed in shootouts with the police and with the newly created Harbor Patrol. Scores of other Daybreak Boys were arrested and sent to jail.

By 1859, the Daybreak Boys basically ceased to exist, when its remaining members took up with other gangs in the Bowery and in the other Five Points areas.

Dead Rabbits – Irish Street Gang

The Dead Rabbits Irish Street gang was as vicious as any gang in the history of New York City. In the mid 1800's, the Dead Rabbits prowled the squalid area of Lower Manhattan called the Five Points. If a member of any other gang dared to set foot in the Dead Rabbits' territory, bad things happened to them fast.

There is some dispute as to how the Dead Rabbits got their name. One version is that the word "Rabbit" sounds like Irish word "ráibéad," meaning a "man to be feared." "Dead" was an 1800's slang word that meant "very." So a "Dead Rabbit" was a "man to be very feared."

Another version is that the Dead Rabbits were an offshoot of an older gang called the "Roach Guards." Two factions within the Roach Guards constantly quarreled, and during a fistfight at an especially violent gang meeting, someone threw a dead rabbit into the room. When the fighting subsided, one group took the name "Dead Rabbits," while the other kept the name "Roach Guards." Predating the present street gangs, the Crips and the Bloods, by more than 125 years, to mark which gang a man belonged to, a Dead Rabbit wore a blue stripe on his pants, while a Roach Guard wore a red stripe on his pants.

Besides the Roach Guards, the Dead Rabbits' archenemy was the Bowery Boys. On July 4 1857, the Dead Rabbits and the Bowery Boys squared off at the corner of Bayard and the Bowery. The incident started when an embattled policeman, being chased out of the Five Points by a group of Dead Rabbits, ran for safety into a Bowery Boys' saloon. The Dead Rabbits followed the policeman into the dive, and they were beaten back by an angry group of Bowery Boys.

Taking offense at their turf being invaded, a large group of Bowery Boys marched into the Five Points area, looking for trouble. They were cut off by a battalion of the Dead Rabbits, and a two-day war started, with as many as a thousand combatants fighting with hatchets, knives, stones, and even guns. The police sent in reinforcements, but they were beaten back by both gangs, and told, in no uncertain terms, to mind their own business. The war swayed back and forth into both territories, with Canal Street being the boundary line.

By the end of the second day, the two gangs were near exhaustion, and the Seventh Regiment of the National Guard was called in by New York City Mayor Fernando Wood. The National Guard, joined by the New York City

Police, busted into what was left of the skirmish, and they started cracking the heads of the weary warriors. When the dust settled, eight gang members were dead and hundreds more were injured.

This did not end the animosity between the Bowery Boys and Dead Rabbits. In August 1858, on the corner of Worth and Centre Street, a small group of Bowery Boys were pummeled by a larger group of Dead Rabbits. As the Bowery Boys ran off licking their wounds, two unsuspecting men exited a house at 66 Centre Street, and they walked right into the path of the angry Dead Rabbits. Thinking these two men were Bowery Boys coming back for more, the Dead Rabbits descended upon them with a vengeance. One man was able to escape, but Cornelius Rady was not so lucky. Rady was hit in the back of the head with a rock from a slingshot, and he died soon afterwards. Dead Rabbit Patrick Gilligan was arrested for Rady's murder, but it is not clear if he was ever convicted.

The Civil War started two years later, and many of the gang members were drafted, against their wills, into the war and sent to faraway places, mostly in the South. When the war ended, the Dead Rabbits were either dead themselves, or in no physical condition to continue tormenting the streets of Lower Manhattan.

However, in New York City, the creature that it was, and in some cases still is, other street gangs soon followed to take the ignominious place of the Dead Rabbits.

Diamond, Jack "Legs"

Jack "Legs" Diamond was shot and injured so many times he was dubbed "The Gangster Who Couldn't be Killed."

Diamond was born on July 10 1897, of parents from Kilrush, County Clare, in Ireland. Diamond spent the early years of his life in Philadelphia. When Diamond was 13, his mother died from a viral infection. Soon, Diamond, and his younger brother Eddie, fell in with a group of toughs called "The Boiler Gang."

Diamond was arrested more than a dozen times, for assorted robberies and mayhem, and after spending a few months in a juvenile reformatory, Diamond was drafted into the army. Army life did not suit Diamond too well. He served less than a year, then he decided to go AWOL. Diamond was soon captured and sentenced to three-to-five years in the Federal Penitentiary in Fort Leavenworth, Kansas.

Diamond was released from prison in 1921, and he decided that New York City was the place he could make his fortune. Diamond and his brother Eddie relocated to Manhattan's Lower East Side, where they fell in with an up-and-coming gangster named Lucky Luciano. Diamond did various odd jobs for Luciano, including a little bootlegging, in conjunction with Brooklyn thug Vannie Higgins. Diamond's marriage to Florence Williams lasted only a few months (he was never home). However, Diamond's luck changed when Luciano introduced Diamond to Arnold "The Brain" Rothstein, a notorious gambler and known financial wizard. This was the break Diamond was waiting for, and he made the most of it.

After starting out as a bodyguard for Rothstein, Rothstein brought Diamond in as a partner in his lucrative heroin business. When his pockets were full with enough cash and his need for Rothstein diminished, Diamond, in concert with his brother Eddie, decided to branch out on their own.

The Diamond Brothers figured they could make a bundle, hijacking the bootlegging trucks of other mobsters, including those of Owney Madden and Big Bill Dwyer. This was not a very good idea, since Madden and Dwyer were part of a bigger syndicate of criminals that included Luciano, Dutch Schultz, and Meyer Lansky. In no time, Diamond was persona-non-grata in the gangster world and free pickings for anyone who wanted to get rid of him.

In October 1924, Diamond was driving a Dodge sedan up Fifth Avenue, when at 100th Street a black limo pulled up alongside him. A shotgun was fired at Diamond from the back window of the limo, but Diamond was too quick to be killed. He ducked down and hit the accelerator, without looking where he was going.

Miraculously, Diamond was able to escape his shooters and drive himself to the nearby Mount Sinai Hospital. The doctors removed pellets in his head, face, and feet, and when the cops arrived to question him, Diamond dummied up.

"I dunno a thing about it," Diamond told the fuzz. "Why would anyone want to shoot me? They must of got the wrong guy."

Soon, Diamond became friends with a gangster not looking to kill him. His name was "Little Augie" Orgen. Orgen installed Diamond as his chief bodyguard. In return, Orgen gave Diamond a nice share of his bootlegging and narcotics businesses. This friendship went just fine, until October 15, 1927, when Louis "Lepke" Buchalter and Gurrah Shapiro gunned down Orgen on the corner of Norfolk and Delancey Street, with Diamond supposedly standing guard over Orgen.

Diamond was shot in the arms and legs (probably by accident), necessitating another trip to the hospital. Upon his release, Diamond made nice with Lepke and Shapiro, and as a result, the two killers gave Diamond Orgen's bootlegging and narcotics businesses as a reward for being stupid enough to get in the way of bullets meant for Orgen.

Now, Diamond was on top of the world. He had plenty of cash to throw around, and he became a mainstay in all of New York City's top nightclubs, usually with showgirl Kiki Roberts on his arm (despite the fact he was still married to his second wife Alice Kenny). Diamond was seen regularly at the Cotton Club, El Fay, and the Stork Club, and his picture was frequently in the newspapers, which portrayed Diamond not as a gangster, but as a handsome man-about-town.

Soon, Diamond was part owner of the Hotsy Totsy Club, located on Broadway between 54th and 55th Street, with Hymie Cohen as his fronting partner. The Hotsy Totsy Club had a back room where Diamond frequently settled business disputes, usually by shooting his adversaries to death, then carrying them out as if they were drunk.

Diamond's downfall started on July 13, 1929, when three unruly dockworkers got loaded and started a ruckus at the Hotsy Totsy Club's bar.

Diamond jumped in, with his gang member Charles Entratta, to stop Diamond's manager from being throttled.

"I'm Jack Diamond and I run this place," Diamond told the dock workers. "If you don't calm down, I'll blow your (expletive) heads off."

The talking didn't work and soon the shooting started. When the smoke cleared, two dockworkers were dead and the third one was injured. As a result, Diamond and Entratta took it on the lam.

While they were in hiding, Diamond decided that before he could go back to doing what he was doing before, the bartender and three witnesses had to be killed. And soon they were, Cohen turned up dead, too, and the hat check girl, the cashier, and one waiter disappeared from the face of the earth.

Diamond and Entratta, with everyone out of the way who could possibly harm them, calmly turned themselves into the police and said, "I heard we were wanted for questioning."

No charges were ever brought against Diamond and Entratta for the Hotsy Totsy Club murders, but Diamond realized New York City was no longer safe for him. As a result, Diamond closed the Hotsy Totsy Club, and he relocated to Greene County in upstate New York.

From upstate New York, Diamond ran a little bootlegging operation. However, after a few months of impatience, Diamond sent word back to gangsters in New York City, namely Dutch Schultz and Owney Madden (who had scooped up Diamond's rackets in his absence), that he was coming back to take back what was rightfully his. This put a target in the middle of Diamond's back, and he soon became known as the "clay pigeon of the underworld."

Diamond was sitting at the bar of the Aratoga Inn, near Arca, New York, when three men, dressed as duck hunters, barreled into the bar and filled Diamond with lead. The doctors gave him little chance for survival, but four weeks later, Diamond walked out of the hospital and told the press, "Well, I made it again. Nobody can kill Jack 'Legs' Diamond."

A few months later, as Diamond was leaving an upstate roadside inn, he was shot four times: in the back, leg, lung, and liver. Yet again, Diamond beat the odds the doctors gave him, and he survived.

In December 1931, Diamond was not so lucky, when after a night of heavy drinking at the Kenmore Hotel in Albany, Diamond staggered back drunk to his nearby boarding room and fell asleep. The landlady said afterwards, that she heard Diamond pleading for his life, then she heard three shots. Apparently two gunmen had burst into Diamond's room, and while one held him by his two ears, the other put three slugs into his brain.

The killers escaped in a red Packard, putting an end to the myth that Jack "Legs" Diamond was the "gangster who couldn't be killed."

Eastman, Monk

Monk Eastman was born Edward Osterman, in 1875, in the Williamsburg section of Brooklyn. Edward's father owned a restaurant, and to keep the young Osterman busy, his father bought him a pet shop. Osterman's business venture failed, reportedly because he kept fighting with customers who wanted to purchase pets he became especially fond of. Out of business, young Osterman relocated to lower Manhattan, and to make money, he dived headfirst into a life of crime. He operated under several aliases, before finally settling on the last name of Eastman.

The short and stocky Eastman was nicknamed "Monk," because he resembled a monkey stalking the streets. He had an unkempt appearance, and his pumpkin-sized head and frazzled hair were covered by a derby two sizes too small. Eastman became known as a feared brawler, and he was the bouncer at one of the roughest nightclubs on the Lower East Side, the New Irving Social Club on the Bowery.

While he patrolled the club keeping the peace, Eastman carried a four-foot stick, which he used to crack the heads of any patron who was not behaving properly. In just a few short months, Eastman had whacked the heads of 49 near-do-wells, and not liking crooked numbers, he conked the skull of an innocent man just to make it an even 50. Eastman sent so many people to Bellevue Hospital, the hospital staff jokingly called their emergency room, "The Eastman Pavilion."

Yet Eastman apparently had a soft spot for women. If anyone of the female persuasion needed to be reckoned with, he reportedly dropped his stick, took off his brass knuckles, and hit the woman just hard enough to give her a black eye. No hospital visit was necessary for the lucky young lady.

Eastman also was a willing killer; for hire, or for just plain fun, especially when he was drunk, which was often. Eastman believed in "Dead Man's Eyes," which is the concept that when a person dies, the last thing that person he sees is permanently imprinted on the retina of their eyes. When Eastman killed someone, he truly believed he was leaving proof on the victim's eyes that he was the killer. So Eastman, being the cautious bloke that he was, after he shot someone dead, not to leave any incriminating evidence, he shot out his victim's eyes out, too.

Eastman assembled a rough and tumble gang that reportedly numbered close to 2,000, mostly Jewish men. Eastman curried favor with politicians by doing them "little favors," like patrolling polling places during elections, to make sure each voter cast their vote for the proper man. The politicians returned the favor by springing Eastman out of jail, whenever an ambitious policeman decided to do something foolish, like actually arresting Eastman for one of his many crimes. However, Eastman was so out-of-control with his thievery, thuggery, and killings, he soon ran out of political favors.

In 1904, Eastman was finally sent to prison for robbing and beating a man uptown. He was sentenced to 10 years at Sing Sing Prison, but he was released after serving only five.

When Eastman got back to his old hunting grounds, he discovered his gang had been dismantled, and his former men were now working for other scattered ringleaders. Eastman was reduced to performing petty crimes in the streets for a while, until he had the bright idea of joining the army. Eastman wound up serving in World War I, in France, with the 106th Infantry Regiment of the 27th Infantry Division. Eastman was honorably discharged in 1919, and he immediately went back to the streets of the Lower East Side, causing his usual mayhem.

Eastman soon became involved with a crooked Prohibition agent named Jerry Bohan. On the night of December 26, 1920, the two men got into a drunken argument, and Bohan, knowing full well about Eastman's reputation for killing easy, shot Eastman dead, in front of 62 East 14th Street.

Fein, Benjamin "Dopey"

Benjamin "Dopey" Fein was born on the Lower East Side of Manhattan in 1889. He was nicknamed "Dopey" because an eye condition made his eyelids droop, and he seemed either to be falling asleep, or under the influence of a narcotic: in the street vernacular, "dope."

Fein dropped out of school at an early age, and he became involved is various street crimes, like pickpocketing and petty robberies. Fein enlisted groups of youngsters, particularly from the school he dropped out of (PS 20 on Essex Street), and soon he had scores of preteen criminals terrorizing the streets of the Lower East Side.

In 1905, Fein's luck turned sour, when he was arrested for assault and robbery, and sent upstate to the Elmira State Penitentiary, where he cooled his heels for three years. Fein was released and arrested twice more, before he finally hit the streets in 1910 and joined "Big" Jack Zelig's notorious gang.

After Zelig was murdered in 1912, Fein embarked on an upwardly horizontal career move. Fein started working for the bosses of several labor unions, especially the Garment Workers Union (GWU). Fein and his men became "schlammers," which meant they broke the heads of any union members who did not toe the line the union bigwigs had laid out for them.

After the Triangle Shirtwaist Factory Fire in 1911 (which killed 146 people, 123 of them women), Fein became involved with the ILGWU: the

International Ladies Garment Workers Union. Fein had a reputation of making sure the woman in his union got paid the exact same salary for their work as did the men in the GWU, which was contrary to the common practice at the time.

Being on the ladies' side was a Machiavellian maneuver, which allowed Fein to use these ILGWU women as "toters," or carriers of concealed weapons, to which Fein and his gang had ready access whenever needed. Fein's female accomplices hid guns, knives, and brass knuckles, in mufflers, or in their hair puffed up high on their heads, in a unique hairdo called the "Mikado Tuck-up."

Fein's main foe at the time was Jack Sirroco. Sirroco was also heavily involved in the labor movement; not with the unions, but rather with the manufacturers, which put him at cross purposes with Fein. Fein and Sirroco's gangs fought numerous battles, especially when both sides showed up representing opposing parties at a labor strike.

In January 1914, Fein and his gang ambushed Sirroco's gang at a party at Arlington Hall, on St. Mark's Place. Only one person was killed, and it turned out to be an innocent bystander named Fredrick Strauss, who just happened to be a County Clerk officer. This put another nail in Fein's quickly closing coffin.

The final nail was inserted in the fall of 1914, when Fein threatened to kill B. Zalamanowitz, an official from the butchers union, who refused to pay Fein $600 to protect his striking butchers. Zalamanowitz, knowing Fein's murderous reputation, ran frightened to the police. On Fein's next meeting with Zalamanowitz, hidden cops watched as Fein repeated his intentions to harm Zalamanowitz if he did not pay up right away. The police arrested Fein on the spot; on first-degree extortion charges.

After a few days in the slammer, Fein, realizing his union influence was on the wane, decided to become a canary for the cops. Unknown to his associates in the labor unions, Fein had kept meticulous records on all his "labor transactions." He had written down everything, including who was involved in what, when, where, and how. This led to the arrest and convictions of dozens of people, including high-ranking officials of the

Garment Workers Union and the International Ladies Garment Workers Union.

Fein was set free, but because he was considered a rat, he lost all of his union partners-in-crime, and any political influence he may have had. Fein was reduced to committing petty crimes in the streets, until he was arrested in 1931 for throwing acid in the face of a competitor: Mortimer Kahn. That set Fein up in Sing Sing Prison for a few more years.

In 1941, Fein was arrested again for stealing over $250,000 worth of clothing and fabric from the Garment Center. Fein was tried, convicted, and sentenced to life imprisonment. However, Fein, for some unknown reason, had his sentence reduced to 10-20 years.

When Fein was released from prison for the last time, he went right back into the garment industry, but this time as a legitimate tailor, a skill he had learned from his father. Fein moved from the Lower East Side of Manhattan to Brooklyn, where he married and raised a family.

Fein, unlike most of his contemporaries, who were either killed in the streets or fried in the electric chair, died of cancer and emphysema in 1962.

Forty Thieves

Based on "Ali Baba and the Forty Thieves," the Forty Thieves were considered to be the first organized street gang in New York City.

In 1825, the Forty Thieves originated at a produce store located on Centre Street, just south of Anthony (now Worth Street), in an area called The Five Points. The proprietor of the store was Rosanna Peers, who sold rotted vegetables out front and ran an illegal speakeasy in the back, where she sold rotgut liquor at prices much cheaper than licensed establishments. Soon, the joint became a haven for pickpockets, murderers, robbers, and thieves, and a dour gentleman named Edward Collman rose as their leader.

Collman gave out strict assignments to his men, with quotas on which and how many crimes he expected each man to commit. If after a period of time, a man did not meet his quota, he would be banished from the gang and sometimes even killed, as a message to others about the importance of meeting quotas.

Collman's downfall was precipitated by one of the gang's few legal ventures: the Hot Corn Girls.

Collman would send out scores of pretty young girls onto the streets, carrying baskets filled with hot roasted ears of corn. The Hot Corn Girl, dressed in spotted calico and wearing a plaid shawl, would walk barefooted in the streets, singing; "Hot Corn! Hot Corn! Here's your lily white corn. All you that's got money. Poor me that's got none. Come buy my lily hot corn. And let me go home."

The Hot Corn Girls were not allowed off the streets by Collman until every single ear of corn in their basket was sold.

All the Hot Corn Girls were fairly attractive and the pretty ones were fought over by the amorous young men mingling on the streets. The best looking one of the lot was called "The Pretty Hot Corn Girl" and Collman fell for her hard. After fighting off several other suitors, Collman married "The Pretty Hot Corn Girl," and then he put her back out on the streets selling corn.

However, after his wife consistently did not meet her quotas, Collman felt, in order to save face and be consistent with his orders, he had no other choice but to kill her. And that he did. As a result, Collman was arrested and convicted of murder. On January 12, 1839, Collman became the first man ever to be hanged at the newly constructed Tombs Prison.

After Collman's death, the men in the Forty Thieves drifted into other street gangs: including the Plug Uglies, the Dead Rabbits, and the Bowery Boys.

In the early 1850's, a juvenile street gang sprung up in the Five Points called the Forty Little Thieves, which consisted of homeless children of both sexes, from the ages of 8 to 12, who emulated the escapades of the old

Forty Thieves. The head of the gang was Wild Maggie Carson, only 12-years-old herself.

The Forty Little Thieves soon outgrew their gang, and their members became assimilated into the older and more famous gangs; all except for Wild Maggie Carson, who was taken off the streets by Reverend Lewis Morris Pease, founder of the Five Points House of Industry. Under Pease's guidance, Little Maggie got a legitimate job sewing buttons. According to Pease, when she was 15, Little Maggie met and married a well-to-do gentleman. And she lived happily ever after.

That is, according to Pease.

Flour Riots of 1837

The flour problem began with the 1835 Great New York City Fire, which destroyed almost 700 downtown buildings. Nearly the entire New York City financial center, including the city's lifeblood - the banks - was burned to the ground. Unable to obtain loans, owners of factories and other downtown businesses were not able to rebuild, putting tens of thousands of New Yorkers out of work.

By 1837, New York City had sunk into the depths of a recession. With no jobs and no money, people's diets sometimes consisted of little more than simple buttered or jammed bread. The poor of the city began to panic, when they discovered that flour, needed to make their daily bread, would become so expensive they would not be able to afford to buy it.

Matters were made worse, when reports from Virginia and other wheat producing states said there was a scarcity of wheat, from which flour was made, and a rise in price was inevitable. At the beginning of January 1837, wheat started at $5.62 cents a barrel. Within days, it had risen to $7 a barrel; then to $12 a barrel. There were rumors that in a few weeks, wheat would go to an incredible $20 a barrel.

The hardest hit were the poor people, who lived in the slums of the Five Points, Bowery, and the Fourth Ward areas on the Lower East Side of Manhattan. Besides the increase in the price of wheat, meat prices had doubled and coal to heat their hovels rose to $10 a ton. People became desperate, and poor souls who were not normally crooks felt they had no choice but to commit petty crimes in order to put food on their family's table.

On February 1, 1837, news circulated that New York City had only four weeks supply of flour left and that the large flour and grain depot in Troy, New York, contained only 4,000 barrels of flour, rather than the usual 30,000 barrels. The newspapers began sensationalizing the issue, when they stated in their editorials that certain merchants were hoarding wheat and flour in anticipation of the rising prices.

The Tammany Hall politicians were adept at causing unrest between the poor Irish, who populated the slums of Lower Manhattan, and anyone with either money or prestige. Never letting a crisis go to waste, Tammany Hall began spreading unfounded rumors that England was refusing to send flour to the United States. The message was compounded by the untruth that the Old Mother Country's intention was to starve the poor Irish in America, as a repayment for the rancor between Ireland and England which had existed for centuries.

On February 10, 1837, a crowd of nearly 6,000 slum-dwellers, from the Five Points, Fourth Ward, and Bowery areas, met at City Hall Park. Running the meeting from atop the steps of City Hall were Tammany Hall titans like Moses Johnson, Paul Hedle, Warden Hayward, and Alexander Ming Jr. There it was decided that two businesses in particular - Hart and Company on Washington Street, and SH. Herrick & Company on Coenties Slip - were packed with both flour and wheat, and were holding back distribution, hoping for future monetary gain when the prices rose.

One of the speakers said, "Fellow citizens, Mr. Eli Hart has 53,000 barrels of flour in his store. Let us go there and offer him $8 a barrel, and if he does not take it......"

The speaker stopped in mid-sentence, but his implication was clear.

When the talking was over, the crowd stampeded from City Hall Park, and they headed down Broadway, west on Cortland and onto Washington Street. When the watchmen protecting Hart's Store saw the surging mob, they quickly ran inside, and they locked the three huge iron doors. But they forgot to insert the inside bar on the center door.

Eli Hart was viewing the mob unrest from a safe distance, and he immediately ran to City Hall, asking for police protection. Twenty policemen rushed to the scene, but they were beaten back by the rioters and their clubs taken away from them. The newly elected mayor of New York City, Aaron Clark, hurried up the steps of the store, and he tried to quell the angry mob. However, after he was showered with stones and bricks, Clark was forced to run for this life.

The rioters then rushed into the building and wrenched one of the iron doors from its hinges. Using it as a battering ram, they bashed down the other two iron doors, then they busted inside. Once inside, the mob entered the storerooms, then rolled approximately 1,000 bushels of wheat and 500 barrels of flour into the street. They smashed the bushels and barrels, until thousands of rioters were knee deep in the flour and wheat.

People started to sing, "Here goes flour at eight dollars a barrel!"

Women filled their apron and skirts with flour, while men used their hats and pockets to pilfer the goods. Even young children got into the act, scooping up what they could carry on their frail bodies.

Suddenly, the 27th Regiment of the National Guard arrived, and they confronted the rioters. Using bayonets and clubs, the National Guard stabbed and clubbed as many rioters as they could lay their hands on. Eventually, they captured scores of the worst offenders, and they started marching them to the Tombs Prison. However, before they got very far, more rioters attacked the National Guard, and they rescued dozens of prisoners, and in the process, tore the police commissioner's coat right off his back. Forty rioters were finally hustled to the Tombs, where they were tried and convicted, and sent to Sing Sing Prison.

While the rioters carted off their dead and wounded from in front of Hart's store, another contingent headed to the store of S.H. Herrick & Company.

There the mob smashed the doors and windows with stones and bats, and within ten minutes, they were able to destroy an additional 30 barrels of flour and 100 bushels of wheat.

Then, without any apparent reason, the mob suddenly disbursed and headed back to their slums, their thirst for destruction finally sated.

The very next day, the price of flour increased one dollar.

Gallus Mag

Dating back to the 1700's, the waterfront of the 4th Ward was a haven for robbers, killers, and pirates. Vicious gangs like the Daybreak Boys, Buckoos, Hookers, Swamp Angels, and Slaughter Houses, prowled the streets, robbing and murdering any poor fool with cash in their pockets who was stupid enough to wander into their sacred domain. Yet, the most feared denizen ever to set foot in the 4th Ward of the mid-19th Century was not a man, but an amazon woman named Gallus Mag.

Gallus Mag was an Englishwoman who stood over 6-feet-tall. She was the bouncer at a Dover Street dive called the Hole-In-The-Wall Bar. The Hole-In-The-Wall Bar was originally built in 1794, and is now the site of the famed Bridge Cafe. The Hole-In-The-Wall Bar was owned by one-armed Charlie Monell, and ruled by Mag, who got her nickname "Gallus" because she kept her skirt from falling down with suspenders, or galluses, as they were called at the time.

Mag stalked the bar looking for troublemakers, with a pistol stuck in her belt and a bludgeon strapped to her wrist. If anyone was dumb enough to challenge her mettle, Mag would hit them with her club, then clutch their ear in her teeth, drag them to the front door and throw them out into the gutter. If the patron put up a stink, Mag would bite off their ear and store it in a large bottle of alcohol that she kept in plain sight behind the bar (They called it "Gallus Mag's Trophy Case"). The New York City police of that time proclaimed Gallus Mag the "most savage female they had ever encountered."

Mag was challenged one day by another woman, Sadie the Goat, a member of the Charlton Street Gang. Sadie the Goat got her name because her preferred manner of robbery was slamming her head into the stomach of her victim, whereas her male companion would then nail the sucker in the head with a rock from a slingshot, then rob him of all his valuables. One day in the Hole-In-The-Wall Bar, Sadie, three sheets to the wind, foolishly challenged Mag to a fight and was beaten to a pulp. As was her wont, Mag severed one of Sadie the Goat's ears with her teeth, and she deposited it into a liquor jar behind the bar. Sadie was glad to escape with her life, and she fled the 4th Ward for the foreseeable future. She then prowled the West Side piers, looking for other suckers to rob.

Years later, after she had made considerable cash performing her specialty on the streets of the West Side, Sadie returned to the Hole-In-The-Wall Bar and made her peace with Mag. Mag was so touched by Sadie's gesture, she immediately went into a liquor jar, removed Sadie's severed ear and returned it to its rightful owner. The legend is that Sadie was so overjoyed by the return of her ear, she wore it in a locket around her neck until her final days.

In 1855, after a slew of seven murders were committed on the premises in the space of three months, the Hole-In-The Wall Bar was closed down for good by the authorities.

There is no record of the year of Mag's demise, but her ghost is said to haunt the Bridge Cafe to this very day.

Gophers

The Gophers street gang was formed in the 1890's from a conglomerate of other Irish street gangs that patrolled the west side of Manhattan. The Gophers were given their name, because after they performed one misdeed or another, to avoid arrest, they hid themselves in the cavernous cellars that snaked throughout the neighborhood. The Gophers originally ruled the area west from Seventh Avenue to 11th Avenue, and north from 14th Street to

42nd Street. However, later they moved as far north as 57th Street. The Gopher's numbers swelled and eventually reached over 500 men, all murderous hooligans of the worst kind.

The Gophers' first base of operations was a notorious saloon called Battle Row, also the name of the area on 39th Street, between 10th and 11th Avenue, where the Gophers committed most of their mayhem. Battle Row was owned by a thug named Mallet Murphy, who was given his nickname because he corrected drunks and other miscreants with a wooden mallet instead of a bludgeon, which was the weapon of choice of that day.

Due to the death or imprisonment of their bosses, the Gophers went through several leaders. The most famous Gopher boss was Owney "The Killer" Madden. Madden's reign ended in 1913, when he was sent to the slammer for 10 years for killing Little Patsy Doyle, his girlfriend's ex-boyfriend and an ambitious man intent on replacing Madden as the leader of the Gophers.

Another such boss was One Lung Curran, who originated a practice that determined the fashion wear of his gang. One day Curran, dismayed that his girlfriend did not have a proper winter coat, snuck up behind a passing policeman, clubbed him over the head and stole his winter police coat. Curran gave the coat to his girlfriend, and after a few alterations, she produced a swell model with a military cut.

Other Gophers followed this trend, and soon there was an epidemic of police officers staggering back to their station house on West 47th Street, blood dripping from their heads and dressed only in their shirts, shoes, and trousers. This prompted the police captain of that precinct to send groups of four and five cops into the Gophers' domain. They bludgeoned enough Gophers that their sartorial vogue soon ended.

Another Gophers leader was Happy Jack Mulraney, called Happy Jack because his face was set in a permanent smile. Mulraney's smile was not intended, but, in fact, caused by a quirky paralysis of Mulraney's face muscles. His cohorts enjoyed inciting the psychopathic-killer Mulraney into a rage, by telling him someone had made fun of his unintentional grin.

One day, Paddy the Priest, a bar owner on 10th Avenue and a close friend of Mulraney's, made the horrible mistake of asking Mulraney why he didn't smile out of the other side of his face. Mulraney immediately shot Paddy the Priest in the head, killing him instantly. Then adding insult to injury, Mulraney emptied Paddy the Priest's cash register. For his temporary lapse in judgment, Mulraney was sentenced to life in prison.

In August of 1908, several Gophers wandered out of their West Side domain, and smack into the middle of a shootout on the Lower East Side between Monk Eastman's gang and Paul Kelly's Five Pointers. Not wanting to miss out on the fun, the Gophers opened fire, shooting at members of both warring gangs.

One Gopher later said, "A lot of guys were poppin' at each other, so why shouldn't we do a little poppin' ourselves?"

For years, the Gopher's main source of income was plundering the freight cars and the train depot of the New York Central Railroad, which ran along 11th Avenue. The New York City police was unable, and sometimes unwilling, to stop these shenanigans. So, the railroad organized its own "police force," which was comprised mostly of ex-cops, who had been brutalized by the Gophers in the past and were looking for revenge. This "police force" went into Hell's Kitchen, beating the Gophers from one end of the neighborhood to the other, or as a member of the "police force" said, "From hell to breakfast." Sometimes they used clubs, and if needed, they fired guns. Being former policemen and well-trained in firearms, they were much better at gunplay than were the Gophers.

In 1917, after the arrest of One Lung Curran, and with Madden still in jail and Mulraney in prison for life, the Gophers gradually dissipated. By 1920, the Gophers street gang ceased to exist, only to be replaced in later years by another murderous group called "The Westies."

Great New York City Fire of 1835

It was the worst fire in New York City's history. But that didn't stop the poor Irish, living in the slums of the Five Points, from going on a dazzling display of looting, which led to one of the biggest free champagne parties in the history of America.

The city was in the throes of one of the coldest winters on record. On the days preceding "The Great Fire," the temperature had dropped as low as 17 degrees below zero. By the night of December 16, 1835, there were two feet of frozen snow on the ground and the temperature was exactly zero frigid degrees. It was so cold, both the Hudson River and East Rivers had completely frozen.

Around 9 p.m., a watchman (the precursor to a New York City policeman) named Warren Hayes was crossing the corner of Merchant (now Beaver Street) and Pearl Street, when he thought he smelled smoke. Hayes looked up at the last floor of a five-story building at 25 Merchant Street, rented by Comstock and Andrews, a famous dry-goods store, and he spotted smoke coming out of a window. Unbeknownst to Hayes, a gas pipe had ruptured and had ignited some coals left on a stove.

Hayes immediately ran through the streets yelling "Fire!!" In minutes, the great fire bell that stood above City Hall began peeling loudly, summoning what was left of the New York City Fire Department. The bell at the Tombs Prison, about a mile north, also started ringing, summoning the volunteer firemen in that area.

In 1832, New York City was stricken with the worst case of cholera in the city's history. Four thousand people died, and more than half of the city's quarter million population fled the city in fear. This decimated the New York City Fire Department, and by 1835, the Fire Department had less than half of its previous members.

The volunteer fire department that responded on December 16, 1835, had spent the previous night fighting a fire on Burlington Street, on the East River, and they were now near exhaustion. By the time the local fire department arrived 30 minutes later, due to 40 mile-a-hour winds, the fire had already spread to 50 structures. Buildings were going up in flames on Water Street, Exchange Place, Beaver, Front, and South Streets. By midnight, the fire had also consumed Broad and Wall Street, which was the heart of the business and financial center of New York City, if not the entire country. Most of the city's newspaper plants, retail and wholesale stores, and warehouses, were also engulfed by the conflagration.

The call went out to every fire department in the city, but it was of no use. 75 hook and ladder companies were at the scene less than two hours after the fire had started. Hundreds of citizens pitched in, carrying water in buckets, pails, and even tubs. Unfortunately, because of the cold weather, the fire hoses were mostly useless.

In addition, the entire city's cisterns, wells, and fire hydrants were frozen too. Whatever water did stream thinly from the hydrants through the hoses, only went 30 feet into the air, then quickly turned into ice. What made matters worse, due to the high winds, this ice/water mixture, feebly coming out of the hoses, was blown back onto the fireman themselves, and soon scores of firemen were living ice structures. Many firemen poured brandy into their boots to keep their feet from getting frostbite. Some drank the brandy, too, in order to keep the rest of their body warm.

Other firemen raced to the East River, and they started chopping the ice to reach the water below. Black Joke Engine No. 33 was dragged onto the deck of a ship, and it started pumping water through the holes in the ice. Engine No. 33 directed the water though three other engines, until it finally reached the fire on Water Street. However, in just a few hours, those four engines were frozen too and were no longer of any use.

Two buildings were saved in an extremely odd way. Barrels of vinegar were rolled out of the Oyster King Restaurant, in the Downing Building on Garden Street. This vinegar was poured into several fire engines and used to douse the fires in the Downing Building, and in the Journal of Commerce Building next door. However, the vinegar soon ran out and could not be used to save any more structures.

As the city was engulfed in mayhem, a man ran into a church on Garden Street, and he began playing a funeral dirge on an organ, which could be heard all throughout Lower Manhattan. Minutes later, that church caught fire too, and the organist was seen sprinting from the flaming church.

Soon, the fire spread to Hanover Square, Williams Street, Hanover Street, and Exchange Place. Burning cloths and twines from various buildings were blown into the air, and they flew across the East River, igniting the roofs of homes in Brooklyn. The city's blaze was so intense, smoke could be seen as far south as Philadelphia and as far north as New Haven. New York City was so desperate, Philadelphia firemen were summoned from 90 miles away to help fight the blaze.

After consulting with experts, New York City Mayor Cornelius W. Lawrence agreed that the fire could be stopped, if they blew up certain buildings in strategic places, so that the flames could not travel from building to building. The only problem was, the sale of gunpowder was forbidden in New York City. The nearest ample supply was in the Brooklyn Navy Yard, in Red Hook, Brooklyn, as well as on Governors Island.

Mayor Strong sent word that the gunpowder was needed immediately, but it did not arrive until noon on December 17, accompanied by 80 marines and a dozen sailors. The military, with the help of James Hamilton, the son of former Secretary of the Treasury Alexander Hamilton, began blowing up buildings. In a few hours, the blaze was contained at Coenties Slip.

As downtown Manhattan continued smoldering, hundreds of Irish men, women, and children, from the slums of the Five Points area, rushed into the devastated area, eyes sparkling, and hands a-grabbing. For a full 24 hours, the hoodlums looted whatever they could get their hands on: stealing cloaks, frock coats, plug hats, and silk and satin of the finest quality.

Cases and kegs of booze, beer, and wine were smashed open, and the mob drank heartily in the smoky frigid streets. Fights broke out between the drunk and delirious rioters, over who had the right to steal what. Ten thousand bottles of the finest champagne were stolen, too, and what the mob could not guzzle on site, they lugged back to their slums for later consumption.

Noted diarist and future Mayor of New York City, Philip Hone, later wrote, "The miserable wretches, who prowled around the ruins, and became beastly drunk on the champagne and other wines and liquors, with which the streets and roads were lined, seemed to exult in the misfortune of others."

Finally, the area was placed under martial law, and patrolled by the marines from the Navy Yard, and from the Third and Ninth Military Regiments. However, this did not completely stop the looters from continuing their felonious frenzy. Dozens rushed to unaffected areas outside the burn zone, and they torched buildings, so they could loot those buildings too. Five arsonists were arrested by the Marines. But a sixth one, who was caught torching a building on the corner of Stone and Broad, was captured by angry citizens and immediately hung from a tree. His frozen body stood dangling there and was not cut down by the police until three days later.

From the start of the fire, three days had passed until the last spark was extinguished. By then, 17 blocks of lower Manhattan, covering 52 acres and consisting of 693 buildings, had burned to the ground. Two people were killed, and the damages were assessed at $20 million, almost a billion dollars by today's standards.

There was 10 million dollars in insurance money owed for the damages, but only a scant amount of that money was ever paid, since the insurance companies, and the banks, had also burned to the ground, forcing them out of business. Not being able to collect on their insurance, and not being able to get loans from banks that no longer existed, hundreds of businesses that burned to the ground during "The Great New York Fire of 1835" never re-opened.

In 1836, the downtown area was rebuilt, with structures made of stone and concrete, which were less susceptible to spreading fires. Some of those buildings are standing to this day.

Hicks, Albert E.

Albert E. Hicks, called "Hicksey" by his pals (if he had any) and "Pirate Hicks" by the police, was the last man to be executed for piracy in the United States of America.

Hicks was a freelance gangster, who lived with his wife and son at 129 Cedar Street in downtown Manhattan, only two blocks from the East River. Hicks felt his criminal enterprises were better served if he worked alone, and as a result, Hicks never joined any of the other gangs that prowled the waterfront in the treacherous 4th Ward. Working solo, the police suspected Hicks committed scores of robberies and over a dozen murders.

However, Hicks scoffed at that notion. "Suspecting it and proving it are two different things," he said.

In March 1860, Hicks tied on a big one at a Water Street dive, and he became so drunk, he could not walk the two blocks home. Instead, he staggered into a Cherry Street lodging house, figuring he'd sleep until he was sober enough to walk the rest of the way home. The owner of the establishment was a known crimp, or a man who specialized in shanghaiing, which was the practice of "kidnapping men into duty as sailors on ships, against their will, by devious techniques such as trickery, intimidation, or violence." Hicks asked the crimp for a nightcap, and that he got, as the crimp, not aware of Hicks's reputation, laced Hicks's rum with laudanum, which is an alcohol solution containing opium.

The nightcap knocked Hicks out cold and when he awoke the next morning, he found himself at sea, on the ship the *E. A. Johnson*, which was bound for Deep Creek, Virginia, to pick up a load of oysters. Five days later, the *E. A. Johnson* was found abandoned at sea, a few miles off the coast of Staten Island. The ship seemed to have collided with another vessel, and when it was finally secured, Coroner Schirmer and Captain Weed of the Second Precinct Police Station, boarded the boat to examine the cause of its condition. No one was on board, but in the ship's cabin they found the room ransacked, and the floor, ceiling, and bunks filled with blood. On the deck, they found four human fingers and a thumb lying under the rail.

The next day, two residents of the Cedar Street house, where Hicks lived with this family, told the police that Hicks had returned home with a considerable sum of money, and was now gone, with no trace of him, or his family. In fact, Hicks had packed his belongings and escaped with his family to a boarding house in Providence, Rhode Island.

New York City Patrolman Nevins traced Hicks, and with the help of the Providence police, he arrested Hicks's entire family. When Patrolman Nevins searched Hicks's belongings, he found a watch and a daguerreotype (an early version of a camera), which belonged to Captain Burr, the captain of the *E. A. Johnson*. The two other missing seamen were brothers, Smith and Oliver Watts, but nothing could be found belonging to them and their fate remained a mystery.

As a result, Hicks was arrested and locked up in the Tombs Prison. At his trial in May, it took the jury only seven minutes to convict Hicks of piracy and murder on the high seas. He was sentenced to be hanged at Bedloe's Island on Friday the 13th, which was certainly a double-bad-luck day for Hicks.

A week after his trial, Hicks decided to become downright chatty. Hicks summoned the warden and several newspapermen to his cell, and he began spilling the beans about the whole sordid affair.

"I was brooding about being shanghaied," Hicks said "And I decided to avenge myself by murdering all hands on the ship."

Hicks told the assembled crowd that he was steering the ship, while Captain Burr and one of the Watts brothers was sleeping in the cabin below. The other Watts brother was on lookout at the bow. Hicks lashed the steering wheel to keep the ship on course, then he picked up an iron bar, sneaked to the bow of the ship, and hit the lookout over the head with the bar, knocking him out cold.

The other Watts brother heard the noise, and he rushed topside. By this time, Hicks had found an ax, and when the boy climbed onto the deck, Hicks decapitated him with one mighty blow. Hicks then rushed down to the cabin and confronted Captain Burr, who had just awakened from a deep sleep. The Captain put up a brave battle, but in the end, he too was decapitated.

Hicks said he then heard rumblings from up top. Hicks rushed up to the deck, and he found the first Watts boy staggering around in obvious pain. Hicks knocked him down with a heavy blow. Then he picked him up, carried him to the rail and tried to throw the boy overboard. The boy clutched at the railing, and Hicks used the ax to chop off the boy's five fingers, after which the lad toppled into the murky waters below.

Hicks threw the other two bodies overboard. Then he rushed below and ransacked the cabin, looking for money and valuables. When he saw the coast of Staten Island, Hicks lowered a small boat, and he rowed the rest of the way to land.

Hicks's confession made him an instant celebrity. Hundreds of gawkers paid the prison guards small fees to see Hicks shackled in his cell. And for a few pennies more, they were allowed to speak with the condemned man himself.

Among Hicks's many visitors was circus owner P.T. Barnum, who offered Hicks $25, a new suit of clothes, and two boxes of cigars, in exchange for a plaster cast of Hicks's head, which Barnum, the enterprising chap that he was, had planned to display in his circus, after Hicks's execution. Hicks agreed, but later on his way to the gallows, he complained to the warden that the suit was cheap and it did not fit properly. The warden told Hicks it was too late for alterations.

On the morning of July 13, Hicks, led by Marshall Rynders and a crowd estimated at 1500 people, started a procession to the docks. Rynders and Hicks boarded the boat accompanied by several policemen, and they sailed for Bedloe's Island, where a gallows had been erected 30 feet from the water. Hundreds of boats followed the doomed man, and it was estimated that 10,000 people came to witness Hicks's execution.

After the noose was slung around Hicks's neck and the ground removed from beneath his feet, Hicks struggled for a full three minutes before he stopped moving. Hicks was then cut down and pronounced dead.

Hicks was buried at Calvary Cemetery. However, a few days later, Hicks's body was stolen and sold to medical students, intent on studying the brain of a man who could commit such vile atrocities without much remorse.

Holstein, Caspar – The Harlem Policy King

He was considered a genius; a compassionate man who gave freely to the poor. However, Caspar Holstein made his fortune in the Harlem numbers policy racket, a game of chance he helped invent.

Casper Holstein was born on December 7, 1876, in St. Croix, Danish West Indies. His parents were of mixed African and Danish descent, and his father's father was a Danish officer in the Danish West Indies Colonial militia. In 1894, the Holstein family moved to New York City. Holstein, an extremely bright teenager, graduated from high school in Brooklyn, which was no mean accomplishment for a black man before the turn of the century. After graduation, Holstein enlisted in the Navy, and during World War I he visited his homeland, which, by then, was known as the West Virgin Islands.

When Holstein was discharged from the Navy, he worked at various odd jobs, including being a doorman in an Upper East Side building. He also became a personal assistant to a wealthy white couple, and years later, after he had made his fortune and they had lost theirs, Holstein supported this couple, then paid for their funeral.

Looking to better himself, Holstein wandered down to Wall Street, where he got a job, first as a messenger, and then as head messenger for a commodities brokerage firm. Holstein became enamored of gambling, especially the horses. But he also dabbled in the stock market, perusing the daily figures from the Boston and the New York City Clearing Houses.

One day, an idea came to Holstein that would improve his lot dramatically. Holstein knew that people in black neighborhoods, such as Harlem, loved to gamble, but most didn't have enough spare cash to do so. When he had saved enough money to start his new endeavor, Holstein devised a scheme where people could bet as little as a dime on a random set of three digit numbers which would appear daily in the New York City newspapers.

Using the Boston and New York City Clearing House figures, Holstein took the two middle digits of the New York number and the one middle digit from the Boston number. So if the two clearing house totals were $9,456,131 and $7,456,253 respectively, the winning number would be 566: the "56" being the two digits before the last comma of the first figure, and the "6" being the last digit before the last comma of the second figure.

This system was so random, it could not be manipulated; like it would be later by gangster Dutch Schultz, after he muscled in on the Harlem numbers rackets and began using race track figures which he manipulated to decrease his losses. By the early 1920's, Holstein's system was the rage in Harlem. Holstein became known as the "Bolita King," earning an estimated $5000 a day.

Using his newfound wealth, Holstein contributed generously to worthwhile causes. He gave huge amounts of money to the St. Vincent Sanitarium and to the nationalist Garvey Movement. Holstein also funded prizes for *Opportunity Magazine's* literary awards, which discovered much of Harlem's young artistic talent. Holstein built dormitories at black colleges, and he financed many of Harlem's artists, writers, and poets. Holstein also helped start a Baptist school in Liberia, and he established a hurricane relief fund for his native Virgin Islands. The *New York Times* said that Holstein was, "Harlem's favorite hero, because of his wealth, his sporting proclivities, and his philanthropies among the people of his race."

Seeing how Holstein and Stephanie St. Clair had turned Harlem into a financial bonanza due to their numbers rackets, gangster Dutch Schultz barged in and took over their games. Just like that. Schultz had big politicians, including the disgraced Jimmy Hines, in his back pocket. Schultz also bought off the cops, and he killed, or had killed, black numbers runners who did not work for him. Schultz eventually forced St. Clair to work under him, but Holstein refused Schultz's offers to consolidate their numbers rackets.

In 1928, Holstein was kidnapped for $50,000 ransom, by five white gangsters, whom were presumed by the Harlem public to be goons sent by Schultz. The news of Holstein's kidnapping made national headlines. The *New York Times* reported that Holstein had been seen at Belmont Racetrack just days before his abduction, betting more than $30,000 on the ponies.

Holstein was released by his captors after three days in custody; insisting he had paid his kidnappers no ransom. Holstein's explanation was that his abductors had felt sorry for him and had freed him with $3 cab fare in his pocket.

However, Holstein's tale carried very little weight, since he soon mysteriously cut down on his policy activities. A few years later, Holstein completely stopped his street operations, and he operated only as a lay-off better.

In 1935, despite the fact that he was barely in the game, Holstein was arrested for illegal gambling. Holstein was tried and convicted, and he spent one year in prison. Holstein claimed he was framed, possibly by Schultz, but he did his time in jail uneventfully. When he was released from prison, Holstein got involved in the real estate business, and he provided mortgages for people in Harlem whom the regular banks shunned.

Casper Holstein died on April 5, 1944, at the age of 68. More than 2,000 people attended Holstein's funeral at Harlem's Memorial Baptist Church. A scholarship at the University of the Virgin Islands and a housing development in St. Croix are named in Holstein's memory.

Hudson Dusters

The Hudson Dusters were an unruly street gang, which, starting in the late 1890's, ruled the Greenwich Village area of New York City. They were formed by the trio of Kid Yorke, Circular Jack, and Goo Goo Knox, who was a former gang member of the Gophers, a homicidal group that ran Hell's Kitchen a few blocks to the north.

Knox had tried to take control of the Gophers, failed, and then moved south to terrorize a different neighborhood, which was open to whichever gang could take control. The Hudson Dusters crushed local gangs like the Potashes, and the Boodles, and then they took command of the rackets in Greenwich Village. The Hudson Dusters also made big scores, plundering the docks along the Hudson River, a few blocks to the west.

After the Hudson Dusters committed one of their varied crimes, the snakelike streets of Greenwich Village were perfect for their getaways. Their most accomplished thief was Ding Dong, who would roam the streets with a dozen or so youths. When the opportunity arose, Ding Dong would direct the kids to jump on passing wagons, and to toss to him any valuables they could get their hands on. Before the police could respond, Ding Dong was long gone, having disappeared through the maze of streets that comprised Greenwich Village.

The Hudson Dusters became street legends, but they were not particularly famous for their fighting prowess, as were other brutal New York City gangs. The Hudson Dusters hung out in the taverns and gin mills of the Village, mingling with the famous writers and artists of their time. The print journalists also favored the Hudson Dusters, whom they portrayed in the newspapers as nothing more than a fun-loving bunch, who drank more than they committed crimes. One of Hudson Dusters' party pals was playwright Eugene O'Neil, who frequented the gang's hangout - the Hell Hole on Sixth Avenue and 4th Street. It was there that O'Neil garnered most of his characters for his most famous play: *The Iceman Cometh*; the Iceman meaning "death."

At their inception, the Hudson Dusters moved their base of operations frequently, finally settling on a house on Hudson Street, just below Horatio Street, later the site of the Open Door Mission. More interested in partying than pillaging, the Hudson Dusters installed a piano, and they danced the nights away, in a cocaine-induced stupor, with the prostitutes who prowled the West Side piers a few short blocks away. This annoyed the neighboring homeowners and business owners to no end, but they all were afraid to make a complaint to the police, because the Hudson Dusters had the reputation of seeking revenge in a hot moment against anyone who dared rat them out. After a night of carousing, the Hudson Dusters were known to parade in the streets, boozed out and hopped-up on coke, looking to cause mayhem on anyone or anything in their path.

One night, the Hudson Dusters asked a local saloon keeper to provide them with a few kegs of beer for a party, on the arm, meaning they did not expect to pay the man for his stock. The saloon keeper refused, and the Hudson Dusters descended up his establishment. They wrecked the joint and carried away every ounce of booze on the premises. The saloon keeper ran to his friend, Patrolman Dennis Sullivan. Patrolman Sullivan opted to declare war on the Hudson Dusters. He rounded up ten Hudson Dusters, including their then-leader Red Farrell, and arrested them for vagrancy.

The Hudson Dusters decided to retaliate, and with the blessing of a Greenwich Village politician who used the Hudson Dusters for intimidation on Election Day, they ambushed Patrolmen Sullivan, as he was about to arrest one of the Hudson Dusters on a robbery charge. The Hudson Dusters attacked Patrolman Sullivan from behind and stole his jacket, gun and shield, while beating him with stones and blackjacks. As many as 20 Hudson Dusters took turns kicking and punching the distressed policeman after he was down. When Patrolman Sullivan was finally unconscious, four Hudson Dusters rolled him onto his back, and then they ground the heels of their boots into his face, causing permanent scars. Patrolman Sullivan was finally taken to the hospital, where he stayed, recuperating for over a month.

The Gophers Street Gang congratulated the Hudson Dusters on their cop-beating accomplishment. Gopher leader, "One Lung" Curran, felt moved enough to write a poem praising their actions. The poem reads:

Says Dinny "Here's me only chance

To gain meself a name;

I'll clean up the Hudson Dusters,

and reach the Hall of Fame."

He lost his stick and cannon,

and his shield they took away.

It was then he remembered,

Every dog had his day.

The Hudson Dusters loved this poem so much, they printed up hundreds of copies, and distributed them on the streets of Greenwich Village, even dropping one off at the Charles Street Station House where Patrolman Sullivan was assigned.

By 1916, the Hudson Dusters had dissipated, as most of their gang members were either coke addicts, dead, or locked up in jail. Another Greenwich Village gang, the Marginals, led by Tanner Smith, took over the Hudson Dusters' rackets. The Marginals controlled the Village, until Tanner was killed by Chicky Lewis, inside the Marginal Club on Eighth Avenue, on July 29, 1919.

For all practical purposes, that was the end of a street gang presence on the Lower West Side of Manhattan.

Ida "The Goose"

Ida "The Goose" Burger was a strikingly beautiful dance hall girl, and sometimes prostitute, who was the favorite of several members of the five-hundred-strong Gophers gang, which controlled New York City's Hell's Kitchen. The Gophers passed Ida the Goose around from boss to boss, and even down to the low-level members of their gang. Make no mistake, Ida belonged to the treacherous Gophers, and anyone who thought otherwise would be dealt with severely.

Jack Tricker was a saloon keeper/gangster, whom, after Monk Eastman was sent to prison for armed robbery, headed up one faction of the Eastman gang on the Lower East Side. Tricker owned a bar on Park Row in downtown Manhattan. But after it was closed by authorities (for basically being a den of iniquity), Tricker decided to branch out of the Lower East Side and into Hell's Kitchen, which was enemy territory. Tricker decided, that maybe, because of the Gophers' internal battles, they were not so tough anymore. In an act of defiance, Tricker bought the Old Stag Bar on West 28th Street, smack in the middle of Gopher territory, and he renamed it the Maryland Cafe.

One of Tricker's men, Irish Tom Riley, somehow won the affections of the glorious Ida the Goose. Riley spit in the Gophers' face, when he took Ida away from the Gophers and brought her to the Maryland Cafe, where they immediately installed Ida as the main attraction - the "Belle of The Ball," so to speak.

The Gophers sent an emissary to Tricker, demanding the return of Ida the Goose. Tricker told the emissary that he would not get involved, one way or another, and that it was their problem, not his. Immediately, threats spewed from the Gophers to Tricker's gang, who armed themselves heavily in anticipation of a street war. However, after weeks had passed and nothing happened, Tricker's gang relaxed a bit, thinking the Gophers were all talk and no action.

In October of 1910, four Gophers, one of whom was Ida's former boyfriend, swaggered into the Maryland Cafe. They approached the bar and ordered four beers, which they were quickly served. Six Tricker gangsters, who were sitting at a large round table nearby, were so surprised by the bold move, they sat transfixed and said not a word, let alone try to evict the invaders.

Outraged, it was Ida the Goose who spoke first. She screamed at the Gophers, "Say!! Youse guys have some nerve!"

The Gophers calmly finished their beer, then one turned around slowly, and said, "Well, let's get at it."

The four Gophers each drew two guns, and they began spraying the bar's walls, mirrors, and tables with bullets. The two bartenders, who were not part of Tricker's gang, dived behind the bar for cover. Five of Tricker's men were shot and disabled. The sixth, who was Ida's newfound lover, Riley, was so far untouched and un-bloodied. Seeking refuge, Riley dived under Ida's flowing skirt.

Nonplussed, Ida stared down at Riley in disdain.

Then she shrugged her shoulders and said, "Say, youse! Come on out and take it."

Ida stepped back, and she shoved Riley into the center of the floor. Smiling broadly, the four Gophers pumped four bullets into Riley's torso. Then Ida's former boyfriend stepped forward, and he put one final bullet into Riley's brain.

Proud of their accomplishments, the four Gophers strode out of the Maryland Cafe, followed closely by Ida the Goose, glowing with pride that such a battle had been fought over her affections.

As a result, Ida the Goose was again the exclusive property of the Gophers, never to stray from their embrace.

Johnson, Ellsworth (Bumpy)

Ellsworth "Bumpy" Johnson was known as a murderous policy numbers baron in Harlem during the 1930's, but he was, in addition, the conduit between the Italian Mob and the Harlem rackets for almost three decades.

Ellsworth Johnson was born in Charleston, South Carolina, on October 31, 1905. He got the nickname "Bumpy" because as a child he had received a huge dump on the back of his head. Johnson was a brilliant youth, and by the time he was eight years old, he had already skipped two grades.

When Johnson was 10, his brother Willie was accused of killing a white man. Knowing a lynch mob was looking for Willie, Johnson's parents sent Willie to live up north.

Growing toward adulthood, Bumpy Johnson was a proud black man, defiant of the segregation and the violence perpetrated against blacks in the deep south. Johnson's parents were worried Johnson, who had a violent temper, would follow in his brother Willie's footsteps. So, in 1919, they sent Johnson to Harlem to stay with his Aunt Mabel.

After graduating from Boys High in Brooklyn and attending City College for a few semesters, Johnson got involved with a wild element in Harlem. As a result, he made several trips to prison, for such crimes as armed robbery and burglary. In a 10-year stretch of prison life, Johnson, because of his penchant for violence, spent a full three years in solitary confinement. When he was released in 1932, Johnson had spent more than half of his life behind bars.

Back on the streets causing mayhem, Johnson caught the eye of Stephanie St. Clair, called "Madame Queen" in Harlem. Johnson became chief lieutenant to St. Clair. But it was rumored they were also lovers, even though St. Clair was 20 years Johnson's elder.

St. Clair was a numbers baron, who was being squeezed out of the rackets by crazed gangster Dutch Schultz. Schultz used every trick in the book to drive St. Clair out of Harlem, including killing her numbers runners and paying off the cops to arrest St. Clair's numbers runners on sight.

Johnson, knowing Schultz was not a reasonable man, went to Italian mob boss Lucky Luciano, and he asked Luciano to intercede on St. Clair's behalf. Luciano was impressed with Johnson's gumption and intelligence. But he told Johnson there was not much he could do as far as Schultz was concerned, since he and Schultz were partners in several other illegal activities. Johnson decided to take the war to Schultz, and for the next three years, the two gangs shot each other on sight, resulting in numerous casualties on both sides.

In 1935, Johnson and St. Clair caught a break, when Luciano, tired of the murderous Schultz's unpredictable violence, had Schultz gunned down in a

New Jersey steakhouse. Luciano gave Schultz's numbers rackets to "Trigger" Mike Coppola, a captain in what was later to be called the "Genovese Crime Family."

However, Luciano, remembering Johnson's capabilities, cut a deal with Johnson, allowing Johnson and St. Clair to keep their independent Harlem numbers business intact. This made Johnson an instant hero to the black people in Harlem, and it also gave Johnson respect and credibility with the Italian mob. Soon, St. Clair opted for retirement, and she turned over her number business to Johnson.

With the backing of the Italian mob, Johnson became "The Man" in Harlem. Johnson rubbed elbows with many Harlem celebrities, including Bill "Bojangles" Robinson, Lena Horne, Billie Holiday, and World Middleweight Champion Sugar Ray Robinson. Johnson was also the uncrowned "Crime Boss of Harlem," and no one could run an illegal operation in Harlem without clearing it with Johnson first and cutting him in for a piece of the pie.

From 1940 until 1968, Johnson acted as a "middleman," between the Genovese Crime Family, who operated out of Italian Harlem (the area surrounding East 116th Street), and the black gangsters operating out of the main section of Harlem. Johnson brokered numerous drug deals between black drug dealers and the Italian suppliers, who were importing the drugs from overseas. Johnson was also known as a "persuader," or a high-level gangster, who could settle mob disputes before they erupted into violence. It is estimated that during the time he was in power in Harlem, Johnson brokered deals, mostly drug affairs, involving tens of millions of dollars with the Genovese Crime Family.

In 1952, Johnson was indicted for conspiracy to sell heroin. He was convicted and sentenced to 15 years in prison. While he was at Alcatraz, it was rumored Johnson helped three fellow inmates escape. Although he stayed put himself, Johnson was said to have arranged to have a boat to pick up the three escapees, once they slipped out of prison and made it to San Francisco Bay.

Johnson was released from prison in 1963, and when he returned to Harlem, the local folk threw him a ticker tape parade. In December 1965, Johnson led a sit-down strike in a police station, refusing to leave, as a protest against the cops conducting unreasonable surveillances on his crew. Johnson was charged with "refusal to leave a police station," but at trial he was found not guilty.

On July 7, 1968, Johnson, under indictment by the feds for drug conspiracy, was at Wells Restaurant in Harlem at 2 a.m., munching on a meal of chicken legs and hominy grits, washed down with coffee. Suddenly, Johnson grabbed his chest, and he toppled to the floor.

With two lifelong friends at his side, Ellsworth "Bumpy" Johnson died of a heart attack at the age of 63, forever to be known as the "Harlem Godfather."

Kaplan, Nathan (Kid Dropper)

Nathan Kaplan was born on the Lower East Side of Manhattan in 1891. Kaplan took to the streets as a youth, and soon he became engaged in petty swindles, such as the "dropper" scheme.

When no one was watching, Kaplan would conveniently "drop" a wallet full of counterfeit money on the sidewalk. Then he would immediately "find" the wallet, and look for a sucker, whom he told, "Lookit, I don't have time to locate the owner. You take the wallet and find the owner. Give me half of what you think the reward money will be."

Dupes constantly fell for this scheme, hence Kaplan was given the nickname "Kid Dropper."

Because of his expertise in making an illegal buck, Dropper joined Paul Kelly's (Paolo Vaccarelli) Five Points Gang, which was quite unusual for the Jewish Dropper, since the vast majority of Kelly's gang members were of Italian descent.

Yet, Dropper did not last too long with the Five Pointers. In 1911, he was arrested for armed robbery and sentenced to seven years in Sing Sing Prison. By the time Dropper was released in 1917, Kelly's gang had been disbanded. Dropper, considered a minor criminal before he went to jail, fancied himself as successor to Kelly, and he grabbed Kelly's labor rackets business.

In his past life, Dropper was a habitual wearer of slovenly attire, in other words, he dressed like a bum. Now as a boss, Dropper started to dress accordingly. He threw away his normal rags, and started prancing around the streets in loud checkered suits, pointed shoes, shirts and ties with loud colors and outlandish designs, and a straw hat or a derby tilted rakishly over one eye.

Dropper soon compiled a motley crew of low-level gangsters. He called his gang, "The Rough Riders of Jack Dropper." However, Dropper soon found himself in a war for control of Kelly's old rackets with an old foe who had just been released from prison himself.

Before his incarceration, Dropper had made a very bad enemy in fellow Five Pointer Johnny Spanish, a Spanish Jew; real name Joseph Weyler. The two men had been pals, until 1911, when Spanish had to take it on the lam for a shooting which resulted in the death of an innocent eight-year-old girl. Spanish split town for a few months, and when he came back he found Dropper had stolen his girlfriend. Spanish, who carried four guns with him at all times, proceeded to pepper his former lover with multiple gunshots. Somehow the woman survived, but Spanish got seven years in prison for his actions.

When he was released in 1917, Spanish took dead aim at Dropper and every illegal activity Dropper controlled. Each man had approximately three dozen shooters under their wings, and these shooters went to work, resulting in the deaths of several men on both sides. The war ended, when Dropper got the drop on Spanish, so to speak, after he and two of his men ambushed Spanish as Spanish exited a restaurant at 19 Second Avenue. When the dust settled, Spanish was dead, and Dropper was now in charge of all the strong-arm tactics used by several unions to control their men.

Between 1920 and 1923, Dropper and his gang were responsible for more than 20 murders. However, in these rackets, when you kill one competitor, another one usually emerges from the shadows intent on doing to you what you did to the other guy, to gain control of whatever illegal activities you dominated. This person emerged in the name of Jacob "Little Augie" Orgen.

Little Augie had in his stable a crew of every capable killers, which included Jack "Legs" Diamond, Louis "Lepke" Buchalter, and Gurrah Shapiro. In 1922 and 1923, Dropper's gang and Little Augie's gang turned Manhattan into one big shooting gallery. The result was 23 murders, including the death of one innocent man who just happened to be in the wrong place at the wrong time.

In 1923, Dropper was arrested on a concealed weapons charge. He was soon released outside the Essex Market Court, on Second Avenue and Second Street. There were rumors that a death squad was awaiting his release, so as he stepped into a waiting taxi, Dropper was surrounded by a phalanx of cops.

Dropper was sitting in the back seat of the taxi next to Detective Jesse Joseph, when a minor thug working for Little Augie, named Louis Kushner, rushed from behind the cab and shot Dropper through the closed window, twice in the head.

Dropper's wife rushed to her mortally wounded husband, and said, "Nate! Nate! Tell me you were not what they say you were."

Dropper gasped, and with his last breath he said, "They got me."

Then he keeled sideways, dead, his head nestled on Detective Joseph's shoulder.

Kushner, restrained by several burly cops, was obviously proud of his handiwork. He smiled at the coppers, and snapped, "I got him! Now give me a cigarette!"

Kelly, Paul (Paulo Vaccarelli)

In the early 1900's, Paul Kelly was the most high-profile gangster in New York City. Real name Paulo Vaccarelli, Kelly was born in Sicily in 1879. He immigrated to America in the early 1890's, and soon became a bantamweight boxer of some repute. He changed his name from the Italian Vaccarelli to the Irish-sounding Kelly, in order to get more fights, at a time when being Italian in America was considered being a low-class citizen of ill repute.

Unlike most gangsters of his day, Kelly was an intelligent, erudite man, who could speak three languages. Kelly was a dapper dresser and an easy person to like, which is why he was able to recruit so many quality gangsters to work for him.

After Kelly retired from boxing, he formed the notorious Five Points Gang in Lower Manhattan. The 1,500-member Five Points Gang was the breeding ground for some of the most famous gangsters ever to set foot in America. Their members included Johnny Torrio and Al Capone (both of whom later emigrated to control Chicago), Meyer Lansky, Bugsy Siegel, Lucky Luciano, and Frankie Yale.

While Kelly's gang was almost entirely comprised of Italians, his main nemesis was Monk Eastman, who headed a 2000-strong, mostly Jewish gang. Kelly and Eastman's crew fought often and violently. The dividing line between their territories was the Bowery. Kelly's domain was west of the Bowery, and Eastman ruled to the east of the Bowery. Everything else was neutral territory, and that's where the trouble began, resulting in disputes over who controlled what and where.

Both Kelly and Eastman worked for Tammany Hall as head-busters on Election Day, when either one group, or the other, would stand guard at all the polling places, making sure that the Tammany Hall-backed candidate won the election. Finally, the two gangs became so out-of-control dangerous to the community, the Tammany Hall bosses ordered Eastman and Kelly to duke it out, mano a mano, with the winner getting control of the prized neutral territories.

The two men went at it for a full two hours, and even though the ex-boxer Kelly was 50 pounds lighter than the hulking Eastman, neither man was able to knock the other man out. The fight was ruled a draw, and Kelly and Eastman went back to their usual violent territorial disputes.

Kelly's base of operations was his fancy New Brighton Athletic Club on Great Jones Street, just north of Houston Street. In April 1905, police raided the club, and they arrested several members, including Kelly. Even though four policemen testified they had witnessed illegal activities in the club, due to the false testimony of a police captain named Burke and a Tammany Hall-appointed judge named Barlow, Kelly's case was summarily dismissed, to the roar of a cheering crowd of hundreds of Kelly's supporters assembled in the courtroom.

In November 1908, Kelly's luck ran out, when two of his former henchmen, Biff Ellison and Razor Riley, barged into the New Brighton Athletic Club, with guns blazing. Kelly was sitting at a table with his two bodyguards, Bill Harrington and Rough House Hogan. Kelly dove under the table, but not before he was shot three times. Harrington took a bullet in the head, and he died instantly. Kelly fired back from under the table, and he injured both Ellison and Riley.

Even though he recovered from his injuries, Kelly's clout was never the same after the shooting incident. Within days, since Kelly's new-found notoriety had cost him the favor of Tammany Hall, police shut down the New Brighton Athletic Club. Kelly relocated to Italian Harlem, and he toned down his criminal activities, to a point. Kelly became intimately involved in union activities, some legal and some not-so-legal. Through intimidation and strong-arm tactics, Kelly was eventually elected vice president of the International Longshoremen Association.

Unlike his arch enemy Eastman, who was shot to death on the streets in 1920, Kelly died in 1936 of natural causes.

Lansky, Meyer

Born Majer Suchowlinki on July 4 1902, in Grodno, Poland, Meyer Lansky was considered one of the great masterminds of the modern day mob.

In 1911, Lansky's family immigrated to New York City, and they took up residence at 6 Columbia Street on the Lower East Side of Manhattan. As a boy, Lansky learned the trade of tool and die making. He also dabbled as an auto mechanic, and for a short time he worked in a factory. Tired of the 9-5 drag, Lansky hooked up with fellow Lower East Sider, Benjamin "Bugsy" Siegel (no one called him Bugsy to his face), and they started an auto-theft racket. Siegel would steal the cars. Lansky would get them in good working order, and then sell them.

They soon formed the violent "Bugs and Meyer Mob," which delved heavily in the illegal booze business. When Lansky and Siegel weren't hired as muscle to protect other bootlegger's shipments, they were hijacking liquor trucks themselves, sometimes even the trucks of the bootleggers which they were supposed to be protecting.

The "Bugs and Meyer Mob" was also intimately involved in violent "schlammings" (beating up people for a fee) and a few murders, as long as the price was right. The murder business was so lucrative, several of the "Bugs and Meyer Mob" alumni eventually became key members of "Murder Incorporated," which terrorized the streets of New York City in the 1930's. These killers included Joe "Doc" Stacher, Joe Adonis, Abner "Longie" Zwillmen, and Arthur "Dutch Schultz" Flegenheimer.

As a young man, Lansky became fast friends with Italian mobster Lucky Luciano. Lansky and Luciano joined forces with men like Arnold "The Brain" Rothstein, and they began to run their crime enterprises like a business, with violence used only as a last resort.

In 1931, after the deaths of Mafia bosses Salvatore Maranzano and Joe "The Boss" Masseria (both were ordered killed by Luciano), Lansky and Luciano transformed the mob into one National Crime Syndicate, with men of assorted nationalities on their "Board of Directors." Not only did this Crime Syndicate engage in illegal activities, such as gambling, hijackings, shakedowns, and loansharking, but they also controlled the labor unions, which oversaw the shipping and trucking industries, as well as public works projects. Lansky also partnered with mob boss Frank Costello, to corner the illegal slot-machine markets throughout the country.

Even though most of his mob boss associates were in the Italian Mafia, Lansky had as much say as the Italians. In fact, most people considered Lansky "the brains of the operation," while the Italians mostly provided the muscle. Because he was short in stature, Lansky was dubbed "The Little Man," However, this was not a derogatory term. Lansky's vote on any crime issue usually took precedence over anyone else's vote.

After Luciano went to jail on a trumped-up prostitution charge, Siegel convinced Lansky that there was money to be made in the desert of Las Vegas, Nevada, which was then little more than a "comfort station" for weary travelers. Lansky formed the Nevada Projects Corporation, and Las Vegas was born.

Unfortunately, Siegel did not live long enough to reap the mob's Las Vegas profits. Siegel was suspected of skimming the mob's construction cash, and in 1947, Siegel was shot through the eye, as he sat in the living room of his girlfriend Virginia Hill's mansion in Beverly Hills. Rumors arose that Lansky voted against killing his longtime pal Siegel, but in fact, Lansky agreed, saying, "I had no choice."

Lansky invested heavily in the casino gambling operations in Cuba. However in 1959, Lansky lost everything, when Fidel Castro took over the rule of Cuba from Fulgencio Batista in a military coup.

With the United States government cracking down on the mob in Las Vegas, Lansky fled to Israel to avoid arrest. He tried to claim Israeli citizenship under "The Law of Return," a rule that gave citizenship to anyone born of a Jewish mother. After lengthy court battles, Lansky's pleas for citizenship in Israel were turned down, and he was sent back to America. In 1973, law enforcement officials tried to jail Lansky on tax evasion charges, like they had done with Al Capone four decades earlier. However, Lansky was acquitted at trial, which gave the government a big black eye.

After undergoing open heart surgery in 1973, Lansky spent the rest of his life as a sickly man. Stricken with lung cancer, Meyer Lansky died at his home in Miami Beach, Florida, in January 1983, at the age of 80.

Leslie, George Leonidas

George Leonidas Leslie started out in life as one of the privileged class. However, Leslie soon became a criminal, known by the New York City Police as "King of the Bank Robbers."

Leslie was born in Cincinnati in 1840. His father owned a brewery, and Leslie started out as an academic, graduating from the University of Cincinnati with honors and a degree in architecture.

After both his parents had died, Leslie sold his father's brewery. He gave up his architectural career, and he moved to New York City. There Leslie fell in with a bad crowd, and he decided he could make a darn good living by robbing banks. It is estimated, that in the 10-year period spanning 1874-1884, Leslie was responsible for 80 percent of all bank robberies committed in the United States; swiping cash estimated to be between 7-12 million dollars.

In New York City, Leslie posed as a man-about-town of considerable means. He belonged to the most exclusive clubs, and he was a regular theatergoer and a patron of the arts. Leslie used this false pretense to gain access to valuable bits of information, that made his bank-robbing life most profitable.

Leslie would often spend as much as three years planning a bank job. When he found a bank to his liking, Leslie would try to get the blueprints of the interior of the bank. If that were not possible, Leslie would visit the bank posing as a depositor. With his experience in architecture, Leslie would then draw up rough plans, detailing the intricacies of the inside of the bank. Sometimes, Leslie would have one of his gang members get a job at the bank, either as a night watchman, or a porter. These "inside men" would provide Leslie with the exact specifications of the inside of the bank, and the make and model of the bank vault.

After obtaining all this valuable information, Leslie would then buy a duplicate of the bank's safe. Leslie spent days, and sometimes weeks, perfecting the art of opening that safe. Leslie shied away from using dynamite to crack the safe, having decided that an explosion would cause too much noise and lead to them being detected.

Leslie method of opening safes included boring a hole underneath the dial, then using a thin piece of steel to manipulate the tumblers into place. To cover almost any contingency in robbing a bank, Leslie had a set of burglar tools specially created for him, which cost the staggering sum of $3,000 - more than most people, at that time, earned in several years.

To perfect the job he was planning, Leslie sometimes set up a room in a loft he had rented downtown to resemble the inside of the bank he was planning to rob. There Leslie, and the men whom he had selected for that particular bank job, would spend considerable amounts of time practicing exactly how the bank robbery should develop. Leslie would darken the lights, and watch his men go through their maneuvers in the dark. He would then critique their work.

Leslie's cohorts consisted of various known criminals, such as Jimmy Hope, Jimmy Brady, Abe Coakley, Shang Draper, Red Leary, Johnny Dobbs, Worcester Sam Perris, Bill Kelly, and Banjo Pete Emerson.

In May of 1875, Leslie decided to rob the Manhattan Savings Institution at 644 Broadway. Leslie, through his "inside man" at the bank, Patrick Shelvin, found out the make and model of the lock on the bank's vault. Leslie procured an exact model from the manufacturers: Valentine & Bulter. Then, Leslie spent six months perfecting the opening of the lock.

On October 27, 1875, Shelvin let Leslie and Leslie's crew into the bank at night. When their work was done, they had stolen $3.5 million in cash and securities, almost $50 million in today's money. No one was arrested until May 1879, and as a result, Jimmy Hope and Bill Kelly were convicted and sent to prison. Abe Coakley and Banjo Pete Emerson were also arrested, but they were acquitted at trial. Leslie was never arrested, and his involvement in the bank robbery was not discovered until after his death.

Leslie's reputation grew to such gigantic proportions, he was often called in as a "consultant" by other bank-robbing gangs. It is believed, Leslie received more than $20,000, just to travel to San Francisco to look over plans for a local bank heist.

Yet, if Leslie had one weakness, it was for the affections of a woman. Leslie began an affair with the girlfriend of one of his cohorts: Shang Draper, a murderous thug of the worst sort.

On June 4, 1884, Leslie's decomposed body was found lying at the base of Tramps Rock, near the borderline between Westchester and the Bronx. He was shot twice in the head. Police speculated that Leslie was killed by the jealous Draper in a house at 101 Lynch Street in Brooklyn. Then, Leslie's body was carted to Tramps Rock by three of Draper's associates, who had been seen near Yonkers at the time Leslie's body was discovered.

However, there was little evidence of the crime, and no one was ever arrested for Leslie's murder.

Luciano, Lucky

Lucky Luciano was born Salvatore Luciana on November 24, 1896, in Lercara Friddi, a tiny town near Palermo, Sicily. Luciano immigrated with his family to America in 1907, and they settled in an apartment building at 265 East 10th Street. The rumor was that as a 10-year-old Luciano was a terror in Sicily, and he convinced a customs officer at Ellis Island to change his name from Luciana to Luciano, in order to avoid detection by several enemies he had made in the old country.

Luciano was not a model student. As a result, Luciano decided to work a racket in which he would confront skinny Jewish kids on their way to the public school he attended, and offer them, for a penny or two, protection from him not beating them up. Some kids paid, and some kids Luciano beat up badly. However, one skinny Jewish kid fought Luciano tooth and nail in an all-out street fight. The Jewish kid's name was Meyer Lansky, and they started a lifelong friendship that would be extremely profitable to both.

Luciano dropped out of school at the age of 15, and he worked in a hat factory for a while. Unfortunately, that was not the life for him. Looking for a different kind of work, Luciano started hanging out on Mulberry Street, and soon he became a charter member of the Five Points Gang, under the tutelage of their leader, Paul Kelly, with top-notch hoods Johnny Torrio and Frankie Yale as his mentors. Luciano became a "leg-breaker" for the Five Points Gang, and he was suspected of many beatings and maybe even a few murders. However, the Five Points Gang had their hooks into crooked cops and politicians, so Luciano was never brought up on any criminal charges.

By 1920, the Five Points Gang had splintered into several smaller gangs. Luciano saw potential in the rackets of Joe "The Boss" Masseria, who himself saw potential in the rough-and-tumble Luciano. Masseria treated Luciano like a son, and he made Luciano his top gun and second in command in all Masseria's operations.

However, Masseria didn't like the fact that Luciano did business with Jews like Lansky and Lansky's partner Bugsy Siegel; or even with Italians like Frank Costello, who was from Calabria, and didn't have Masseria's required Sicilian bloodlines.

Finally, Luciano decided Masseria had to go, and because Masseria was now involved in the Castellammarese War with rival Salvatore Maranzano, Luciano threw in with Maranzano with the intention of killing Masseria. To finalize his double-cross, Luciano lured Masseria to a Coney Island restaurant, and while Luciano was taking a bathroom break, Siegel and three other men barged in and shot Masseria to death.

After a few months under the strict rule of Maranzano, Luciano decided Maranzano, and his old-world ways, had to go, too. Furthermore, Maranzano felt the same way about the ambitious Luciano. As a result, Maranzano invited Luciano to a meeting in Maranzano's midtown office, where he planned to have Vincent "Mad Dog" Coll shoot Luciano into Swiss cheese.

Luckily for Luciano, he was one step ahead of Maranzano. Luciano sent four men, led by Samuel "Red" Levine, to Maranzano's office, where they shot and stabbed Maranzano to death. As they left the scene of the crime, the four men passed Coll in the ground floor hallway. They told Coll that Maranzano was already dead and not to bother going up to Maranzano's office. Coll shrugged, did an about-face and quickly exited the building, quite content in the fact that he had been paid in advance for doing absolutely nothing.

Luciano's next move was to unite all the disjointed mobs into separate, but equal groups; Italians and otherwise. With the assistance of Lansky, Luciano formed a National Crime Syndicate. However, Luciano's reign was short-lived.

In 1936, ambitious special prosecutor, Thomas E. Dewey, arrested, tried, and convicted Luciano on a trumped-up charge of prostitution. The key evidence against Luciano was provided by several pimps and prostitutes, who were more interested in staying out of prison than they were about giving truthful testimony. As a result, Luciano was sentenced to 30-50 years in prison.

However, after the end of World War II, Dewey, now Governor of New York, offered Luciano parole, for his "wartime services to his country." These services included Luciano's men providing protection on the New York City docks, most likely from themselves. The catch was, Luciano could never return to the United States and would instead be exiled forever to Italy. From Italy, Luciano still kept his fingers in mob affairs, even sneaking into Cuba to help Lansky run his lucrative casino businesses.

By the early 1960's, Luciano, due to several heart attacks, was an extremely ill man. Knowing his days were numbered, Luciano was contemplating providing details for a movie concerning his longtime connections to organized crime. Lansky and his pals were not too happy about this new turn of events. But before they could stop him, on January 26, 1962, Charles "Lucky" Luciano died of a heart attack at a Naples airport. He was on his way to meet an arriving scriptwriter to discuss the details of that never-made biographical flick.

Madden, Owney

Owney "The Killer" Madden was an anomaly in the world of the 1920 New York City gangsters, mainly because Madden was not Italian or even Jewish. Madden was British, the son of a relocated Irish dockworker, born and bred and dedicated for life to his homeland: merry old England. In fact, even though Madden was an American criminal for six decades, he didn't give up his English passport until 1950, after he was threatened with deportation.

Owen "Owney" Madden was born at 25 Somerset Street, in Leeds, England, on December 18, 1891. In need of work, his father moved the Madden family to Liverpool. In 1903, when young Madden was only 12, his father died, and his mother re-located her family to America, settling on the West Side of Manhattan in a treacherous neighborhood called "Hell's Kitchen."

Madden fell in with a rough-and-tumble gang known as the Gophers, and he became proficient in the favored crimes of the era: robberies, muggings, and labor racket beatings. Madden was adept at using a myriad of weapons, including a slingshot and brass knuckles. However, Madden's favorite weapon was a lead pipe, wrapped in newspaper.

Madden's main source of income was the "insurance business," where Madden sold "bomb insurance" to scores of local merchants who were worried about having their businesses bombed, of course, by none other than Madden himself. As a member of the Gophers, Madden was arrested 44 times, but managed to stay out of prison every time.

When he was 17, Madden earned his nickname "The Killer," after he shot to death an unarmed Italian in the street, for no reason, other than the fact that he could do so. After the killing, Madden stood over the dead body, and he announced to the assembled crowd, "I'm Owney Madden!"

By the time he was 23, Madden had at least five other murders to his credit.

One time, Madden's braggadocio almost cost him his life. On November, 6, 1912, at the Arbor Dance Hall, which was in the heart of the territory controlled by the Gopher's rivals, the Hudson Dusters, Madden strolled into the hall by himself during a dance given by the Dave Hyson Association. Madden was watching the proceedings from the balcony, when 11 Hudson Dusters surrounded him and filled his body with six pieces of lead. Madden was rushed to the hospital where a detective asked Madden who had shot him.

"Nothin' doin,'" Madden said. "It's no business but mine who put these slugs into me. My boys will get them."

By the time Madden was released from the hospital, six of his 11 assailants had already been shot dead.

While Madden was recuperating, one of his fellow Gophers, Little Patsy Doyle, thought he could use Madden's weakened condition as a reason to take control of the gang. However, the main cause of Doyle's ire was that Madden had stolen Doyle's girlfriend, Freda Horner, away from him.

When word got back to Madden about Doyle's intentions, Madden used Miss Horner to lure Doyle to a saloon on Eighth Avenue and 41st Street, where Madden and two of his gunmen shot Doyle dead. Madden was arrested three days later, and at his trial, Miss Horner turned the tables and testified against Madden. Madden was sentenced to 10-20 years in Sing Sing Prison, but he did only eight years, being released in 1923.

When he hit the streets again, Madden found his Gophers gang had dissipated, so he threw himself headfirst into the bootlegging business. As a result of his great bootlegging success, Madden moved up in class and was considered the equal of mobsters like Lucky Luciano, Frank Costello, Louis Lepke, Bugsy Siegel, and Meyer Lansky. Madden also dabbled in the night club business, opening the legendary Cotton Club in Harlem, which he bought from former heavyweight champion Jack Johnson.

His relationship with Johnson segued Madden into the boxing business, where he nurtured the career of Italian carnival freak, the 6-foot-6-inch, 285-pound Primo Canera. Madden fed Canera so many stiffs and setups, the no-talent Canera was able to win the heavyweight championship of the world. Canera did so by landing an invisible punch against champion Jack Sharkey in the 6th round at the Madison Square Garden Bowl, in Long Island City. Sharkey obviously took a dive and was reportedly paid handsomely to do so.

The first time Madden put Canera in a tough match, against Jewish heavyweight sensation Max Baer, Canera was knocked down 10 times, before the referee mercifully stopped the fight in the 11th round. Of course, Madden made big money betting on Baer, who, because of Canera's feared reputation, went into the fight as a slight underdog.

In 1932, Madden was arrested on a parole violation, and when he was released a few months later, he decided he had accumulated enough cash in a lifetime of crime to relocate to Hot Springs, Arkansas. There, Madden opened several casino/hotels, which were used as hideouts for New York City mobsters on the lam. To perpetuate his guise of respectability, Madden even married the Postmaster's daughter. In 1943, Madden was granted United States citizenship.

In 1965, after being stricken with emphysema, Madden died in his own bed, at the ripe old age of 74. He was said to have amassed a fortune of $3 million, but not surprisingly, none of that money was ever found after his death.

Mandelbaum, Fredericka "Marm"

Fredericka "Marm" Mandelbaum was born in 1818 in the country of Prussia. In 1848, she immigrated to the United States with her husband, Wolfe Mandelbaum. A big woman, tipping the scales at over 250 pounds, Mandelbaum opened a dry-goods store at 79 Clinton Street on the corner of Rivington. The dry-goods store was located on the ground floor of a three-story building, which Mandelbaum later purchased with her ill-gotten gains.

By 1854, the dry-goods store was a front for the biggest fencing operation in the history of New York City. Mandelbaum lived on the top two floors of the building with her husband, son, and two daughters. Their apartments were as lavishly furnished as any in New York City; furnished, of course, with stolen goods. Among the famous crooks Mandelbaum dealt with on a regular basis, were Shang Draper, George Leonidas Leslie, Banjo Pete Emerson, Mark Shinburn, Bill Mosher, and Joe Douglas.

Mandelbaum was known for throwing lavish parties in her apartment, attended by every known criminal, of both sexes, in New York City, including judges and politicians, whom she had in her back pocket. Knowing women were as good, or even better crooks than men, Mandelbaum became fast friends with female criminals like Black Lena Kleinschmidt, Big Mary, Ellen Clegg, Queen Liz, Little Annie, Old Mother Hubbard, and the notorious pickpocket and shoplifter Sophie Lyons. Lyons, along with her bank-robber husband Ned, moved right over the Hudson River to New Jersey, and she later became known as the "Queen of Hackensack."

In 1862, Mandelbaum first caught the eye of the police, and it is estimated that from 1862 to 1884, she handled between 5-10 million dollars of stolen property. Her business was so good, Mandelbaum decided to put some of her best crooks on salaries. However, Mandelbaum abandoned that idea quickly, when she caught a few of them peddling their stolen goods to other fences. (What did she expect, honest crooks?)

As her business grew, Mandelbaum, imitating the Dickens character Fagin, decided to start a school for children on Grand Street, where little tykes could learn the noble profession from the ground up, starting as pickpockets and sneak thieves. For the older children, Mandelbaum offered courses in burglary, safe-breaking, blackmailing, and confidence games. Mandelbaum's school became so well-known, the son of a prominent police official applied for admittance, compelling Mandelbaum to shut down her school immediately and permanently.

Whenever Mandelbaum did get herself into trouble, she could always count on Little Abe Hummel and Big Bill Howe, from the law firm of Hummel and Howe (not to be confused with the law firm of Dewey, Screwem, and Howe), to find whatever loophole they could find, legal and illegal, to keep Mandelbaum out of jail. Hummel and Howe were of such good service to Mandelbaum, she placed them on an annual retainer of $5,000.

In 1884, the New York District Attorney, Peter B. Olney, hired the Pinkerton Detective Agency to infiltrate Mandelbaum's criminal organization. One of the detectives sold her a stolen shipment of silk, and when her house was raided the next day, Mandelbaum was arrested, along with her son Julius and clerk Herman Stroude. Mandelbaum was charged with grand larceny and receiving stolen goods (pieces of silk and satin worth $633). However, the wily Hummel and Howe arranged for Mandelbaum's release on bail. Resorting to form, Mandelbaum jumped bail, and she moved to Toronto, Canada, where she lived the rest of her life in comfort.

To add insult to injury, the state of New York got hoodwinked by Hummel and Howe, and a crooked bondsman, who was supposed to have held the property Mandelbaum had pledged for bail. Using backdated checks, these three gyp-artists transferred the property to Mandelbaum's daughter, along with other properties the state was in the process of putting liens on.

Jabbing her finger in the eye of the New York City police, Mandelbaum, still wanted for her numerous crimes, traveled several times to New York City, in disguise, to take up with her old criminal pals, helping them plan several heists.

In 1894, after having screwed the American government as much as any woman in American history, Marm Mandelbaum died of natural causes in Canada at the age of 76.

Big Bill Howe died peacefully in his own bed in 1903. However, in 1905, Little Abe Hummel was sent to prison after being convicted of several counts of legal malpractice.

To paraphrase Meat Loaf, one out of three ain't bad.

Maranzano, Salvatore

Salvatore Maranzano was the Mafia leader who organized the first Cosa Nostra in America.

Maranzano was born in Castellammare del Golfo, Sicily, in 1886. As a young man, the college-educated Maranzano studied to become a priest, but then he did a 180-degree turn and became a Mafioso instead. Maranzano came under the influence of Sicilian Mafia Boss, Don Vito Cascio Ferro, who groomed Maranzano to be his second-in-command.

In 1925, Ferro sent Maranzano to America to organize the Sicilian crime families into one powerful group. Ferro eventually planned to come to America himself and assume the title of "Capi de Tutti Capi" (Boss of All Bosses). Unfortunately, Ferro was arrested in 1926 by Sicilian prefect Cesare Mori, on a trumped-up charge and sentenced to life in prison. This opened the door for Maranzano to take Ferro's place at the top of the Mafia heap in America.

When Maranzano arrived in America, he worked ostensibly in the real estate business, when in fact, he was a major bootlegger, who specialized in "homebrew." Maranzano employed hundreds of people to produce illegal booze in their homes, which Maranzano's men distributed throughout New York and New Jersey, and even as far as Pittsburgh.

Maranzano's long-range plan was to unseat New York's top Mafia chief, Joe "The Boss" Masseria, then reorganize the fractured crime families, including non-Italians, into one large organization with several "Bosses" leading their individual families. Of course, Maranzano envisioned himself as the "Boss of All Bosses." Masseria did not exactly agree with Maranzano's vision, and the result was the Castellammarese War, where the casualty count, in both Masseria and Maranzano's ranks, totaled over 50 dead bodies.

In 1928, in order to achieve his goal, Maranzano tried to recruit Masseria's top lieutenant, Charles "Lucky" Luciano, to take out Masseria. Luciano balked at first, but in 1931, Luciano, tired of Masseria's greed, and also tired of Masseria's ban on Luciano working with non-Sicilians, switched sides and agreed to take out Masseria. Luciano lured Masseria to an Italian Restaurant in Coney Island, and with Luciano conveniently in the men's room, four men, led by deranged killer Bugsy Siegel, filled Masseria's belly with lead, to go with the Chicken Parmesan he had eaten earlier.

With Masseria out of the way, Maranzano was now on top of the American Mafia world. Or so he thought.

Maranzano summoned more than 500 Mafioso to a meeting in the Bronx. At this meeting, Maranzano outlined a Roman Empire-style organization, with the entire New York Mafia divided into five families, each with a boss, an underboss, lieutenants, and soldiers. Maranzano dubbed his new organization the "Cosa Nostra," or "Our Thing." Of course, Maranzano officially anointed himself "Boss of All Bosses," which did not sit well with Luciano and his Italian pals, which included Frank Costello, Vito Genovese, and Joe Adonis; nor with Jewish gangsters Meyer Lansky, Louie "Lepke" Buchalter, and Bugsy Siegel.

Maranzano, ever the wily fox, knew Luciano had the adulation of many of the top New York City mobsters and would eventually try to wrest control of the organization from Maranzano. As a result, Maranzano compiled a "death list" of guys who had to go. Luciano's name stood right at the top of the list.

Maranzano struck a deal with kill-crazy, Vincent "Mad Dog" Coll, to murder both Luciano and Genovese, while they were present at a meeting in Maranzano's midtown office. Maranzano gave Coll $25,000 down, with $25,000 more, due upon the completion of his task. However, Luciano caught wind of the plot, and on the same day Luciano and Genovese were supposed to be killed, Luciano sent his own execution squad to Maranzano's office, which consisted of four Jewish gangsters led by capable killer, Red Levine.

On September 10, 1931, while Maranzano was awaiting the arrival of Luciano and Genovese, four men barged into Maranzano's outer office, flashing badges. They threw Maranzano's bodyguards against the wall, frisked them, and relieved them of their weapons. Then the four killers strode into Maranzano's inner office, where they stabbed and shot him to death.

The killers rushed from Maranzano's office, bypassed the elevator, and hurried down the emergency stairwell. They were followed by the two Maranzano bodyguards, who were now out of work, and seeking employment. The killers crossed paths with "Mad Dog" Coll, who was ready to enter the stairwell to do in Luciano and Genovese, who were nowhere near the premises.

When Levine informed Coll about Maranzano's demise, Coll did an immediate about-face, and then rushed out of the building, whistling a happy tune. Due to the unexpected turn of events, Mad Dog Coll was $25,000 richer, without having to kill anyone.

Masseria, Joe (The Boss)

Joe "The Boss" Masseria was an uncouth mobster who enjoyed killing as much as he enjoyed eating, and he enjoyed eating a lot.

In 1903, the 5-foot-2-inch Masseria fled Sicily, because he had murdered someone and was not cool about cooling his heels in a Sicilian prison for the rest of his life. Masseria landed in New York City, and he immediately became part of the vicious Morello Gang, America's first Italian organized crime family.

The Morello gang was headed by Joe Morello and his brother Nick; killers so proficient, they were reportedly responsible for scores of murders themselves. The Morello Brothers also employed two other vicious henchmen: Lupo "The Wolf" (real name Ignazio Saietta, of the Black Hand fame), and half-brother Ciro Terranova, who later became the "Artichoke King" in New York City.

However, the greedy, ambitious, and treacherous Masseria did not like taking a back seat to anyone. As a result, after Lupo the Wolf, Joe Morello, and Terranova were sent to prison for various crimes, including a counterfeiting charge, Masseria planned to snatch the reins of the organized crime family from the Morello brothers. Masseria joyfully pulled the trigger himself, killing several Morello loyalists. After Nick Morello was killed by men from the Neapolitan Camorra (Naples' version of the Mafia) in Brooklyn, it left Masseria in charge of all the local Manhattan rackets.

For the next few years, there were several hit attempts on Masseria's life, but Masseria always emerged unscathed. In 1922, Masseria left his apartment at 82 Second Avenue, protected by two bodyguards. He was met by a hail of bullets, fired at close range by two men, one of whom Masseria recognized as Rocco Valenti. Masseria's two bodyguards were shot dead, but Masseria fled into a millinery shop next door. Amazingly, even though the two gunmen had emptied their guns at Masseria, Masseria was able to bob and weave, and avoid any contact with the lead.

Soon after, Masseria set up a meeting with Valenti at a restaurant on East 12th Street, ostensibly to make peace. Valenti arrived with two bodyguards, but three of Masseria's men were waiting in ambush. Seeing imminent danger, Valenti made a mad dash across the street, looking for cover. After Masseria's men wounded Valenti's bodyguards, Valenti jumped on the running board of a passing taxi. Valenti was firing back at his assailants, when he was shot dead, reportedly by a young Lucky Luciano, a hood who would later play an important part in Masseria's demise.

To keep his empire running smoothly, Masseria hired young gangsters like Luciano, Vito Genovese, Joe Bonanno, and Thomas Lucchese to do his dirty work for him. Masseria was so fond of Luciano, he eventually made him his second-in-command.

The relationship between Masseria and Luciano became strained, when Luciano started doing business with two Jewish gangsters, Meyer Lansky and Bugsy Siegel, and also with Frank Costello, an Italian from the mainland of Italy. Masseria had one strict rule. He and his men could only do business with fellow Sicilians. Period. This did not go over too well Luciano, and he waited for the right time to take out Masseria, and gain control of Masseria's rackets.

In 1927, Masseria encountered a new threat to his supremacy in the name of Salvatore Maranzano, who came over from Sicily, as the underboss to Don Vito Cascio Ferro, the most powerful Mafia leader in Sicily. What happened next, was the Castellammarese War: a two-year bloody confrontation between Masseria's and Maranzano's men. During this time, Luciano, and his pals, ostensibly stayed loyal to Masseria. However, reading the writing on the wall, they finally decided to throw their lot in with Maranzano.

On April 15, 1931, Luciano lured Masseria to the Nuova Villa Tammaro Restaurant, in Coney Island. After Masseria had stuffed his belly with an enormous amount of Italian food (Masseria was said to have the eating habits of a "drooling mastiff"), Masseria and Luciano sat down to play cards.

At 3:30 p.m., Luciano excused himself to go to the bathroom. While he was taking care of business, four gunmen busted through the front door: Vito Genovese, Bugsy Siegel, Albert Anastasia, and Joe Adonis. The four men fired repeatedly at Masseria, hitting him six times, before he dropped dead to the floor holding the Ace of Spades in his right hand.

Minutes later, when the police arrived, Luciano told them, since he had been busy in the bathroom, he had not seen who had killed Masseria; nor did he have the slightest idea who would do such a terrible thing.

The police doubted the sincerity of Luciano's statement, but since Masseria was held in such high contempt by the law, no one was ever arrested for Masseria's murder.

Mock Duck

No, Mock Duck is not an item on the menu of a Chinese restaurant, but rather the name of one of the most notorious Chinese gangsters ever to set foot in America.

Real name, Sai Wing Mock, Mock Duck was born in China in 1879. In the late 1890's, Mock Duck traveled to the United States. He immediately took residence in New York City's Chinatown, where he joined the Hip Sing Tong, a small group of Chinese gangsters led by Lem Tong Sing.

At the time, Chinatown was controlled by the powerful On Leong Tong, whose boss was the murderous Tom Lee. Soon, Mock Duck pushed aside Lem Tong Sing as leader of the Hip Sing Tong, and he took control of the Tong himself. Mock Duck's first act as boss of the Hip Sing Tong was to demand fifty percent of the profits from Tom Lee's On Leong Tong. This did not sit well with Lee, and as a result, the Tong Wars of the early 1900's started in full force.

Mock Duck, knowing his Hip Sing Tong couldn't compete in terms of total gang members against the On Leong Tong, joined forces with the Four Brother's Society to even up the numbers a bit. Still, the Tong Wars became a bloody mess for three decades, with many casualties on all sides.

On January, 24, 1906, as a group of On Leong Tong members exited a building at 32 Pell Street, a dozen Hip Sing Tong members jumped from an alley on Doyers Street, and the fired as many as hundred rounds of ammunition at their rivals. Two On Leong Tong members were killed, and two were badly injured. This rampage was reportedly planned by Mock Duck, who ordered murders to be done, but very rarely got his hands dirty doing the actual killings himself.

The one exception was in 1900, when Mock Duck allegedly murdered a New Jersey tailor named Ah See, in front of 23 Mott Street. Mock Duck was tried three times for See's murder, but was never convicted.

Mock Duck lived in a top floor apartment with his family at 21 Pell Street, in the heart of Chinatown. The rest of the apartments in this building also housed Hip Sing Tong members. There had been several attempts on Mock Duck's life, so he was forced to wear a "chain mail" vest, in addition to always carrying two guns and a small hatchet for protection, just in case.

On January 12, 1912, Mock Duck narrowly escaped death, when two On Leong Tong members casually entered an apartment at 21 Pell Street. They opened fire at a group of Hip Sing Tong members, as the Hip Sings played a game of fan-tan, killing Lung You, one of Mock Duck's top henchmen. Luckily for Mock Duck, he was out of the building at the time and was not a victim of the shooting, which was obviously intended for him.

Mock Duck was finally arrested by the police in 1912 for the minor crime of running a "policy game," more commonly known as the "numbers racket." Mock Duck was convicted and sentenced to two years in Sing Sing Prison. When Mock Duck was released in 1914, he returned to Chinatown, and he assumed a very low profile in the Hip Sing Tong.

In 1932, Mock Duck briefly resurfaced in the news, when he, in conjunction with the American and Chinese governments, arranged a truce, officially ending the Chinatown Tong Wars.

Unlike most of his fellow Chinese Tong members, who were killed in the streets of Chinatown, Mock Duck died of natural causes, at the age of 72, in his Brooklyn home in 1941.

Morrissey, John (Old Smoke)

John Morrissey started out as a feared bare-knuckle boxer, but later became a street-gang member and a leg-breaker for the Tammany Hall politicians.

Morrissey was born in Templemore, County Tipperary, Ireland in 1831. The famed potato famine was in its infancy, but Morrissey's parents saw the writing on the wall. They immigrated to America in 1833 and settled in Troy, New York. Not being educated, but good with his fists, Morrissey was relegated to working as a collection agent for the local Irish crime bosses. While working as a bouncer in a Troy brothel, Morrissey taught himself how to read and write. Realizing his future was limited in Troy, Morrissey made the short trek to New York City. There, Morrissey made a name for himself as a rough hooligan, fighting often in bars and on the piers, just for sport.

One day, Morrissey engaged in an impromptu fight with Tom McCann, at the indoor pistol gallery under the St. Charles Hotel. McCann was getting the best of Morrissey, when a powerful McCann punch drove Morrissey over burning coals from a hot stove, which had been overturned during the fight. Morrissey's clothes and flesh were on fire, and with smoke comes from his backside, Morrissey leaped forward, and he immediately battered McCann senseless. Hence, Morrissey was awarded the nickname "Old Smoke."

After winning a few more battles, inside and outside the ring, Morrissey challenged world heavyweight champion Yankee Sullivan to a fight for the World's Heavyweight Title. The fight took place on October 12, 1853, at Boston Corners, on the border of Massachusetts and New York. Morrissey was battered throughout the fight, but he won by disqualification in the 37th round, when Sullivan hit Morrissey while he was down.

Buoyed by his newfound fistic fame, and now a member of the Dead Rabbits, a feared street gang, Morrissey was hired by the Democrats from Tammany Hall to protect the polling places from the Bowery Boy's gang, led by Butcher Bill Poole. Poole and his pals terrorized the polling places on election days, in favor of the Native American, or Know-Nothing political party.

On Election Day 1854, Poole announced that he and 30 of his Bowery Boys were headed to a certain local election site to destroy the ballot boxes. Tammany Hall called on Morrissey to protect their interests, and with John A. Kennedy, who later became New York City's Superintendent of Police, they assembled a gang of over 50 Dead Rabbits. Itching for a fight, they stood in wait inside the polling place for Poole and his gang's arrival.

A man of his word, Poole arrived at the polling place looking to do as much damage as possible. However, as Poole scanned the inside of the polling place, he immediately realized his group was vastly outnumbered by Morrissey and the Dead Rabbits.

Not a good thing for Poole.

Poole met Morrissey in the center of the room, and after staring menacingly at each other for a few moments, without saying a word, Poole abruptly turned and left, taking his gang with him. Tammany Hall was so overjoyed by Morrissey's heroics, they gave him a free gambling house (under the protection of the New York City police, of course).

In 1855, Morrissey challenged Poole to a bare-knuckles fight, on a pier near Christopher Street. Poole accepted, but once the two men squared off, instead of fighting with his fists, Poole tried to crush Morrissey to death by squeezing Morrissey in a mighty bear hug. When Morrissey was nearly unconscious, a group of men barged into the ring, and they stopped the murder attempt.

A few months later, Poole was shot and killed by Morrissey's close friend Lew Baker at Stanwix Hall, a bar on Broadway near Prince Street. Both Baker and Morrissey were arrested for Poole's murder, but after three mistrials (rumor had it that Tammany Hall influenced some jurors in Morrissey and Baker's favor), the charges were finally dropped.

In 1857, Morrissey retired from boxing, and he went full-throttle into the gambling business. Morrissey eventually opened 16 gambling houses throughout the state of New York, including an exceptionally profitable one in Saratoga Springs.

From 1867-71, and with the backing of Tammany Hall, Morrissey was elected United States Congressman from New York. In 1873, tired of Tammany Hall's illegal tactics, which were only surpassed by the illegal tactics Morrissey employed himself, Morrissey testified against Tammany Hall chief and thief, William "Boss" Tweed. Based on Morrissey's testimony and the overwhelming evidence of Tweed's treachery, the jury convicted Tweed on several counts of misappropriating government funds. As a result, Boss Tweed was sent to prison, where he subsequently died.

In 1875, as a reward for his service to his country, Morrissey was elected to the New York State Senate. Morrissey was still a Senator, when he died of pneumonia in 1878 at the age of 47.

In 1999, John Morrissey, A.K.A., "Old Smoke," was elected to the International Boxing Hall of Fame.

Orgen, Jacob (Little Augie)

Jacob "Little Augie" Orgen was born on the streets of the Lower East Side of Manhattan in 1896. He quickly ditched school and became known as a "schlammer," for the Benjamin "Dopey" Fein mob. "Schlammers," or "Sluggers" were basically head-breakers, who kept the union workers in line, by "schlammin'" them on the side of the head, with a club, or with a baseball bat, if they went against what their union leaders decreed. Orgen formed a little side gang call the "Little Augies," but he was strictly a small-time player under Fein.

After Fein was arrested for improprieties concerning the Amalgamated Clothing Workers of America, rather than go to jail for a long period of time, Fein, not as dopey as his name, cut a deal with the cops. As a result of being a rat, Fein lost his job and his influence with the labor unions.

Enter rival gangsters Johnny Spanish and Kid Dropper, who while Orgen was cooling his heels in prison on a robbery charge, spent the next several years fighting over control of the labor unions. In 1919, Dropper eliminated Spanish with a few bullets, and Little Augie, fresh out of prison, put his eyes on Dropper's domain.

Orgen's gang of mostly Jewish criminals joined forces with the gang of Solomon Schipiro, whose men, strangely enough, consisted mostly of Italians. Orgen and Schipiro were fighting a losing battle against Dropper's forces, so they decided to cut off the head: Dropper himself.

As Dropper was being released from prison on a gun charge at the Essex Market Court on Second Avenue and Second Street, Little Augie and his gang stood anxiously in the street outside the court, mayhem on their minds. A dozen cops surrounded Dropper, with their eyes on Orgen, who was rumored to be there to kill Dropper. The police pushed Dropper into a waiting cab, when out of nowhere, a nobody named Louis Kushner rushed the cab from the back and shot Dropper twice in the head. Kushner denied all involvement with Orgen (but the cops knew better), and he was sentenced to 20 years-to-life in prison for the murder of Dropper.

Orgen immediately took over Dropper's rackets, and he enlisted a dangerous crew of killers, including "Jack Legs" Diamond, Louis "Lepke" Buchalter, and Jacob "Gurrah" Shapiro, to keep in line people who needed to be kept in line.

Pressure from the police (who were embarrassed Dropper was killed right under their noses), forced Orgen to abandon the labor rackets. Dropper segued right into the bootlegging business, supplying illegal hooch to various speakeasies around town. This did not sit too well with the bootleggers whom he had displaced in those joints.

Orgen was told, in no uncertain terms, by Arnold Rothstein and by Meyer Lansky, to get out of the bootlegging business, or bad things would happen to him real quick. Orgen ignored these warnings, so the offended bootleggers struck a deal with Louie "Lepke" Buchalter and Jacob Shapiro, offering them employment in their vast operations if they murdered Orgen.

On October 16, 1927, Orgen was walking in front of 103 Norfolk Street, with his new bodyguard Jack "Legs" Diamond, when a black touring car pulled up alongside him, guns a-blazing. Orgen was killed and Diamond severely wounded, but Diamond lived to die another day.

Orgen was buried by his estranged father, in a huge cherry-wood coffin, lined with white satin. On the top of the coffin was a silver plate that simply said: "Jacob Orgen – Aged 25 years."

Orgen was 33 at the time of his death, but his father, a legitimate, God-fearing man, considered his son dead eight years earlier when he could not convince Orgen to get out of the rackets.

P ioggi, Louis (Louie the Lump)

Louis Pioggi, affectionately called Louie the Lump, was a diminutive and dapper Italian-American Five Points Gang member. Pioggi thrust himself into the spotlight one starry night in Coney Island, when he snuffed out the life of Kid Twist, the boss of the former Monk Eastman Jewish Lower East Side gang.

Kid Twist's gang and the Five Pointers were in a constant battle for control of the Lower East Side rackets. Under Kid Twist's reign, Twist and his gang had made great inroads into the Five Pointer's territory. The ire was so great between the two gangs, they made the Hatfields and the McCoys look like choir boys singing in church.

Born in 1889 on the Lower East Side, Pioggi was basically a footnote in the history of the American gangster. Pioggi was a small-timer, who as fate would have it, fell in love with the same dancehall girl the more illustrious Kid Twist (Maxwell Zwerbach) was seeing on the side.

It was the custom at the start of the 20th Century, for gangsters who had more than a few bucks in their pockets, to break free from the dumps and dives on the Lower East Side and "go out on the town," to the wondrous expanses of Coney Island in Brooklyn. On May 14, 1908, Pioggi took a trip out to Coney Island to see Carroll Terry, a gorgeous Coney Island dancehall girl who was the regular squeeze of Kid Twist.

Unknown to Pioggi, Kid Twist was also in Coney Island to see Miss Terry, and he was accompanied by his bodyguard, Cyclone Louie, real name Vach Lewis. Cyclone Louie was a killer for Kid Twist, but he was better known as a Coney Island circus strongman who bent large pieces steel around his neck for a living.

Pioggi visited the dancehall Terry worked in, and he enticed her to have a few dances with him, which was her job anyway. Pioggi became hopelessly lovesick, and before he left he begged Terry to promise him, after her shift ended, she'd come back to New York City with him. Saying anything to get rid of Pioggi, Terry said she would, but only if Pioggi left at once so she could do her job without his interference.

The real reason Terry gave Pioggi the bum's rush was because she expected to see Kid Twist shortly. And that she did, when just moments after Pioggi left, Kid Twist and Cyclone Louie made their grand entrance into the dancehall. Terry joined them at a table, and after a few drinks her lips loosened, and she told Twist about Pioggi's amorous advances.

Soon after, Pioggi returned to the dancehall, and he saw Kid Twist holding hands with Terry, with Cyclone Louie standing guard nearby. Knowing he had been had, Pioggi wandered into a dive on Surf Avenue, to drown his sorrows on the second floor of the saloon. Minutes later, Kid Twist and Cyclone Louie burst into the saloon and climbed the stairs. They confronted Pioggi.

"I just seen Carroll," Kid Twist told Pioggi. "And she said youse is the biggest bum she knows. So she says you are an active cuss, always jumpin' around. Let's see how active youse is." Kid Twist pointed to the open window. "Take a jump out of the window."

Pioggi was in no mood for the 25-foot jump, but when Kid Twist made a move for the revolver in his belt, Pioggi, as requested, quickly jumped out of the window. Pioggi landed on all fours, but he later found out he had fractured his ankle. Pioggi limped to a telephone and called Paul Kelly, the boss of the Five Points gang. Pioggi told Kelly what had transpired concerning Kid Twist.

"I've got to cook him," Pioggi told Kelly.

"Sure you got to cook him," Kelly said. "I'll send a fleet down. When my boys get there, you get these bums on the street and open up with your cannons."

Kelly's boys arrived an hour later, and when they did, they saw Kid Twist and Cyclone Louie having a grand old time in Terry's dancehall, laughing and talking loudly about Pioggi's daring jump. Terry had vacated the premises for a while and was nowhere to be seen. Pioggi sent a kid inside with a note, telling Kid Twist that Terry was waiting for him outside.

As soon as Kid Twist and Cyclone Louie made it to the sidewalk, Kid Twist heard a voice call him from the side.

"Over this way, Kid," Pioggi yelled.

Before Kid Twist could react, Pioggi put a bullet in his head, killing him instantly. Cyclone Louie stood with his mouth open for an instant, then he started to run for his life. Pioggi and the Five Pointers chased Cyclone Louie, pumping bullets at him at a dazzling rate. Finally, shot five times in the chest and back, Cyclone Louie fell dead as a rock to the pavement.

Pioggi, still outraged, refused to stop shooting. As luck would have it, Terry showed up seconds later, and just for the fun of it, Pioggi pumped a slug into her hip. Terry fell on top of the dead Kid Twist, but she lived to dance another day.

As Pioggi jumped into a getaway car, a cop showed up at the scene. Pioggi fired again. This bullet knocked the cop's helmet off his head, but otherwise did him no harm.

Pioggi finally made his getaway, and he went into hiding, while Kelly contacted Tammany Hall to see if he could negotiate Pioggi a favorable deal.

A few days later, Pioggi turned himself in and pleaded guilty to manslaughter. He also testified that he had acted completely alone, which was quite disingenuous of him, since scores of people had seen the Coney Island executions.

Pioggi was sentenced to 11 months in Elmira State Prison. He left the courthouse sneering. "What's 11 months?" Pioggi said. "I could do that standin' on me head."

Rogers, Mary, "The Beautiful Cigar Girl"

She was known as "The Beautiful Cigar Girl," but the 1841 murder of 20-year-old Mary Rogers remains one of the most baffling unsolved murders in New York City's history.

Rogers was a clerk in the upscale John Anderson's Tobacco Shop in downtown Manhattan. She was an amazingly beautiful girl, and famous writers like Edgar Allen Poe, James Fennimore Cooper, and Washington Irving, became her regular customers. Poet Fitz Green-Halleck was so smitten by Rogers, he wrote a poem in Rogers's honor. Many of the top newspaper editors and beat writers were also frequent customers at Anderson's; some just to get a brief glimpse of Rogers's beauty.

On Sunday morning, July 25, 1841, at a Nassau Street boarding house owned by her mother, Rogers told one of the boarders, her fiancé Daniel Payne, that she was going out for the afternoon to visit her sister, a Mrs. Downing. That night, New York was hit by a severe thunderstorm, and Rogers did not return to the boarding house. Both her mother and Payne figured, that because of the storm, Rogers was spending the night at her sister's house.

Yet on the next day, Rogers's sister told them that Rogers had never shown up at all, nor had she expected Rogers to visit. Joined by Rogers's ex-fiancé, Alfred Crommelin, they searched the city, but could find no trace of Rogers.

Unfortunately, this was not the first time that Rogers had disappeared. In October 1838, Rogers's whereabouts were unknown for several days. When she returned, she said she had visited a friend in Brooklyn, even though she had not told her mother, or her employers, of her intentions to do so.

After Rogers's second disappearance, Rogers's mother placed an ad in the *New York Sun* daily newspaper, asking if anyone knew "the whereabouts of a young lady, aged 20, last seen on the morning of the 25th, who was wearing a white dress, black shawl, blue scarf, Leghorn hat, light colored shoes, and light-colored parasol."

No one responded to the ad.

On Wednesday, July 28, at Sybil's Cave in Hoboken, New Jersey, three men spotted something floating and bobbing on the New Jersey side of the Hudson River. The men jumped in a rowboat, and they quickly rowed to the area where the object was located. When they got there, they found the dead body of a young woman. They tired pulling the body onto the rowboat, but after a few unsuccessful attempts, they tied a rope under the dead woman's chin and rowed toward shore.

When the coroner examined the body, in addition to severe discoloration all over her once- beautiful face, he found a red mark, the shape of a man's thumb, on the right side of her neck. There were also several marks on the left side of her neck, the size of a man's finger, indicating Rogers had been strangled and her body dumped in the river. Crommelin, after reading the accounts in the newspapers of the body found in the Hudson River, traveled to Hoboken, and he identified the body as that of Mary Rogers.

Because of her popularity with the press, Rogers's death became front-page news in all the New York City newspapers. Members of the press cast suspicion on her fiancé Daniel Payne, who had told the police, that on the day of Rogers' disappearance, he had visited his brother and had spent the day bouncing to and from several bars and restaurants in New York City. To prove his innocence, Payne produced sworn affidavits from witnesses, saying he was indeed where he said he was on the day Rogers had disappeared.

The mystery of Rogers's death soon disappeared from the daily newspapers. The New York City police then consisted of motley night-time Watchmen and day-time Roundsmen, who were untrained and lowly paid commoners, with little incentive to solve crimes. These pseudo-policemen decided not to investigate any further, since the body of Rogers was found in New Jersey. The New Jersey police felt Rogers had most likely been killed in New York City and that the murder investigation was not their problem.

Frederica Loss owned a tavern called Nick Moore's House, near Hoboken, New Jersey, not far from where Mary Rogers's body had been found. On August 25, 1841, two of Loss's young sons, who had been playing in the woods, found various articles of women's clothing, including a handkerchief with the initials "M.R." on it. Mrs. Loss immediately notified the police of her sons' findings

This new discovery ignited an investigation by the New Jersey police, since they now decided Rogers had indeed been killed in New Jersey. However, nothing became of the investigation and it soon ended.

Throughout the years, several criminologists tried to explain who killed Mary Rogers, and why. Yet no credible evidence has ever materialized and no one was ever charged with the crime.

A year after Rogers's death, Edgar Allen Poe, obviously saddened by the tragedy of "The Beautiful Cigar Girl," wrote his famous novel, "The Mystery of Marie Roget." The novel was set in Paris, and it duplicated the events that had occurred surrounding Rogers's death. In the novel, Poe's famous detective, Austin Dupin, concluded that the murderer was a naval officer of dark complexion, who had previously attempted to elope with Marie (Rogers), which explained her first disappearance in 1838. This mysterious Naval officer then killed Rogers in 1841 after she refused to marry him a second time.

Poe's novel closely mirrored the most credible explanation of Mary Rogers's death, which was put forth by author Raymond Paul in the early 1970s. Paul's theory was that Daniel Payne had murdered Rogers, but not on the Sunday she disappeared (for which Payne had a solid alibi), but on the following Tuesday. Because Rogers's body was still in rigor mortis when she was found, she could not have been dead for more than 24 hours. Rigor mortis starts scant hours after a person dies, but then after 24 hours it gradually dissipates.

Paul concluded, from the evidence compiled more than 130 years earlier, that Payne had gotten Rogers pregnant, and on Sunday July 25, 1841, he ferried her off to Hoboken to have an abortion. While her mother and former fiancée were looking for Rogers, Rogers was recuperating from the abortion in a Hoboken inn.

Payne then returned to Hoboken on Tuesday, July 27, to pick up Rogers and bring her back to New York City. When Rogers told Payne she was breaking off their relationship, Paul concluded Payne strangled Rogers, then dropped her body into the Hudson River. Paul also deduced from the circumstances that Rogers's brief disappearance in 1838 was for the same reason: to have an abortion.

After Rogers's death, Payne started drinking heavily. On October 7, 1841, Payne, after making the rounds of several New York City bars, purchased the poison laudanum. He took the ferry to Hoboken, then went to Nick Moore's House, where he got properly drunk. Soused, Payne staggered, holding a bottle of brandy, to the very spot in the woods where Rogers's clothing had been found.

There, Payne wrote on a piece of paper, "To the world, here I am on the very spot. May God forgive me for my misspent life."

Payne put the note in his pocket, drank the laudanum, and washed it down with the brandy. Then he laid down and died.

The newspapers, and the New York City police, thinking Rogers had been killed on Sunday, for which Payne had an airtight alibi, figured Payne had committed suicide because the love of his life had been murdered. Yet, the police investigation had been so cursory, incomplete, and totally inefficient, they never considered the fact that it was impossible for Rogers to have been killed four days before she was found, because her body was still in the state of rigor mortis.

Although the murder of Mary Rogers has never officially been solved, her death was not in vain. The complete incompetency of the New York City police force, combined with pressure from an outraged New York City press and populace, compelled the city to totally revamp its policing procedures.

Starting in 1845, Watchmen and Roundsmen became obsolete, as New York City finally created a police force, comprised of men specifically trained to prevent and investigate crimes.

Rothstein, Arnold (The Brain)

Arnold Rothstein was the most notorious gambler of his time; a bootlegger of great proportions and a master-fixer of everything imaginable. Rothstein was so adept at what he did, he reportedly fixed the 1919 World Series.

Rothstein was born on January 18, 1882, on the Upper East Side of Manhattan. His father, Abraham Rothstein, owned a dry-goods store and a cotton processing plant. Rothstein's father, a devout Jew, was also a mover and shaker in New York City politics, and he was called by his friends, "Abe the Just." Abe Rothstein was so popular with the New York City politicians, in 1919 a dinner was staged in his honor, which was attended by New York Governor Al Smith and Judge Louis Brandeis.

Yet, young Arnold wanted no part of his father's life. At the age of 15, Arnold began sneaking away from his fancy Upper East Side home to mingle with the fast-moving crowd on the Lower East Side of Manhattan. Rothstein loved to gamble, and soon he was a fixture at downtown card and dice games.

Having limited funds at that age, Rothstein would "borrow" money from his father in outlandish ways. As the Sabbath approached, Abe Rothstein would stash his money and jewelry in a dresser drawer in his bedroom. Young Rothstein, knowing his father's habits, would take the money from his father's drawer, spend all day gambling, then replace the money before sundown. One time, he even stole his father's watch and pawned it. That day, Rothstein won big at poker. Then before sundown, Rothstein redeemed his father's watch from the pawnbroker and put it back into his father's drawer, without his father being any the wiser.

Rothstein later explained his passion for gambling. He said, "I always gambled. I can't remember when I didn't. Maybe I gambled just to show my father he couldn't tell me what to do. When I gambled, nothing else mattered. I could play for hours and not know how much time had passed."

Successful gamblers sometimes make enemies, and Rothstein was no exception. In 1911, several gamblers, he had regularly taken to the cleaners, decided to teach Rothstein a lesson. As good as he was with dice and cards, Rothstein was even better with a pool stick. So his "pals" imported pool shark Jack Conway from Philadelphia to show Rothstein he wasn't the pool player he thought he was.

After Conway challenged him to a match, Rothstein got to pick the pool parlor in which they would play. Rothstein picked John McGraw's Pool Room, owned by the legendary former manager of the New York Giants. Every known New York City gambler was in the pool room that night, mostly betting against the cocky Rothstein. After Rothstein lost the first match to 100 (probably on purpose), he and Conway engaged in a 40-hour marathon, in which Rothstein won every 2 out of 3 matches they played. During that two-day period, Rothstein won thousands of dollars, and he earned a reputation of being cool and collected under pressure.

Rothstein's prowess at gambling caught the eye of local politician and a mighty fine crook himself: Big Tim Sullivan. Sullivan hired Rothstein, now called "The Brian" by his associates, to manage his gambling concession at the Metropole Hotel on 43rd Street. That was the big break Rothstein had been waiting for.

Rothstein parlayed his stint at the Metropole into owning his own gambling joint on Broadway, in the glitzy Tenderloin section of Manhattan. Rothstein's reputation attracted such known gamblers as Charles Gates (son of John W. "Bet a Million" Gates), Julius Fleischmann (the Yeast King), Joseph Seagram (Canadian Whiskey baron), Henry Sinclair of Sinclair Oil, and Percival Hill, who owed the American Tobacco Company. Playing poker, Hill once lost $250,000 in one night to Rothstein.

In 1919, after Prohibition was enacted, Rothstein became a major bootlegger. He fell in with several young criminals, including Lucky Luciano and Meyer Lansky, both of whom looked up to the classy Rothstein as their mentor. Rothstein made sure all his young Turks made money, by cutting them into every whiskey deal he was involved with. It was during this period, that Rothstein received his second nickname: "The Fixer."

Rothstein had sucked up to Tammany boss Charley Murphy, and using Murphy's clout, Rothstein fixed thousands of bootlegging criminal cases.

Out of 6,902 liquor-related cases that made it to court, with Rothstein's influence, 400 never made it to trial and an incredible 6,074 were dismissed completely.

In 1919, through former featherweight champion Abe Attell, several Chicago White Sox baseball players approached Rothstein about fixing that year's baseball World Series against the Cincinnati Reds. It's not clear whether Rothstein actually bankrolled the fix, or turned them down completely. However, what is clear, is that Rothstein bet $60,000 on the Reds, and he pocketed a cool $270,000.

In 1928, the wear and tear of all his dealings and double-dealings had a severe effect on Rothstein. He started to lose more often than he won at cards. Rothstein's downfall started when he got involved in a marathon poker game, that began at the Park Central Hotel on September 8, and ended on September 12. Among the gamblers involved were Nate Raymond and Titanic Thomson. When the dust settled, Rothstein had lost $320,000 to Raymond and Thomson, which he refused to pay because he claimed the game was fixed.

On November 4, 1928, Rothstein was eating at Lindy's Restaurant, when he received a phone call requesting his presence at the Park Central Hotel to discuss the payment of his gambling debt. Before he left Lindy's, Rothstein told the waitress, "I don't pay off on fixed poker."

Because guns are traditionally not allowed at such meetings, Rothstein gave his gun to an associate to hold until he got back.

A few hours later, the Park Central doorman found Rothstein slumped over a banister in the hotel.

"Please call a taxi," Rothstein told the doorman. "I've been shot."

Rothstein was taken to the Polyclinic Hospital with a bullet in his gut. When the police asked him who had shot him, Rothstein replied, "Don't worry. I'll take care of it myself."

Rothstein fell in and out of delirium for several days. One afternoon, his estranged wife came to the hospital to see him. Rothstein told her, "I want to go home. All I do is sleep here. I can sleep at home."

Rothstein died a few hours later at the age of 46. No one was ever arrested for Rothstein's murder.

Arnold "The Brain" Rothstein's funeral was attended by every card-shark and gangster in New York City. Lucky Luciano said later about Rothstein, "Arnold taught me how to dress. He taught me how not to wear loud things, how to have taste. If Arnold had lived longer, he could have made me real elegant."

Schultz, Dutch (Arthur Flegenheimer)

Mob bosses come in all shapes and sizes. Some are brilliant. Some are just plain dumb. Almost all are homicidal maniacs. However, only one was a certified lunatic, and his name was Dutch Schultz.

In 1902, Schultz was born Arthur Flegenheimer to German/Jewish parents in the Bronx. His father abandoned the family at an early age, and young Flegenheimer took assorted jobs, including one at the Schultz Trucking Company. Despite his legitimate work at the trucking company, young Flegenheimer took up with a gang of crooks, who during Prohibition, did a little illegal importing of hooch (from Canada to New York City) on the side.

When he was pinched for the first time by the cops, Flegenheimer gave his name as Dutch Schultz, which was the name of the son of the boss of the Schultz Trucking Company. Later, the headline-happy Schultz would tell the press that he changed his name to Dutch Schultz because it fit in the newspaper headlines better than Arthur Flegenheimer did.

"If I had kept the name of Flegenheimer," Schultz said. "Nobody would have ever heard of me."

Schultz quit the trucking business, and he decided he could make a mint off the Harlem numbers rackets, where it was reported that the locals bet a staggering $35,000 a day. Schultz set up a gang that included crazed killer Bo Weinberg, mathematical genius Otto "Abbadabba" Berman, and Lulu Rosenkrantz, who could kill with the best of them too. Schultz and his crew invited the black gangsters, who ran the numbers show in Harlem, to a meeting. When the black gangsters arrived, Schultz put a 45 caliber pistol on the table and told them, "I'm now your partner."

And that cemented the deal.

Yet Schultz was not satisfied with just making a ton of cash off the Harlem numbers racket. He wanted to make 100 tons of cash; maybe even more. So, he enlisted the genius mind of Abbadabba Berman to rig the Harlem numbers game so that he could achieve his goal.

The *Harlem Age* newspaper, instead of using the *New York Clearing House Reports* for its daily three-digit number, used Cincinnati's Coney Island Race track to determine the winning numbers. The only problem was Schultz owned that particular racetrack. So all Berman had to do was go over the thousands of slips bet that particular day, and before the seventh race at the track, he knew which numbers Schultz did not want to win. Then one phone call to the race track, and like magic, the final numbers were altered for Schultz's monetary benefit.

Schultz had one simple rule that helped propel him to the top: if someone stole a dime of his cash, that person would soon die. His longtime lawyer, J. Richard "Dixie" Davis, Schultz's conduit to the crooked politicians who protected Schultz's flank, once said, "You can insult Arthur's girl. Spit in his face. Push him around. And he'll laugh. But don't steal a dollar from his accounts. If you do, you're dead."

Two such men, who were deposited into the hereafter by Schultz, were Vincent "Mad Dog" Coll and Jack "Legs" Diamond. After Schultz's men pumped several bullets into Diamond's head in an upstate hotel, Schultz said, "Just another punk caught with his hands in my pocket."

The killings of Diamond and Coll propelled Schultz into the big time, and soon he became an equal in a syndicate of gangsters, which included Lucky Luciano, Louie "Lepke" Buchalter, Meyer Lansky, Albert Anastasia, and Joe "Adonis" Doto. While the rest of the crew were immaculate dressers, Schultz dressed one step above a Bowery bum. Even though he was raking in millions, Schultz never spent more than $35 for a suit, or $2 for a shirt.

Lucky Luciano once said of Schultz, "Dutch was the cheapest guy I ever knew. The guy had a couple of million bucks, and he dressed like a pig."

As for his insistence on not dressing up to his mob stature, Schultz said, "I think only queers wear silk shirts."

As time passed, the rest of the syndicate grew weary of Schultz's erratic ways. One such example of his lunacy was when Schultz, in order to beat a tax-evasion case in upstate Malone, New York, converted to Catholicism in order to butter up the all-Catholic jury. His scheme worked, and Schultz was acquitted on all counts.

Another time, at a syndicate meeting, Schultz became upset over a wisecrack Joe Adonis made about Schultz's chintzy clothes. Schultz, who had a bad case of the flu, grabbed Adonis in a headlock, and he blew hard into his face.

"See you (expletive) star. Now you've got the flu too."

Adonis did indeed catch the flu from Schultz, which did not make him and the rest of the syndicate particularly happy.

Schultz's downfall was his insistence that the syndicate kill New York City Special Prosecutor Thomas E. Dewey, who was on a mission to crack down on all the mobs, especially Schultz's. Schultz called a meeting of the nine-member syndicate, and he demanded Dewey's head on a plate. The other members thought killing Dewey was a terrible idea, because they were convinced, if Dewey was offed, an avalanche of criminal investigations would surely fall down on their heads. Schultz's proposal was voted down 8-1.

Schultz stormed from the meeting, saying, "I still say he ought to be hit. And if nobody else is going to do it, I'm gonna hit him myself. Within 48 hours."

The other syndicate members, knowing Schultz was not one to bluff, immediately voted unanimously that Schultz was the one who had to go; and quickly, before Dewey was dead.

On October 23, 1935, the day following the fateful votes, Schultz, Berman, Lulu Rosenkrantz, and Abe Landau were in the Palace Chop House and Tavern in Newark, New Jersey, ostensibly to discuss how best to do away with Dewey. Schultz was in the bathroom, when Charlie "The Bug" Workman and Mendy Weiss slipped quietly through the front door.

With Weiss standing guard outside the bathroom door, Workman quietly entered the bathroom, looking for possible witnesses. Instead, he found a started Schultz just zipping up his pants. Workman plugged Schultz once, right in the middle of the chest. Satisfied Schultz was dead, Workman and Weiss rushed into the main dining room, and they shot numerous holes into Berman, Rosenkrantz, and Landau, killing all three men.

Schultz was rushed to the hospital, and he lay delirious for two days. While lying in his hospital deathbed, Schultz spouted such idiocies as: *Oh Duckie, see we skipped again.* And, *Please mother, crack down on the Chinaman's friends and Hitler's commander.* And, *Louie, didn't I give you my doorbell?*

Schultz's temperature rose to 106 degrees, and on October 25 he fell into a coma and died. His former pals in the syndicate, overjoyed and more than little relieved, divided Schultz's prosperous operations equally amongst themselves.

Siegel, Benjamin (Bugsy)

Benjamin "Bugsy" Siegel is the man most responsible for the birth of the city of Las Vegas, which became the gambling capital of the world.

Siegel was born Benjamin Siegelbaum on February 28, 1906, in the Williamsburg section of Brooklyn. As a teenager, Siegel crossed the bridge to Manhattan, and he started a gang on Lafayette Street, which skirted the border of Little Italy, with another thug named Moe Sedway. Their main racket was shaking down pushcart owners for protection money, and if they weren't paid quickly enough, they burnt down the poor owners' pushcarts.

Soon, Siegel teamed up with Meyer Lansky, the man who would shape his life, and eventually, his death. Together they formed the "Bugs and Meyer Gang," which started out in auto theft and ended up handling hit contracts for bootleggers, who were having their shipments hijacked. This tidy little killing business was the forerunner to the infamous "Murder Incorporated," which handled hundreds of contract killings during the 1930's.

In the late 1920's, Siegel and Lansky hooked up with ambitious Italian mobsters Lucky Luciano, Frank Costello, Joe Adonis, Vito Genovese, Joe Bonanno, Albert Anastasia, and Tommy Lucchese. Together they formed a National Crime Commission, which controlled all organized crime in America, for many years to come. Siegel was the main hitman for the group, and in 1931, he led the four-man hit-squad which riddled Joe "The Boss" Masseria's body with bullets in a Coney Island Restaurant. Siegel developed the reputation as a man who not only killed frequently, but enjoyed killing, with the glee of a schoolboy on his first date.

In the late 1930's, The Commission sent Siegel to California to take over their West Coast rackets, including the lucrative racing wire, which transmitted horse race results to thousands of bookie joints throughout the country. Siegel pushed aside West Coast mob boss Jack Dragna, who was told by Lansky and Luciano, if he didn't step down and hand the racing wire reins over to Siegel, bad things would happen to him quickly. Dragna did as he was told, and Dragna soon disappeared from the California organized crime scene.

While in Hollywood, Siegel, who was movie-star-good-looking, was a renowned ladies man, who sometimes bedded down three or four starlets at a time. He hung around with such movie hunks as Clark Cable, Gary Cooper, George Raft, and Cary Grant. The girls he bedded included Jean

Harlow, Wendy Barry, Marie McDonald, Virginia Hill, and Italian Countess Dorothy DiFrasso.

Even though Siegel was busy with the broads, he always found time to do a little killing on the side. In 1939, on orders from New York City Jewish mob boss Louis "Lepke" Buchalter, Siegel whacked Harry "Big Greenie" Greenberg, who was singing like a canary to the feds. Siegel was arrested for Greenberg's murder, but after a witness conveniently disappeared, Siegel was acquitted of all charges.

The bad publicity from the Greenberg trial ruined Siegel's man-about-town reputation in Hollywood. As a result, the Commission sent Siegel to the deserts of Nevada, to scout sites for a hotel/casino they wanted to build. Siegel found the perfect location in Las Vegas, and he convinced the boys from New York City, including his pal Lansky, to invest millions of dollars in an opulent night club, Siegel dubbed "The Flamingo Hotel."

The building of the "The Flamingo Hotel" was a disaster from the start. Siegel's insistence on only the best of everything skyrocketed the costs to a staggering $6 million, which annoyed his partners in New York City more than just a little bit. Furthermore, there were concerns that maybe Siegel was skimming a little construction money off the top, to fund his actions with the ladies.

In December 1946, the opening night of "The Flamingo Hotel" was an unmitigated disaster. Siegel had moved up the opening date from March 1947, while the hotel was still in the late stages of being built. Since "The Flamingo Hotel" did not show well (the lobby was draped with ugly drop cloths), the Hollywood crowd they had depended upon to generate business stayed away.

In a few short months, "The Flamingo Hotel" was more than a quarter of a million dollars in the red. Losing money on gambling was unheard of in the mob, and as a result, Siegel's partners in New York City made a business decision that Siegel's days on earth must end as soon as possible.

Contrary to what has been written in the past, longtime pal Lansky had no problem signing off on Siegel's death warrant. Lansky said that "business is business," and Siegel was bad for business.

On June 20, 1947, Siegel was sitting on the living room couch, in the Beverly Hills home of his girlfriend Virginia Hill, reading the *Los Angeles Times*. Suddenly, two rifle bullets, fired from an open window, struck Siegel in the face. One bullet hit his right cheek and settled in his brain. The second hit him in the nose, then pierced his right eye.

Siegel's unseeing right eye was found on the floor, 15 feet from his lifeless body.

St. Clair, Stephanie (Madame Queenie)

She was chased out of the Harlem numbers rackets by Dutch Schultz, but when Schultz lay dying in a hospital bed from a bullet wound, Stephanie St. Clair had the last laugh.

Stephanie St. Clair was born in 1886, in Marseilles, a seaport in southern France. At 26, she emigrated to New York City, and she settled in Harlem. Almost immediately, St. Clair hooked up with the Forty Thieves, a white gang which were in existence since the 1850's. There is no record of what St. Clair did for the next 10 years, but it's safe to say, considering her ties to the Forty Thieves, a notorious shake-down gang, what she did was anything but legal.

In 1922, St. Clair used $10,000 of her own money, and she started Harlem's first numbers rackets. St. Clair was known for having a violent temper, and she often cursed at her underlings, in several languages. When people questioned St. Clair about her heritage, she snapped that she was born in "European France," and that she spoke flawless French, unlike the French-speaking rabble from the Caribbean. In Harlem, they called her Madame St. Clair, but in the rest of the city she was known as just plain "Queenie."

In the mid-1920's, known bootlegger and stone killer Dutch Schultz, decided he wanted to take over all the policy rackets in Harlem. Schultz did not ask St. Clair to back away too nicely, resulting in the deaths of dozens of St. Clair's numbers runners.

St. Claire enlisted the help of Bumpy Johnson, an ex-con with a hair-trigger temper, to take care of the Schultz situation. Johnson went downtown, and he visited Italian mob boss Lucky Luciano. Johnson asked Luciano to talk some sense into Schultz, before things got downright nasty. However, there was not much Luciano could do, since at the time Luciano was one of Schultz's partners in several illegal endeavors. Luciano suggested that St. Clair and Johnson throw in with Schultz, making them, in effect, a sub-division of Schultz's numbers business. This did not sit too well with St. Clair, and even though Johnson tried to convince her this was the smart move, St. Clair turned down Luciano's offer.

As a result of her refusal to buckle under to Schultz's demands, St. Clair began having trouble with the police, whom she paid off to look the other way. This was the work of Schultz, who through his connections with Tammany Hall, had several politicians in his back pocket, as well as half of the New York City police force. While Schultz's number runners worked the streets of Harlem with impunity, St. Clair's runners, when they were not being killed by Schultz's men, were being arrested for illegal gambling.

St. Clair decided to fight back with the power of the press. In December 1930, St. Clair took several ads in Harlem newspapers, accusing the police of graft, shakedowns, and corruption. That did not go over too well with the local fuzz, and they immediately arrested St. Clair for illegal gambling. St. Clair was tried, convicted, and sentenced to eight months of hard labor on Welfare Island.

Upon her release, St. Clair appeared before the Seabury Committee, which was investigating graft in the Bronx and in the Manhattan Magistrates Courts. St. Clair testified that from 1923-1926, to protect her runners from arrest, she had paid the police in Harlem $6,000. She added that after the police took her money, they arrested her number runners anyway. Schultz had a good laugh over that one, since $6,000 was less than he paid monthly to keep the cops in New York City happy.

Nothing came from St. Clair's testimony before the Seabury Committee, so St. Clair decided to plead her case directly to New York City Mayor Jimmy Walker, who was almost as crooked as Schultz. St. Clair told Walker that Schultz was pressuring her to join his gang, or else. Walker, who was being investigated by the Seabury Committee himself, answered St. Clair by quitting his job as Mayor and relocating to Europe for the next few years, until the heat died down.

At her wit's end, St. Claire pleaded with the other black policy number bankers in Harlem to join forces with her in a battle against Schultz. Knowing that Schultz had too much juice in the government and too many shooters in his gang, the other Harlem policy bankers turned St. Clair down flat.

Bumpy Johnson soon found out that Schultz had put the word out on the streets that St. Clair was to be shot on sight. St. Clair went into hiding, refusing to even go outside to see the light of day. On one occasion, Johnson had to hide St. Clair in a coal bin, under a mound of coal, to save her from Schultz's men. That was the final straw for St. Claire. She sent word to Schultz that she would agree to his demands. Schultz sent word back to St. Clair, that she could remain alive as long as she gave Schultz a majority share of her numbers rackets. St. Clair reluctantly agreed.

Schultz had his own run of bad luck, when he demanded that Luciano and Luciano's pals, agree to the killing of Special Prosecutor Thomas E. Dewey, who was breathing down Schultz's neck. Schultz's proposition was turned down flat, and when he said he would kill Dewey himself, Schultz was shot in the belly, in the bathroom of a New Jersey restaurant.

Schultz lingered in a delirious state in a hospital for a few days before he died. As Schultz was laying there mumbling inanities, a telegram arrived, saying *"As ye sow, so shall you reap."*

The telegram was sent by the Queen of Harlem: Stephanie St. Clair.

Wanting to get away from all the tensions, St. Clair eventually turned over her number business to Bumpy Johnson. Not being the boss "Madame Queenie" any longer, St. Clair faded into obscurity, and she died in her sleep in 1969.

In the 1997 movie "Hoodlum," Lawrence Fishburne played Bumpy Johnson, Tim Roth played Dutch Schultz, Andy Garcia played Lucky Luciano, and Cicely Tyson played Stephanie St. Clair.

Sullivan, Timothy (Big Tim)

"Big Tim" Sullivan was a Tammany Hall hack who gave true meaning to the term "crooked politician."

Sullivan was born in 1863 at 25 Baxter Street, one of the worse slum buildings in New York City. At 25 Baxter Street, the squalor was so intense, in 1866, a *New York Times* article called it, "one of the filthiest tenements in New York City."

Sullivan's parents had emigrated from County Kerry, Ireland, and with them being so poor, Sullivan was thrust into the streets at the age of eight, to shine shoes and sell newspapers. Being the enterprising lad that he was, Sullivan soon saved up enough cash to start his own newspaper delivery service, in which Sullivan employed dozens of poor kids from the neighborhood to do his deliveries. In a few short years, Sullivan had enough cash to purchase four local bars; the first of which he opened on Christie Street, just east of the Bowery.

One of Sullivan's bar customers was Thomas "Fatty" Walsh, a notorious ward leader in Tammany Hall. Sullivan fell under Walsh's political wing, and in 1894, Sullivan was elected to the Third District's State Assembly.

Running roughshod over the rules, Sullivan became a large cog in Tammany Hall's corrupt wheel. Soon, Sullivan was appointed the District Leader of the entire Lower East Side of Manhattan.

That was like giving a vampire the key to the blood bank.

Sullivan bridged the gap between public service and common street thuggery, by recruiting infamous gang leaders, like Paul Kelly and Monk Eastman, to do his dirty work. This work included "voter influence" at election sites, which basically meant their gangs beat up voters who didn't see things exactly Sullivan's way.

In return for using his influence to keep these gangsters out of jail, Sullivan got a piece of all their illegal activities in the Lower East Side, including prostitution, gambling, loan-sharking, and extortion. To keep things looking on the up-and-up, Sullivan also entrenched himself in many legal endeavors, including becoming partners in the MGM and Loews cinema operations.

In Congress, Sullivan did pioneer a couple of key pieces of legislation. In 1896, Sullivan introduced a law that made boxing legal, only to see it made illegal again in 1900 after several boxers were killed in the ring.

In 1911, Sullivan also passed the dubious "Sullivan Act" which made it illegal to carry guns, unless you could afford to pay a hefty registration fee. Needless to say, Sullivan's cronies made so much illegal dough, they all were able to cough up the cash needed to carry guns legally, in order to enforce their illegal activities. Yet, the common schmo on the street was so poor, he had no choice but to walk the mean streets of New York City without a firearm to protect himself.

In late 1911, Sullivan's evil ways finally caught up with him. Sullivan contracted syphilis, probably in one of the many prostitution houses in which he was a partner. As a result of this disease, Sullivan became paranoid and delusional. Sullivan was judged mentally incompetent, and he was removed from his seat in the Senate. In 1912, Sullivan's family placed him in a mental institution, which made his condition worse. While in the sanitarium, Sullivan complained he was being watched and that his food was being poisoned.

In 1913, while the guards were playing cards, Sullivan escaped from the sanitarium. Two weeks later, Sullivan's body was found near the railroad tracks in Pelham Parkway. It appeared, he had been hit by a freight train.

For some unknown reason, Sullivan's body was not claimed until 13 days later. The city declared him a vagrant, to be shamefully interred in a potter's field at Hart Island. As Sullivan's body was being readied for transport to Hart Island, a police officer made a final inspection of the corpse. He was astounded to discover that the dead man was, indeed, the missing Big Tim Sullivan. As a result, Big Tim was finally given a proper send-off.

After a jam-packed funeral ceremony at Old St. Patrick's Cathedral on Mulberry Street, an estimated 25,000 people lined the streets, as Sullivan's funeral reception made its way along Lower Manhattan and over the Williamsburg Bridge.

Sullivan was finally laid to rest at Calvary Cemetery in Long Island.

Torrio, Johnny

Giovanni "Johnny" Torrio, nicknamed "The Brain," "The Fox," and "Terrible Johnny," was born in Italy in 1882. His father died when Johnny was 2-years-old, and his mother emigrated with Torrio to America. They settled on the Lower East Side of Manhattan, where Torrio's mother remarried a grocer.

After working as a porter at his stepfather's grocery store (which was really a front for illegal activities), Torrio embarked on a life of crime. He soon became the boss of the James Street Gang, and with the money he saved from his ill-gotten gains, Torrio opened his own pool hall, which was the base of operations for his assorted crimes, which included burglaries, robberies, gambling, and loan-sharking.

Torrio caught the eye of Paul Kelly, the leader of the 1,500-member Five Points Gang. Kelly inserted the diminutive, but tough-as-nails Torrio as the bouncer at Kelly's nightclub on Pell Street, considered one of the roughest dives in Manhattan. In a short time, Kelly was so impressed with Torrio's business acumen, he made Torrio his second-in-command.

However, Torrio figured he could make more money by branching outside Kelly's gang. As a result, in 1912 Torrio moved his operations to Brooklyn, where he opened a bar with a hidden brothel, near the Brooklyn Navy Yard. His partner was the murderous Frankie Yale and one of their bouncers was a 19-year-old Al Capone.

In 1915, Torrio was summoned to Chicago by his uncle-through-marriage, "Big Jim" Colosimo, to help Colosimo rid himself of treacherous Chicago

Black Hand shake-down artists. In Chicago, Torrio had killed whomever needed to be killed, and soon Torrio was in charge of Big Jim's numerous brothels. In 1919, Torrio brought Capone to Chicago, to help with the muscle he needed to keep things running smoothly in the flesh-peddling business.

In 1920, when Prohibition came into effect, Torrio saw the prospect for tremendous profits by importing, selling, and serving illegal booze. Torrio tried to convince Colosimo to pare down his brothels and to get into the illegal liquor business. However, Colosimo did not see the potential of Prohibition, and he turned Torrio down flat.

Frustrated, Torrio concluded Colosimo was in the way of Torrio making some big money. In late 1920, Torrio imported Yale from Brooklyn, to put Colosimo permanently out of commission. A few bullets did the trick, and Colosimo was erased from the Chicago rackets.

After taking over all of Colosimo's interests, Torrio decided to convince Chicago's other gangs: Italians, Irish, and Poles, to join forces, each with their own exclusive territory. Most fell into line, with the exception of the North Side Gang headed by Irishman Dion O'Banion. Again, Torrio called on his pal Yale, and in November 1924, while toiling in his flower shop, O'Banion was cut down by a barrage of bullets.

"Homicidal" Hymie Weiss took over O'Banion's operations, and his first order of business was to eliminate Torrio. When his limousine was ambushed by Weiss's shooters, Torrio narrowly avoided death. His dog and chauffeur were killed, but Torrio escaped with just two bullet holes in his hat. Torrio was not so lucky a few months later, when he was cornered in front of his apartment building, and shot four times. The shooters were Weiss and George "Bugs" Moran.

For 10 days, Torrio was near death's door, and he was under constant watch by Capone and 30 of his best men. While Torrio was recovering from his wounds, he decided he would live longer if he got out of the Chicago rackets completely. Torrio was 43, and he had accumulated enough cash he could not spend it in several lifetimes.

So Torrio handed over all his operations to Capone, saying "It's all yours, Al. I'm retiring."

Torrio absconded with his wife to live in Italy for a few years, but then he returned to America. Back on his home turf, Torrio became a mentor to such notables as Lucky Luciano and Meyer Lansky, both of whom came to Torrio many times for advice.

In 1973, while sitting in a barber's chair in Brooklyn, Johnny Torrio died of a heart attack at the age of 75. Torrio died facing the door, his eyes wide-open, ever cautious to the very end.

Triangle Shirtwaist Factory Fire

If it weren't for the greed of the sweatshop bosses, this tragedy may never have occurred. However, on March 25, 1911, the Triangle Shirtwaist Factory Fire took the lives of 141 people, most of them women.

At the turn of the 20th century, working conditions in the New York City sweatshops were abysmal. Men, woman, and children toiled in dirty factories, warehouses, and tenements, doing menial tasks, that made the garment industry one of the most profitable businesses in the nation. Labor laws were inadequate and hardly ever enforced. Factory inspections were rare, and if they were done at all, the factory owners knew whose palms to grease to get high inspection marks, when the condemnation of their factory was the proper course of action.

In 1899, a law banning night work for women was declared unconstitutional. The absurd reason given by the courts, whose members were often in the sweatshop bosses' back pockets, was that the law "deprived woman of the liberty to work in factories at night, or for as long as they wished to." In 1907, this ruling was upheld by the New York Court of Appeals. Even though the International Ladies Garment Workers Union was formed in 1900, the sweatshop bosses hired thugs as strikebreakers, to keep the ladies' union in line, by force if necessary.

Of all the greedy sweatshop owners, the worst offenders were Max Blanck and Isaac Harris, who owned the Triangle Shirtwaist Company, located on the 8th, 9th, and 10th floors of the 10-story Asch Building at 22 Washington Place, on the corner of Greene Street. The factory produced women's blouses, known at the time as "shirtwaists." The firm employed around 500-600 people, most of whom were young female Jewish and Italian immigrants, who worked under horrible conditions, for 9 hours a day on weekdays, and 7 hours on Saturdays. The bosses were such tyrants, they charged their employees for needles and for other supplies. They also charged them a fee for using their chairs, and if one of the employees damaged a piece of goods, they had to pay three times the value of the item to replace it.

In 1908, Blanck and Harris formed a sham company union that served their purposes much better than it served their hundreds of employees. Several employees, who tried to join a legitimate union, like the International Ladies Garment Workers Union or the United Hebrew Trades, were quickly fired. The reason management gave for these firings was that because of poor economic conditions, they had to cut staff. Yet strangely enough, new workers were hired almost immediately after the dismissal of the others.

Because Triangle Shirtwaist Company had locked out their dismissed workers, Local 25 of the International Ladies Garment Workers Union called for a strike against them. Blanck and Harris hired union strike breakers, or "schlammers," to beat up the male pickets. They also hired prostitutes to mingle with the female workers in the picket lines, in order to cause disruptions. The police and the judges, obviously working at the behest of the owners, sided with Blanck and Harris. One judge even said at the sentencing of one picketer, "You are on strike against God."

On March 25, 1911, it was a cold and windy day. As the 5p.m. closing time approached, it was estimated that 600 employees, packed in like sardines, were working at the sewing machine at the Triangle Shirtwaist Company. Most were women between the ages of 13 and 23.

After the 5p.m. bell rang, the women scrambled to get their coats and hats, and then they rushed for the elevators.

Suddenly, a fire broke out on the southeast corner of the 8th floor. It was later determined that the fire was inadvertently caused by a cigarette butt that had been thrown into a litter basket, near a sewing machine. An updraft of air sent the flames and smoke shooting upwards towards the roof.

The building had no sprinkler system, and the fire quickly enveloped the entire 8th, 9th, and 10th floors. Girls on the 8th floor ran to a stairwell on the Washington Place side of the building, but the door was locked from the outside. The fire was so intense, all the windows on the top three floors of the building blew out from the heat.

Some workers were able to jam themselves into the elevators, while the elevators were still working. Others, including Blanck and Harris, were saved because they were able to make it to the safety of the roof.

A passerby named Joe Zito, and an elevator operator named Gaspar Mortillalo, used the only working elevator to make five trips up to the 9th floor; taking down 25-30 terrified people at a time. However, that elevator soon became inoperable too.

Within five minutes, the fire trucks had arrived, but there was not much they could do. Their extension ladders only reached the 6th floor and the stream from their hoses only reached the 7th floor. Rather than burn to death, people began jumping out of the windows, sometimes in groups of two, three, and four.

A man and a woman appeared in a 9th floor window, their clothes ablaze. They kissed, then hugged, and jumped together, their bodies smashing on the cold pavement below.

The firemen brought out safety nets to catch the jumpers, but it was hopeless.

One fire chief later said, "Life nets? What good were life nets? The little ones went right through the life nets, and the pavement too. Nobody could hold a life net when those girls from the ninth floor came down."

The fire only lasted 10 minutes, but when it was over, 141 workers had died; 125 were women.

Nine months after the fire, Blanck and Harris were put on trial on manslaughter charges. However, the trial, like the earlier building inspections, was a farce. The judge was Thomas Crain, a Tammany Hall appointee, and he had little interest in justice for the dead workers. Judge Crain manipulated a trial where only an acquittal was possible. It took the jury just 100 minutes to render a verdict of not-guilty.

This did not go down too well with the victims' families. The day after the not-guilty verdicts, hundreds of despondent victim's relatives stood outside the Tombs Courthouse. Blanck and Harris, surrounded by five police officers, tried to slither out of the building through the Leonard Street exit. When the two men were spotted, they were quickly enveloped by an angry crowd.

David Weiner, whose sister had died in the fire, charged at the sweatshop bosses, swinging his fist in the air.

"Not Guilty? Not Guilty?" Weiner screamed. "It was murder! Murder!"

Weiner quickly was subdued by the police, but he was so distraught, he fainted and had to be rushed to the hospital.

In 1913, the victims' families won a lawsuit against Blanck and Harris. The families were awarded a measly $75 per victim, whereas Blanck and Harris were paid by the insurance company $60,000 more than the total reported loss of life and property. Ironically, in late 1913, Blanck was arrested again, for locking the doors to his sweatshop.

The tragedy of the Triangle Shirtwaist Factory Fire did not go for naught.

The New York State Legislature - whose members included future Presidential candidate Al Smith, and Robert Wagner, the father of the future Mayor of New York City by the same name - forced the state to completely rewrite its labor laws. The State Legislature created the New York State Factory Investigating Committee, to "investigate factory conditions in this and other cities, and to report remedial measures of legislation to prevent hazard, or loss of life, among employees through fire, insanitary conditions, and occupational diseases."

As a direct result of the Triangle Shirtwaist Factory Fire, The American Society of Safety Engineers was founded on October 14, 1911.

Tweed, William (Boss)

William "Boss" Tweed, head crook at Tammany Hall, stole so much money from the New York City coffers, by 1870 Tweed had become the third largest land owner in the entire city.

Tweed, a third generation Scottish-Irishman, was born on April 3, 1823, at 24 Cherry Street on the Lower East Side of Manhattan. His father was a chair maker, and the young Tweed tried to follow in his father's footsteps, but the lure of the streets became too much for Tweed to overcome. Tweed ran with a motley crew of juvenile delinquents called the "Cherry Street Gang," who wreaked havoc on local merchants by stealing their wares and selling them on the street's black market.

Soon, Tweed became boss of the "Cherry Hill Gang," and he (as did most gang members of that era) joined various volunteer fire companies, which were a springboard for men with political ambitions. Tweed helped found American Fire Engine Company No. 6, which was called the "Big Six." During his time in the volunteer fire business, Tweed forged friendships with people of all ancestries: Irish, Scottish, Germans - anyone who could help him climb the ladder of public service, with only one thing in mind, steal big and steal often.

In 1850, Tweed ran unsuccessfully for assistant alderman on the Democratic ticket. However, a year later Tweed was elected alderman, a non-paying job, but with unlimited power for anyone smart enough, and crooked enough, to take advantage of its perks. Just scant weeks after he became an alderman, Tweed brokered a deal to buy land on Wards Island for a new potter's field. The asking price was $30,000, but Tweed paid

$103,450 of the city's money for the land, then split the difference between himself and several other civic-minded officials.

In 1855, Tweed was elected to the New York City Board of Elections, which was another cash cow for the money-hungry Tweed. He sold city textbooks for his own profit, and he sold teachers' jobs to whomever had the money to buy one. In one instance, Tweed peddled a teachers' position to a crippled schoolmarm for $75, even though the job only paid $300 a year.

In 1857, Tweed was appointed to the New York County Board of Supervisors, which propelled Tweed into a much more profitable form of thievery. Tweed formed what was known as the "Tweed Ring," which was nothing more than Tweed and his buddies controlling every job and work permit in the entire city of New York. Every contractor, artisan, and merchant who wanted to do business with the city had to cough up the cash, and they coughed up plenty. It is estimated that Tweed's Board of Supervisors pocketed 15 percent of every dollar spent on construction in New York City.

Concerning Tweed and his cronies, American lawyer and diarist George Templeton Strong wrote in 1860, "Our city government is rotten to the core."

By 1865, Tweed's wealth had grown to impressive proportions and so did his girth. Standing 5-feet-11-inches, Tweed's weight ballooned to 320 pounds. His reputation for eating was legendary, and he consumed enormous amounts of the finest foods in the finest restaurants. Tweed floundered around town, like a whale out of water, with a huge diamond stuck right in the middle of his fancy shirt, flouting his tremendous wealth.

It is estimated, from 1865 to 1871, Tweed's gang stole as much as $200 million from the New York City Treasury. They did this by over-billing the city for everything imaginable. They paid out of the city's coffers $10,000 for $75 worth of pencils, $171,000 for $4,000 worth of tables and chairs, and $1,826,000 for the plastering of a municipal building, which actually cost only $50,000 to plaster. Tweed also gave citizenship to over

60,000 immigrants, none of whom could read or write, but who could vote for Tweed and his cohorts on election day.

Tweed's downfall began on December 25, 1869, when *Harper's Weekly* published a cartoon of Tweed and his gang breaking into a huge box, with the caption "Taxpayers' and Tenants' Hard Earned Cash."

Upon seeing the cartoon, Tweed said, "Stop them damned pictures. I don't care so much what the papers say about me. My constituents don't know how to read, but they can't help seeing them damned pictures!"

With the pressure mounting to unveil the extent of Tweed's corruption, a blue ribbon panel, headed by future Presidential candidate Samuel J. Tilden, was formed to investigate New York City's financial documents. When the books were checked, it was discovered that money had gone directly from city contractors into Tweed's pocket. The next day, Boss Tweed was arrested.

His first trial, in January 1873, ended in a hung jury; a jury many people thought was bought with Tweed's money. However, in November of that same year, Tweed was convicted on 204 out of 220 counts and sentenced to 12 years in prison.

Tweed was incarcerated in the Ludlow Street Jail, but, for some unknown reason, he was allowed home visits. During one such visit, Tweed fled the country and traveled to Spain, where he worked as a seaman on a commercial ship. Because his picture had been seen frequently in the newspapers, Tweed was recognized and returned to America. Tweed again was imprisoned in the Ludlow Street Jail, but this time no home visits were allowed.

On April 12, 1878, Boss Tweed died in the Ludlow Street Jail from a severe case of pneumonia. He was buried in Brooklyn's Greenwood Cemetery, and due to Tweed's outlandish treachery, New York Mayor Smith Ely would not allow the City Hall flag to be flown at half-mast in Tweed's memory.

No one could account for what became of Boss Tweed's vast amounts of ill-gotten gains. And not surprisingly, there were no reports of a Wells Fargo stagecoach following his horse-drawn hearse.

Watchmen (Leatherheads) and Roundsmen

The first New York City police force was created in 1845, but before then the streets of New York city were "protected" by a motley crew of incompetents, called Watchmen and Roundsmen.

The Watchmen first came into existence in the late 1600's, when the Dutch ruled New York City. Their job was little more than patrolling the streets at night, looking for any possible disturbances, but mostly avoiding them. They would also call out the hours of the night with such inane declarations as, "By the grace of God, two o'clock in peace." Or, "By the grace of God, four o'clock and a cold, raw morning."

Except for a 33-inch club, the Watchmen carried no arms. And they wore no uniforms, except for a fireman's leather hat, which they varnished twice a year, which made the hat as hard as a rock; hence they received the name - "Leatherheads." They were also called "Old Charlies," which was also not a term of endearment.

Starting in 1829, Watchmen were required by New York City ordinance to call out fires. If they saw smoke, the Watchmen would scream out either the name of his post, or the street name of where the fire was located.

There was also a street curfew, which stated anyone seen outdoors after 9 p.m. was considered to be of "bad morals." It was the Watchmen's duty to arrest anyone they caught wandering the streets at night, and then bring them to the local jail to be locked up until daylight.

The Watchmen's pay was a mere $1 a night. They were also paid an additional fifty cents to attend as witnesses at Special Court Sessions. There, they would testify to the particulars of any crime they may have seen while on duty, which, because of their lack of energy, hardly ever happened.

The criminals and gangs of New York City had very little respect for the Watchmen, who numbered only 30-40 in the entire city. The Watchmen were considered not to be very bright, nor very ambitious and were known to be frequently drunk on duty.

Each Watchmen had a post, or watch-box, which consisted of an unanchored wooden shack, where they would frequently fall asleep on duty, usually after consuming large amounts of whiskey. A favorite activity of the young ruffians throughout the city was to catch a Watchmen sleeping in his watch-box, lasso the watch-box with a rope, and then drag it through the streets, whooping and hollering like banshees. The soon-to-be-famous writer Washington Irving was known to be one of these pranksters.

Whereas Watchmen patrolled New York City at night, the crime solvers, or Roundsmen, were the daytime duty men. Roundsmen were considered the plainclothesmen, or detectives of the era, but solving crimes was certainly not their strong suit. Roundsmen were usually common laborers, or stevedores, who could not find work in their chosen fields of endeavor. As a result, Roundsmen were not especially adept at solving crimes, or catching criminals

Roundsmen were paid no salary, and they derived their income solely by serving legal papers, or collecting rewards from citizens for returning stolen property. This led to some very enterprising Roundsmen forming alliances with groups of criminals. The crooks would steal the goods, and the victims would post a reward for the return of their property. The Roundsmen would then "find" the stolen property, collect the reward, and then split it with the crooks.

Solving murders was very low on the list of the Roundsmen's priorities, since there was usually no reward for finding killers. The only way a Roundsmen could make a profit going after murderers was if the family of the victim posted a reward. And if the Roundsmen was lucky enough to catch the killer, which was very unusual, he would collect the reward and a further stipend from the city for serving a legal summons on the perpetrator.

Because of their outright incompetence, the Roundsmen and Watchmen were fast becoming an endangered species. It was the 1841 murder of Mary Rogers that put the final nail in their coffin. With plenty of clues as to who the murderer was, the Roundsmen dragged their heels, long enough that Rogers's killer was never found.

In 1845, the public was fed up with the archaic system of Watchmen and Roundsmen acting as an incompetent and un-industrious quasi-police force. Spurred on by the fury of the press, New York City reformers disbanded the Watchmen and Roundsmen system, and they replaced it with a functional police department, which was then copied by many cities throughout the United States of America.

Weyer, John (Johnny Spanish)

Johnny Spanish, whose real name was John Weyer, was one of the most feared gangsters in the early part of the 20th century. Weyer took the name Johnny Spanish because he was half-Jewish and half-Spanish. On his Spanish side, Weyer claimed to be a descendant of Butcher Weyer, the last Governor of Cuba. Weyer figured "Johnny Spanish" had much more cache to it rather than plain old John Weyer the Jew, so he claimed the name Johnny Spanish as his very own.

Spanish was born on the Lower East Side of Manhattan, and he quickly immersed himself in various street crimes. The short, frail, and morose Spanish was a loner, whose specialty was robbing saloons. When robbing a dive, Spanish liked to throw in the twist of sending a message to the saloon owners first, telling them of his imminent arrival. Spanish's legend grew immensely, when he performed that feat in a joint on Norfolk Street owned by Mersher the Strong Arm.

On the morning of the robbery, Spanish gave Mersher notice that he would arrive at a certain time. And that he did, armed with his usual four guns and an accomplice lurking behind him. Spanish threw a couple of shots through the mirror behind the bar, and then he emptied the till. To add insult to injury, Spanish lined 10 customers against the wall, and he relieved them of all their cash and jewelry. Spanish's notoriety grew, and soon he was accepted into Paul Kelly's Five Points Gang where he continued his shenanigans.

As an addition to his saloon crimes, Spanish found it quite profitable to steal the proceeds from the lucrative stuss gambling games located throughout New York City (stuss was a game which was a variation of the popular faro). Spanish had his eye on one such game, operated by Kid Jigger on Forsyth Street. One day, Spanish approached Jigger, who was known to be a fierce gunfighter, and he demanded half the take from Jigger's stuss game.

"And why should I give you half my stuss graft?" Jigger inquired.

"Because I'll knock you off if you don't," Spanish said.

Jigger just laughed.

Spanish took offense and told him, "Alright then, I'll knock you off tomorrow night."

Sure enough, being a man of his word, on the following night, as Jigger strode from his stuss game on Forsyth Street, Spanish opened fire with two guns. Jigger ran back into the building to safety, but the bullets struck an 8-year-old girl who was playing in the streets, killing her on the spot.

This necessitated Spanish leaving New York city for several months, until the heat died down. When Spanish returned, he was alarmed to find out that his girlfriend (who happened to be pregnant by who-knows -who), had been stolen by fellow thug Kid Dropper, real name Nathan Kaplan.

Spanish figured he'd settle with his ex-girlfriend first. He grabbed her off the streets, threw her in a taxicab, and then he headed out to the marshes of Maspeth, Long Island. There, Spanish tied her to a tree, and then he emptied five bullets into her pregnant belly. Spanish left the woman there to die, but miraculously, she survived. However, her baby was subsequently born with three missing fingers.

For this atrocity, Spanish was arrested, tried, convicted, and sentenced to seven years in Sing Sing Prison. Upon his release in 1917, Paul Kelly's Five Points Gang had dissolved, so Spanish figured he would take over Kelly's former rackets. The only problem was, Kid Dropper had the same idea.

The two old foes battled over the union protection racket for more than two years. One day in early 1919, the bulkier Dropper cornered Spanish on the street, and he carved him up badly with a knife. Spanish survived, but not for long.

On July 29, 1919, Spanish was entering a restaurant at 19 Second Avenue, when Dropper and two accomplices opened fire, hitting Spanish several times in the chest.

Bullets working better than blades, Spanish died a few days later in Bellevue Hospital.

Wexler, Irving (Waxey Gordon)

In the 1920's, Waxey Gordon was one of the richest, most powerful gangsters in New York City. However, after he was set up by his enemies for a fall, Gordon was reduced to selling junk on the streets like a common two-bit criminal.

Waxey Gordon was born Irving Wexler in 1889 on the Lower East Side of Manhattan to Polish/Jewish parents. Not having a great fondness for the New York City school system, Wexler took to the streets, and he became the best pickpocket on the Lower East Side. Wexler was so good at his trade, he got the nickname "Waxey," because he was so "light fingered," he could pick someone's wallet, like his fingers and the wallet were coated with wax. Waxey Gordon sounded better than "Waxey Wexler," so Waxey Gordon it was, from that point on.

Gordon did what most tough Jewish criminals did in those days. He got involved in the labor rackets (with the Dopey Fein gang), and soon Gordon was "schlammin'," or breaking heads, with the best of them. To supplement his income, Gordon also did a little burglary and minor dope dealings on the side.

One of the men Gordon cracked heads for was the legendary gambler Arnold "The Brain" Rothstein, who was known to do a little investing in other people's illegal enterprises. It was the beginning of Prohibition, and Gordon hooked up with small-time hood, Max "Big Maxey" Greenberg, who had big ideas, but little cash. Greenberg had left his home in St. Louis for the bright lights of Manhattan, because he heard there were certain people who might bankroll his dream of owning his own bootlegging business. Greenberg needed $175,000 to get started, and through Gordon's connection to Rothstein, Maxey and Waxey approached "The Brain" (on a Central Park bench, no less), about loaning them the cash they needed in return for a piece of the action.

At first, Rothstein turned them down flat. Then, Rothstein had a change of heart, as well as a change of plans. Rothstein saw tremendous potential in the bootlegging business, but what Greenberg and Gordon were planning was strictly small-time. Rothstein said he would loan them the money, but with very specific conditions.

First, Rothstein would run the operation; no questions asked. Greenberg and Gordon would act as Rothstein's main men, using their street contacts as secondary employees, who were needed for such a big operation.

And second, instead of smuggling cheap hooch in boats from Canada, Rothstein saw more monetary potential in shipping in top-notch booze from England. Rothstein purchased six speedboats, and when the cargo ship he hired, carrying 20,000 cases of Scotch, arrived in American waters from England, it would stop several miles off the coast of Montauk, Long Island. There it would be met by the six Rothstein speedboats, each of which would carry nearly 1,000 cases of booze back to shore. After the speedboats made three or four trips from ship to shore, trucks would take the booze to a warehouse in Manhattan, where it would be stored, and then distributed to thousands of speakeasies throughout the city.

This continuing operation brought Gordon much wealth. It was estimated, Gordon earned between $1 and $2 million a year, pure profit for himself. With this dough, Gordon bought several office buildings in Manhattan, a string of speakeasies, and illegal gambling houses.

After Rothstein was killed over a bad gambling debt, Gordon purchased his own fleet of motor boats, to keep the illegal flow of booze coming from across the pond. Gordon also bought a townhouse in Manhattan on Central Park West and a castle in New Jersey, complete with its very own moat.

Gordon soon formed bootlegging partnerships with the Italian gangs, headed by Lucky Luciano, who was himself was partnered with Jewish kingpin Meyer Lansky. By this time, Luciano was in the process of organizing Italian gangs throughout the country under one umbrella, and Lansky was doing the same thing with Jewish gangs.

The only problem was, Lansky and Gordon, both Jews, couldn't stand each other and wouldn't even sit at the same table together. Both accused the other of hijacking their bootlegging trucks, and both were right in their assumptions.

What transpired next, was what was known in the press as "The War of the Jews." Lansky killed Gordon's men, and Gordon returned the favor. Luciano tried to step in to settle the dispute, but to no avail.

Gordon had now been declared "Public Enemy Number One" by the FBI, which put him right in the cross-hairs of Special Prosecutor Thomas E. Dewey. In 1930, it was Luciano's idea to feed Gordon to Dewey on an income tax rap, with Lansky's brother Jake leaking information to Dewey's investigators concerning Gordon's financial operations. Gordon was arrested and indicted by Dewey.

At Gordon's trial, Dewey was able to show that Gordon lived high on the hog, raking in almost $2 million a year and only reporting an annual salary of $8,125. One hundred and fifty witnesses testified against Gordon, and they minutely explained to the jury Gordon's illegal moneymaking activities. As a result, the jury took only 51 minutes to come back with a guilty verdict, which sent Gordon to the slammer on a 10-year sentence.

In 1940, when Gordon was released from Leavenworth, all his properties had been seized by the government and his millions had somehow disappeared. He told reporters, "Waxey Gordon is dead. From now on it's Irving Wexler, salesman."

Gordon became a salesman alright, but not in the conventional manner. Gordon moved out to California, and he began peddling dope on the streets. In 1951, Gordon was arrested while delivering $6,300 of heroin to a federal narcotics informant. One of the cops who arrested Gordon was Sgt. John Cottone.

As Cottone was putting the cuffs on Gordon, Gordon started crying "Please Johnny, don't arrest me. Don't take me in for junk. Let me run, then shoot me."

In December of 1951, Gordon, now 63, was convicted of narcotics trafficking and sentenced to 25 years in Alcatraz Prison. Gordon, broke and a broken man, died in prison six months later of a heart attack.

Whyos Street Gang

The Whyos were a vicious Irish street gang which ruled Lower Manhattan, starting right after the Civil War and running through the 1890's. The Whyos started out as an offshoot of a pre-Civil War gang called the Chichesters. Their headquarters was in the 6th Ward on Baxter Street, formerly Orange Street, and named after Mexican War hero Lt. Col. Charles Baxter.

The Whyos got their name from the bird calls they made to each other to identify themselves as members of the gang. When they first appeared on the streets of Lower Manhattan, the Whyos cruised the area called Mulberry Bend, robbing, beating, and killing with ungodly gusto. Soon, they extended their domain to the Lower West Side, into Greenwich Village, and then further north.

Author Herbert Asbury said about the Whyos "The Whyos were the most ferocious criminals who ever stalked the streets of an American city."

The Whyos favorite hangout was a dive on the corner of Mulberry and Worth called "The Morgue"; an apt name, since it was estimated that over 100 murders took place on the premises. The bar owner boasted his booze was powerful and quite tasty, but could also be used an excellent embalming fluid if necessary.

Myth had it, that in order to become a member of the Whyos, an aspiring member had to kill, or at least make an attempt to kill someone. One of the Whyos early leaders was Mike McCoin, who was hanged in the Tombs on March, 8, 1883, for the slingshot murder of a saloon owner on West 26th Street named Louis Hanier. The day after he killed Hanier, McCoin announced to his gang, "A guy ain't tough until he's knocked his man out (killed)."

Some hard men took McCoin's remark to heart and a string of murders followed, precipitating new members being inducted into the gang.

In the 1880's, the Whyos reached the height of their power, when such miscreants as Big Jim Hines terrorized the city. Hines was the first person to hold up stuss games, which were then run by the Italian and Jewish gangs and a great source of revenue. The stuss games were played nightly at numerous locations, from east of the Bowery, up to 14th Street, and then west to Broadway. Almost every night, Hines bounced from one stuss game to another, a huge gun in each hand. Using impending force, Hines extracted a fat percentage of each game, but he always left a substantial cut for the house.

Once, after he was arrested, Hines told a detective, "Them guys must be nuts. Don't I always leave 'em somethin'? All I want is me share."

In 1884, Whyos member Piker Ryan was arrested for one of his numerous crimes. The police found a book on him, containing prices for a laundry list of crimes the Whyos performed for monetary profit. The list read:

Punching -- $2,

Both eyes blacked -- $4

Nose and jaw broke -- $10

Jacked out - - $15

Ear chewed off -- $15

Leg or arm broke -- $19

Shot in the leg -- $25

Stab -- $25

Doing the big job (murder) -- $100 and up

Another prominent Whyos member was Dandy Johnny Dolan, who was fastidious in dress, with oiled and plastered hair, and a penchant for wearing only the finest shoe apparel available.

Dolan was also the inventor of two gruesome weapons. The first was sections of an ax blade, embedded in the sole of his "Fighting Shoes," which he used to stomp and stab a fallen foe. The other was an "eye gouger," made of brass and worn on Dolan's thumb.

On August 22, 1875, Dolan decided to rob a brush manufacturer at 275 Greenwich Street. On the premises, he confronted James H. Noe, and Dolan bashed Noe over the head with an iron crowbar. Then Dolan proceeded to rob Noe of money, a gold watch and chain, and Mr. Noe's walking stick, which had a metal handle formed into the shape of a monkey. However, before Dolan left, he gouged out both of Mr. Noe's eyes with his "eye gouger," and then he proudly showed Noe's eyeballs to his pals.

Mr. Noe died a few days later, and when Dolan was soon arrested, he was walking with Mr. Noe's distinctive cane and carrying Mr. Noe's eyeballs in his pocket. As a result, Dolan was tried and convicted of murder. He was hung in the courtyard of the Tombs Prison, on April 21, 1876.

The most famous of the Whyos leaders were a couple of Dannys; Messrs. Driscoll and Lyons, who co-ran the Whyos in the 1880's. In 1888, Driscoll became involved in a gunfight with Five Points gang member John McCarthy, over the affections of a prostitute named Beezy Garrity. Not being the greatest of gunslingers, Driscoll accidentally shot and killed Ms. Garrity instead.

At his trial, Driscoll swore it was a case of mistaken identity, and that John McCarty had fired the fatal shots at Ms. Garrity. However, Garrity's mother, Margaret Sullivan, said on the witness stand that as her daughter lay dying at St. Vincent Hospital, she whispered into her mother's ear, "Danny Driscoll shot me, mother."

Even though Driscoll was represented by famed trial attorney William Howe, as a result of Garrity's deathbed statement, on October 1, 1887, the jury took only 29 minutes to find Driscoll guilty of first degree murder. Seven days later, Judge Fredrick Smyth sentenced Driscoll to death.

On January 22, 1888, Driscoll was hanged in the Tombs Prison. At the gallows, after the black mask had been pulled over Driscoll's face, his last words reportedly were, "Jesus, have mercy on me!"

Danny Lyons was considered the most vicious gangster of the 1880's. Lyons's downfall was an argument over a young lady, too. It seemed Lyons snatched Pretty Kitty McGown from her paramour Joseph Quinn. Quinn vowed revenge, and on July 4, 1887, the two men squared off with guns, at Paradise Square in the Five Points area. Lyons was better with a gun than his pal Driscoll had been, and he shot Quinn right through the heart, killing him on the spot.

Lyons took it on the lam for a few months, but he was finally captured. Lyons was hung at the Tombs Prison on August 21, 1888, just seven months after Driscoll had met the same fate in the same place.

After the deaths of Lyons and Driscoll, the Whyos fell into disarray. In the late 1890's, Monk Eastman defeated what was left of the Whyos. For the next 20 years, Eastman battled with Paul Kelly, leader of the Five Points Gang, for control of all the rackets in Lower Manhattan.

Wood, Fernando, and the Police Riots of 1857

In 1857, it was chaotic times in New York City, as the city's two adversarial police forces battled over the right to arrest people, and to accept graft from anyone willing and able to pay.

In 1853, under Democratic Mayor Harper, the first uniformed police force in New York City was created. Their uniform consisted of a blue coat with brass buttons, a blue cap, and gray pants. Led by Police Chief George G. Matsell, the police were generally more crooked than the crooks, taking bribes not to arrest people and sometimes taking bribes *to* arrest people. The citizens of New York City complained that their police force, called the Municipal Police, was "the worse in the world."

By the age of 37, Fernando Wood was a millionaire in the real estate business. On January 1, 1855, after buying votes through his wealth, Wood was elected Mayor of New York City. Wood immediately inserted himself as head of the police graft-gravy-train; charging new police captains $200 a year for a promotion to their $1,000-a-year job. Of course, to make up for the shortfall, the police captains charged each patrolman under their command $40 a year. The policemen, in turn, shook down honest citizens and protected dishonest citizens for pay, so everyone on the public law enforcement dole was quite happy to keep things just the way they were.

However, the New York State Legislature would have none of that.

In 1857, the legislature passed an act creating a new Metropolitan Police Force, with Fredrick Tallmadge named as Superintendent of the Force. The legislature also ordered Wood to immediately disband his 1,100 member Municipal Police Force. Wood refused; saying the creation of the new police force was unconstitutional. Thus, the court battle began over which police force would be the one to patrol New York City.

The Supreme Court soon voted that the creation of the new police force was indeed constitutional. Yet Wood, with the backing of Police Chief Matsell, steadfastly refused to cooperate. Eight hundred men, all aligned with the Democratic Party, stayed with Wood and Matsell. However, three hundred men, under respected Police Captain George W. Walling, defected and comprised the new Metropolitan Police Force, which was backed by the Republican Party.

On June 16, 1857, the issue came to a head. The street commissioner Joseph Taylor had died, and Wood, for the sum of $50,000, appointed Charles Devlin as the new street commissioner. On the same day, Republican Governor John A. King appointed Daniel Conover to the same position. As Conover entered City Hall to assume his new post, Wood had his Municipal Police throw Conover out of the building. Conover immediately went to a Republican judge, who swore out two warrants for Wood's arrest: one for assault and one for inciting to riot.

Captain Walling strode to City Hall to arrest Wood on the assault charge, but he was met by a contingent of five hundred Municipals. Captain Walling was allowed to enter the building and Wood's office. However, when Captain Walling told Wood he was under arrest for assault, Wood refused to recognize the legality of the arrest warrant.

Captain Walling grabbed Wood's arm to lead him out of the building, but he was immediately swarmed by 20 Municipals and thrown out of City Hall himself. Captain Walling repeatedly tried to go back up the steps of City Hall, but he was beaten back every time.

Suddenly, a contingent of one hundred Metropolitan Police, wearing their new uniforms of frock coats, and plug hats, arrived to serve the second arrest warrant on Wood. Instead of wearing the gold badges of the Municipals, the Mets wore copper badges, which gave birth to the term "coppers," and then "cops."

The motley Metropolitan Police was described by essayist G.T. Strong as, "a miscellaneous assortment of suckers, soaplocks, Irishmen and Plug-Uglies (an Irish Street Gang)."

Thus, began a horrendous half-hour battle between the two New York City Police Departments. The Mets were vastly outnumbered by the Municipals, and when the fight was over, some Mets were lucky enough to be able to flee unharmed. However, 53 Mets were injured, 12 hurt seriously, and one was crippled for life.

While the fighting was intensifying, Captain Walling rushed over the office of Sheriff J.J.V. Westervelt, and he implored the sheriff to arrest Mayor Wood. After consulting with a state attorney, Captain Walling, Sheriff Westervelt, and the state attorney marched to City Hall, and they pushed their way into Wood's office.

When the three men informed Wood he was indeed under arrest, he shouted at them, "I will never let you arrest me!"

At the same time, a beaten contingent of Mets spotted the Seventh Regiment of the National Guard boarding a boat for Boston. The Mets convinced the National Guard that they were needed to police a state matter.

Recognizing the severity of the situation, Major General Charles Sandford marched his men to City Hall. As his troops stood guard, Sandford strode up the steps of City Hall and into Wood's office, where he announced to Wood that he was under arrest. Wood looked out the window and spotted the National Guard. Realizing his men were no match for the military troops, Wood finally submitted to the arrest.

Yet, this was only the beginning of a long strife. For the rest of the summer, the two police departments constantly conflicted. When a Met cop arrested a crook, a Municipal would step in and set the man free. And vice versa. On numerous occasions, contingents of policemen would raid the other department's station house and free all the prisoners.

In the meantime, the criminals of New York City were having a field day.

While the two police forces battled each other all hours of the day and night, honest citizens were being robbed while walking the streets. Murders were committed with impunity, and still, all the two police departments were interested in was fighting each other.

This total indifference by the two New York City police departments led to a two-day riot on July 4 and July 5, of 1857, when the Bowery Boys and the Dead Rabbits street gangs squared off with fists, knives, stones, and pistols. As many as a thousand gang members were involved. Hundreds were injured, and several gang members were killed. The riots also led to the indiscriminate looting of stores, in the Five Points and Bowery areas and as far north as 14th Street.

Finally, in the fall of 1857, the Court of Appeals upheld the Supreme Court's ruling, that the Metropolitan Police were the only legitimate police department in town. The Municipals were disbanded, and although Mayor Wood had been arrested, he was released on bond and never tried.

The Mets, who were injured in the June 16 fight, sued Mayor Wood for personal damages. They were awarded $250 apiece by the courts, but Mayor Wood refused to pay a dime. Finally, the city of New York was forced to pay the damages from the city treasury, including the injured Mets' legal costs.

Wood was defeated in the 1858 Mayoral race by Daniel F. Tiemann. Yet, in 1860, the rotten Wood was somehow re-elected mayor of New York City, until 1862.

After the Civil War started, Wood floated a trial balloon, whereby New York City would secede from the state of New York, which was run by Republicans, and therefore, become a free city. Wood's proposal was shot down, and *New York Tribune's* editor Horace Greeley, wrote in an editorial, "Fernando Wood evidently wants to be a traitor. It is lack of courage only that makes him content with being a blackguard."

In 1867, Wood found his true calling in the United States House of Representatives, where he served, not too admirably, until his death on February 14, 1881.

A year later, statesman and author John Bigelow, who knew Wood well, said that Wood was, "The most corrupt man who ever sat in the mayor's chair of New York City."

Yale (Uale), Frankie

Frankie Yale, real name Uale, was the number No. 1 mobster in Brooklyn for most of the Roaring 20's.

Yale was born in the Calabrian town of Longobucco, Italy, in 1893. In 1901, he emigrated to the United States, and soon Yale became immersed in a life of crime. Although his stomping grounds were in Brooklyn, Yale met fellow Brooklynite Johnny Torrio, and he became partners with Torrio in the Five Points Gang in Lower Manhattan, under the tutelage of mob boss Paul Kelly.

Torrio and Yale were involved in several illegal endeavors, but their biggest moneymaker was a version of the Black Hand extortion shakedown, in which they threatened to kill Italian immigrants unless the immigrants paid protection money. Most paid, but some didn't. It was reported that Yale had killed a dozen times before he reached the age of 21.

Yale and Torrio decided to split with the Five Points Gang, and they relocated to Brooklyn, where their base of operations was the Harvard Inn, a bar and brothel near the Brooklyn Navy Yard.

In 1919, Torrio moved to Chicago, to work for his uncle-through-marriage, mob boss Big Jim Colosimo. Yale filled Torrio's absence by hiring a friend of Torrio's, the 19-year-old Al Capone, as his main bouncer at the Harvard Inn. Soon afterwards, Torrio summoned Capone to work for him in Chicago, with the eventual intention of killing Colosimo and taking over his rackets.

In 1920, Torrio decided the time was ripe for Colosimo's death, so he asked his friend Frankie Yale if he could make the trip to Chicago to do the dirty deed. Torrio set Colosimo up by telling Colosimo to go to his cafe to receive an illegal shipment of booze. When Colosimo got to the cafe, instead of liquor, Colosimo was greeted by several rounds of hot lead supplied by the reliable Yale.

Torrio's Chicago empire was being threatened by Irish mob boss Dion O'Banion, who ran a flower shop on North State Street. Torrio decided

O'Banion had to go too, and figuring his local shooters couldn't get close enough to O'Banion to kill him, he called on Yale again. The reason Torrio picked Yale for the hit was because O'Banion had never met Yale and wouldn't recognize him.

In November 1924, Yale entered O'Banion's flower shop, and he greeted O'Banion with a firm handshake. O'Banion tried to pull his hand free, but before he could extricate himself from Yale's death grip, two of Torrio's men, John Scalise and Albert Anselmi, busted into the shop and shot O'Banion to death. O'Banion had, up to that point, the biggest funeral in the history of Chicago; costing over $30,000, including a $10,000 coffin.

In 1925, Torrio was ambushed and shot several times in front of his apartment building. After he recovered from his wounds, Torrio decided to retire from the rackets, and he handed over his entire illegal empire to the 26-year old Capone.

Capone worked a deal with Yale, to import his illegal booze from Chicago to New York City, under Yale's protection. Soon, Capone's trucks were being hijacked before they got to New York City. Capone, suspecting Yale was the culprit, sent one his best men, James DeAmato, to survey the truck-hijacking situation in New York City. Soon, DeAmato sent word back to Capone that Yale was indeed hijacking Capone's trucks, and then selling the liquor back to Capone. Six days later, DeAmato was gunned down on a Brooklyn Street.

With Capone safely in Miami, Florida, he sent six of his best shooters to New York City by car. Yale was summoned from his home on a ruse, and while he was driving down 44th Street in Brooklyn, Yale was met with a deadly deluge of bullets fired from the new weapon of choice: a Thompson submachine gun.

Yale had always admired the grandeur of O'Banion's funeral, so he did O'Banion one better.

Yale's funeral procession attracted ten thousand mourners and his funeral cost $50,000, including a $15,000 nickel and silver coffin.

Take that, Dion O'Banion.

Zelig, Big Jack (Zelig Harry Lefkowitz)

Big Jack Zelig was born Zelig Harry Lefkowitz in New York City in 1888. Zelig started his criminal career at the age of nine. By the time Zelig had reached 13, and working for the Crazy Butch Gang on the Lower East Side, he became known as one of the best pickpockets in New York City. By the time he was 15, Zelig was a member of the feared Monk Eastman Gang. As an Eastman, Zelig was respected on the Lower East Side as a feared street fighter, who was especially adept at using a knife. Because of his roughhouse escapades, Zelig was dubbed by the police, "The Most Feared Man in New York City."

While Eastman was in jail for assault and robbery, the Eastman gang was headed by Max "Kid Twist" Zwerbach, who appointed Zelig his No. 1 lieutenant. When Zwerbach was killed in 1908 by a member of the rival Five Points Gang, Zelig took control of Zwerbach's gang.

Zelig's gang robbed casinos, banks and brothels, but their specialty was thuggery for hire. The Zelig gang even had a printed menu of the gang's services.

To have them slash the cheek of someone, it cost anywhere from $1 to $10, according to your ability to pay. A shot in the leg or arm cost $5 to $25. Tossing a live bomb to take down an establishment also cost $5 to $25. And to render someone dead, they charged anywhere from $10 to $100.

Zelig's capable men included such notables as Harry "Gyp the Blood" Horowitz, "Lefty" Louie Rosenberg, and "Dago Frank" Cirofisi.

Zelig's two chief nemeses, who were fighting with him behind the scenes for control of the former Eastman Gang, were gang members Chick Tricker and Jack Sirocco. Tricker and Sirocco tricked Zelig into going on a bank robbery with them. After Tricker and Sirocco were in possession of the bank's cash, they left Zelig behind to take the rap. Zelig was arrested and none too happy with his pals.

To add insult to injury, Tricker and Sirocco refused to bail out Zelig; figuring with Zelig behind bars, they could assume control of his gang. However, Zelig had friends in high places in Tammany Hall, and soon he was set free. Thus commenced a war between Zelig, and Tricker and Sirocco.

On December 6, 1911, Zelig threw a shindig for his gang at Stuyvesant Hall. Tricker and Sirocco were not invited, but they sent their associate Jules Morello to the party, with the expressed intention of killing Zelig.

However, Morello had a few too many drinks at the bar, and he started yelling "Where's that Yid? I'm gonna kill that Yid."

Meaning Zelig.

Zelig heard the commotion, and before Morello could do him any damage, Zelig shot Morello four times, leaving him dead.

On October 15, 1912, Zelig was drinking at Segal's Cafe, at 76 Second Avenue, when he got a phone call from his girlfriend saying she needed company for the night. Delighted at his good fortune, Zelig hopped on the Second Avenue Street Car in front of Siegel's. When the street car reached 13th Street, a junkie thug named Red Davidson snuck up behind Zelig and shot him once behind the ear, killing him.

"The Most Feared Man in New York City" was now dead at the age of 24.

Davidson's motive was never ascertained, but it was reported Davidson killed Zelig because, a few days earlier, Zelig had beaten Davidson to a pulp over a monetary dispute.

Zwerbach, Maxwell (Kid Twist)

"Kid Twist," real name Maxwell Zwerbach, was a ruthless killer who rose up the ranks of the Monk Eastman mob, only to die because he decided to cheat on his wife.

Zwerbach was born in Austria in 1884. His Jewish father, Adolf, and half-Italian mother, Hanna, emigrated to New York City in 1886 to escape the anti-Semitic riots. The family took an apartment on Delancey Street, where Adolph opened a tailor shop. Adolph hoped his son would follow in his footsteps and alter clothes for a living. However, Zwerbach, who was now called Kid Twist on the mean streets of the Lower East Side, had other ideas.

Kid Twist started out as a petty thief. Soon, he hooked up with the famous Monk Eastman gang, made up of Jews who were constantly at war with Paul Kelly's (Paulo Vaccarelli) Italian Five Pointers over the Lower East Side rackets. Kid Twist killed his way up the ranks, until Eastman installed him as his top lieutenant, along with Richie Fitzpatrick, a Jewish killer who took on an Irish last name.

In early 1903, Eastman had the misfortune of getting himself locked up in a Freehold, New Jersey jail, after he beat up a potential witness against a friend of his on the courthouse steps. When Kid Twist heard of his boss's predicament, he rounded up 50 of his best thugs, with the intention of driving to New Jersey to bust Eastman out of jail.

However, before their cars could leave their Christie Street headquarters, a battalion of policemen, led by Inspector McCluskey, descended upon them and beat them with nightsticks back into their club.

Kid Twist decided to change tactics, and he contacted Eastman's cronies in Tammany Hall. The crooked pols used their Jersey connections and Eastman was sprung the following day.

Eastman was not so lucky in 1904, when he was arrested near Times Square for assault and robbery. This time Tammany Hall refused to come to his rescue. Eastman was tried, convicted, and sentenced to 10 years in the slammer.

Kid Twist thought he was now the rightful heir to Eastman's throne, but Fitzpatrick had the same idea. Both men argued over who was the new boss. Finally, Kid Twist told Fitzpatrick, he had a plan on how the rackets could be split down the middle with both men having separate but equal powers. Fitzpatrick thought Twist's idea sounded just swell, and he agreed to a meeting to work out the details.

On November 1, 1904, Kid Twist enticed Fitzpatrick into the back room of the Sheriff Street Saloon (which oddly enough, was located on Christie Street). As soon as Fitzpatrick arrived, the lights went out and so did Fitzpatrick. He was shot twice through the heart by Kid Dahl, real name Harris Stahl, thus installing Kid Twist as the No. 1 man in the Eastman Gang, all by himself.

As a result of Fitzpatrick's sudden demise, Kid Twist took over all of Eastman's operations, which included several brothels and stuss card games. In a show of bravado, Kid Twist announced to the world that "no Wop and no Mick would ever rule the Lower East Side of New York."

As a side moneymaker, Kid Twist championed his own brand of the popular "celery soda," which was the only brand of celery soda allowed to be sold on the entire Lower East Side of Manhattan.

Even though Kid Twist had several stuss games of his own, he coveted the one on Suffolk Street owned by the Bottler, which was under the protection of Paul Kelly's Five Pointers. First, Kid Twist approached the Bottler, and not in a very nice way, Kid Twist told him that he was now the Bottler's partner, not Paul Kelly. Before the ink was dry on Twist's verbal contract, he informed the Bottler that the Bottler was out completely, and that Kid Dahl was now Kid Twist's partner in the Suffolk Street stuss parlor.

This time the Bottler made a stand, and he refused to comply with Kid Twist's demands. As a result, Kid Twist imported Coney Islander Vach Lewis, known as Cyclone Louie, a professional circus strongman, who was famous for bending iron bars around his neck, and sometimes around other people's necks, too.

While Kid Twist was in the Delancey Street police station screaming at the desk sergeant over some trivial matter, and Kid Dahl was in a Houston Street restaurant arguing with the owner over what time of day it was, Cyclone Louie calmly walked into the Bottler's stuss parlor. As 20 customers looked on in shock, Cyclone Louie shot the Bottler twice in the chest, killing him instantly.

With Kid Twist and Kid Dahl eliminated as suspects because of their contrived alibis, a few days later Kid Dahl strode into the Suffolk Street stuss parlor and announced to all that the stuss parlor was now his and Kid Twist's possession. All this did not please Paul Kelly too much, and he waited for the right time to get back what was rightfully his.

On the night of May 14, 1908, Kid Twist and Cyclone Louie decided to travel to Coney Island, to visit the supposedly happily married Kid Twist's girlfriend, dancer Carroll Terry. The two men were sitting inside the dance hall Terry performed in, when a kid rushed inside and told them Terry wanted to see them outside.

As soon as their feet hit the pavement, Kid Twist and Cyclone Louie were blasted with bullets fired by Kelly henchman, Louie "The Lump" Pioggi and several other of Kelly's men. It took only one slug to the brain, shot by Pioggi, to finish Kid Twist, but Cyclone Louie, true to his reputation as a strong man, needed five bullets in his torso to render him deceased.

When Terry showed up seconds later, Pioggi, a jilted suitor of hers, whipped a slug into her hip. Terry fell face forward, and although she would survive, the unconscious Terry landed across the body of her lifeless boyfriend, Maxwell "Kid Twist" Zwerbach, thereby putting a twist in the premise that "true love never dies."

The End

Bonus Feature:

WHITEY BULGER - THE BIGGEST RAT

By - Joe Bruno

Editor – Lawrence Venturato

Published by:

Knickerbocker Publishing Company

*****

"RATS ARE NOT MADE; PEOPLE ARE BORN RATS."
- Mathew J. Mari, New York City Criminal Attorney for 36 years

*****

Chapter One – "You know who I am. I'm Whitey Bulger."

The first time aspiring musician Joshua Bond met "America's Most Wanted Fugitive," Whitey Bulger, Bond knew the spry 77-year-old retiree as plain old Charlie Gasko.

In 2007, the 26-year-old Bond had just moved to Santa Monica, California with plans of getting involved in the in the Hollywood film business or music business, whichever came first. Bond played guitar in a band called the Kings. Since work was hard to come by, Bond needed a way to pay the rent and keep food on the table while he pursued his dreams. As a result, Bond took a job as co-manager of the Princess Eugenia Apartments where he received free living quarters in apartment 304, as one of the perks that came with the job. His next-door neighbor, living in apartment 303, was Charlie Gasko and his wife Carol (real name Catherine Greig).

Bond liked to play the guitar in his apartment, sometimes loud enough to be heard clearly through the walls into apartment 303. One day, after playing a particularly stirring riff, Bond heard a knock on his apartment door. This was the first time this phenomenon had occurred, and Bond figured he was about to get a neighborly complaint about the noise. When Bond opened the door, he came face to face with the man he knew as "Charlie" from next door. Bond recoiled, waiting to receive a string of obscenities.

Instead, he received a gift.

While Bond stood there quivering, Whitey told Bond he was fond of his music, which was a cross between country western and the blues. That said, Whitey handed Bond a black wool Stetson hat, sporting a leather band sprinkled with silver buttons.

"I don't wear this hat anymore," Whitey told Bond. "I think maybe you could use it.

Bond, tickled pink at the lack of a reprimand, eagerly accepted the hat, and then he bid Whitey goodbye.

But it was not goodbye for long.

Whitey developed the habit of knocking on Bond's door at least twice a week, supposedly to make small talk. The truth is, Bulger, on the run for more than a decade, didn't trust anybody, and he wanted to know all he could about everything connected to the Princess Eugenia Apartments. To Whitey, being pals with the co-manager was simply good business sense.

Whitey, being Whitey, found it difficult not to intrude on his young friend without bearing gifts, whether Bond needed them or not. On one visit, Whitey gave Bond a beard trimmer; a subtle hint maybe Bond was looking a little too scruffy, and Whitey didn't like scruffy.

Whitey was a fitness buff, and he thought Bond was a little out of shape for a man fifty years his junior. So, Whitey dipped into his retirement savings and bought Bond a weight set, complete with a bench and a stomach-crunching thingamajig.

Over the years, Whitey was diligent about taking good care of the assistant manager of the Princess Eugenia Apartments. During the Christmas holidays, instead of cash, one year Whitey bequeathed Bond a spiffy decorative plate. Another year Whitey gave Bond an Elvis Presley coffee table (no musician should ever be without one).

However, Whitey was a bit gruff. He insisted on proper decorum when it came to Bond recognizing his benevolence. One holiday season, Whitey left a bag full of Christmas presents at Bond's door. Later, when Whitey and Bonds crossed paths in the underground garage, Bond nary mentioned a word about the gifts. This pissed off Whitey, leading him to reprimand Bond for his lack of respect, even going as far as to "suggest" Bond jot him and Carol a sincere thank-you note. Bond duly complied, kissing off the incident off as nothing more than an old man asking for his due.

During the period from 2007 to 2011, Bond and Whitey maintained a friendly relationship. An uncle/nephew type of rapport developed between the two, where Whitey dispensed advice and Bond made believe he took it. Whitey seemed like a nice elderly man, but Bond was only interested in his music career. Putting up with Whitey was part of the job of being co-manager of the Princess Eugenia Apartments. Bond humored Whitey, and Whitey ate up what seemed to be the young man's deference to Whitey's superior intellect and lifelong experiences.

Bond knew of only one instance where old Charlie Gasko indicated he was capable of violence, and this was because Whitey told Bond about the incident himself.

The Ocean View Manor, a state-licensed residential facility for the mentally disabled, was located a few doors down from Princess Eugenia Apartments. Mentally ill people sometimes do strange things. One resident in particular got his jollies by hiding in the bushes near the facility, and then springing out at an unsuspecting passerby to scare him out of his skin.

One night, as was his wont, Whitey took his moll, Catherine Greig, on a late-night fitness stroll. Suddenly, the eccentric from the Ocean View Manor bounded from the bushes, intending to scare Whitey and Greig.

But Whitey doesn't scare easily.

Whitey told Bond that when the lunatic rushed at him and his wife, Whitey, who always kept a big knife strapped to his ankle, grabbed the man by the neck, pulled out his knife, waved it in the man's face, and said, "If you ever do that to me again, I will cut you to pieces."

Fast-forward to June 22, 2011.

Bond had plans to go to a concert in Hollywood that evening with his pal, Neal Marsh, to see the band, My Morning Jacket. The other co-manager of the Princess Eugenia Apartments, Birgitta Farinelli, had gone on vacation. So, Bond told his assistant, Thea, to substitute for him at the manager's desk, located in the hotel across the street from Princess Eugenia Apartments, while Bond sawed a few afternoon Z's on his apartment couch.

At about 3:30 p.m., Bond's phone rang, rousing him from a deep sleep. Thea was on the line and told him F.B.I. agents were in his office. The feds said they needed to speak to Bond immediately about one of the tenants.

This unwelcome intrusion into his afternoon nap did not please Bond. He planned to motor off to Hollywood in a few hours and didn't appreciate any unnecessary distractions.

Thea handed the phone to F.B.I. agent, Scott Garriola, who told Bond that it was imperative that he come to the office immediately, if not sooner.

"Can't this wait until tomorrow?" Bond asked.

"No, it can't," Garriola said. "I need you here now!"

Knowing you don't argue with the feds, Bond dragged himself off his couch, splashed a little water on his face, and then he exited his apartment. When he reached the manager's office, Bond met Garriola and another federal agent. The agents showed Bond a string of photos of the couple Bond knew as Charlie and Carol Gasko. The feds asked Bond if he could confirm their identities and he did so.

"Yes, I know them," Bond told Garriola. "That's Charlie and Carol from apartment 303."

"Are you absolutely sure?" Garriola asked.

"Definitely; that's them," Bond said.

Garriola told Bond who his neighbors really were, including the information that Whitey was alleged to be a serial murderer. Garriola wanted to arrest Whitey outside his apartment because Whitey's M.O. indicated he kept an arsenal of guns nearby at all times. To facilitate the arrest, Garriola asked Bond if he would be so kind as to go up to apartment 303 and knock on the door.

Bond was not brave. He also was not stupid. Bond didn't mind knocking on apartment 303's door to talk to old Charlie. But confronting a lunatic like Whitey Bulger was not high on Bond's list of things to do.

So, Garriola came up with a plan that would not put Bond in any danger.

Garriola ran down to Whitey's storage locker, located in the garage of the Princess Eugenia Apartments. Using a pair of bolt cutters, Garriola chopped Whitey's lock to pieces, giving the impression petty thieves had stolen Whitey's possessions.

After rushing back to the manager's office, Garriola ordered Bond to phone apartment 303 and tell Whitey his locker had been broken into. By this time, Bond had done a little Googling of Whitey on the office computer. What he saw did not calm his nerves.

Bond later told CBS News, "I went to his (Whitey's) Wikipedia page, and I'm kinda, like, scrolling through, and it's like, murder and extortion, and all this stuff."

Nonetheless, Bond summoned up the courage and phoned apartment 303.

No answer.

Then he tried the cellphone number Carol (Catherine Greig) had given him as a backup.

Still no answer.

Garriola checked with a fellow agent, who confirmed that surveillance definitely showed a man and a woman were present in apartment 303. Garriola tried again to convince Bond to knock on the door of apartment 303.

Bond again refused and who could blame him? He wasn't being paid by the Princess Eugenia Apartments to put his life on the line.

Before Garriola could decide what to do, the phone rang in the manager's office. It was Catherine Greig inquiring if Bond had just called her cell phone. Bond admitted he had, and then told Greig Garriola's malarkey about their storage locker having been broken into.

Grieg hesitated, and then after conferring with Whitey, she said her husband would meet Bond in the garage.

In the underground garage, Whitey didn't get close to his locker. Before he knew what was happening, more than 40 F.B.I. agents in full riot gear, with their guns and rifles pointed his way, surrounded Whitey.

Garriola barked at Whitey, "Get down on your knees!"

Whitey was dressed in white clothes with a white summer hat on his head. (Whitey was a noted Howard Hughes-type neat freak, fearful of the slightest grime.)

"Fuck you!" Whitey said. "There's oil on the floor!"

Garriola told Whitey to move a few steps to his right, and then get down on his knees.

Whitey cursed some more.

Finally, Whitey found a clean spot and got down on his knees, where the agents cuffed Whitey's hands behind his back.

"Please identify yourself," Garriola said.

"I'm Charlie Gasko," Whitey replied.

"You're not Charlie Gasko," Garriola said. "How about we go upstairs and ask your girlfriend to identify you as Charlie Gasko? She's in enough trouble already."

Whitey grunted.

"Okay. You know who I am," Whitey said. "I'm Whitey Bulger."

The 16-year manhunt for the "Most Wanted" criminal in America had finally ended.

*****

If you'd like to read the rest of *Whitey Bulger - The Biggest Rat* go to:
http://www.amazon.com/dp/B00EZCFVNU

*****

I hope you enjoyed reading this book as much as I enjoyed writing it. If you want to be added to my email list, email me at jbruno999@aol.com.

I would also appreciate it if you wrote a short review on Amazon.com at: http://www.amazon.com/dp/B00MBNAKWW

Just click the button that says "Create Your Own Review," and fire away!

All reviews, positive and negative, will be greatly appreciated. Sometimes I learn more from the negative reviews than I do from the positive reviews, so don't be bashful.

*****

Joe Bruno's "Mobsters, Gangs, Crooks, and Other Creeps" was the runner up in the 2013 eFestival of Words Best of the Independent Book Awards in the category "General Nonfiction."
http://www.efestivalofwords.com/2013-efestival-of-words-winners-t473.html

*****

About Joe Bruno:

A Vietnam veteran in the United States Navy, Joe Bruno started out in the newspaper business in the mid-1970s as a sports columnist for the New York Tribune. Bruno's sports articles have also appeared in the Middletown Record, Penthouse Magazine, Razor Magazine, Boxing Today, Boxing World, International Boxing, Referee Magazine, Inside Boxing, the Cyberboxingzone and Travelgolf.com.

In 1997-98, Bruno was the host of a weekday drive-time sports-talk radio show in Sarasota, Florida on WQSA 1220 called "In the Know with Joltin' Joe."

In 2000, Bruno's first novel *Angel of Death* was published by iUniverse.com. Bruno's second novel *Find Big Fat Fanny Fast* was published in 2010. *Snakeheads: Chinese Illegal Immigrant Smugglers - A Screenplay* was published in 2013.

Bruno's true book crime book *Mobsters, Gangs, Crooks, and Other Creeps - Volume 1 - New York City* was published in June 2011.

Other books in this series include, *Mobsters, Gangs, Crooks, and Other Creeps - Volume 2 - New York City* (December 2011*),* *Mobsters, Gangs, Crooks, and Other Creeps - Volume 3 - New York City* (March 2012), *Mobsters, Gangs, Crooks and Other Creeps - Volume 4* (December 2012), and *Mobsters, Gangs, Crooks and Other Creeps-Volume 5 - Girlfriends and Wives (April 2013).*

Other true crime books by Joe Bruno include:

Murder and Mayhem in the Big Apple - From the Black Hand to Murder Incorporated March 2012),

The Wrong Man: Who Ordered the Murder of Gambler Herman Rosenthal & Why (May 2012),

Mob Wives - Fuhgeddaboudit! (August 2012) and

Whitey Bulger - The Biggest Rat (September 2013).

Mob Rats - Gangsters Who Squeal (May 2014)

Abe 'Kid Twist Reles – The Fink Who Took Down Murder Inc. (July 2014)

New York City's Five Points - The Most Dangerous and Decadent Neighborhood Ever! (August 2014)

Famous Murders, Riots, Disasters, and Crooked Politicians - New York City - 1834 to 1938 (September 2014)

Boxed sets written by Joe Bruno include:"

Joe Bruno's Mobsters - Two Volume Set (December 2013)

Joe Bruno's Mobsters - Three Volume Set (March 2013),

Joe Bruno's Mobsters - Five Volume Set (April 2013),

Joe Bruno's Mobsters - Six Volume Set (September 2012), and

Joe Bruno's Mobsters - Eight Volume Set (April 2013).

Mob Rats Two Volume Set - Whitey Bulger - The Biggest Rat and Mob Rats - Gangsters Who Squeal - Volume One (July 2014)

Visit Joe Bruno's Amazon Author Page at: http://www.amazon.com/Joe-Bruno/e/B0047OPD9S/ref=ntt_athr_dp_pel_pop_1

Website: josephbrunowriter.com, or at mobstersgangs.com.

Blog: http://joebrunoonthemob.wordpress.com/.

Facebook page: *Mobsters, Gangs* is at: https://www.facebook.com/mobstersgangs.

*****

What people are saying about Joe Bruno's Books:

5.0 out of 5 stars

Fabulous!!!!!

By **Brenda**
Verified Purchase

I really enjoyed Joe Bruno's *Mobsters, Gangs, Crooks, and Other Creeps, Volumes 1-5*. Joe Bruno's books are easy to get into with the short chapters and out there approach. I love his sarcastic banter and his in depth knowledge of these bad guys. The books are wildly compelling especially since is the real deal. No fictional made up story here. I love that!

These books are thoroughly entertaining, mind blowing and irresistible. If you are interested in mob stories about famous and not so famous crooks, you will love this book and the others that Joe Bruno has written. These books are easy to get into and you can just pick it up and read a chapter at a time. They are a captivating entertain read, to say the least!

5.0 out of 5 stars

A lesson about "The Other" Mob.

By **Rony Barbery**

Verified Purchase

I found all Joe Bruno's books refreshing as a departure from the great books Mr. Bruno has written about what is considered the traditional "Mafia". As always, Joe Bruno has demonstrated that no matter how much or how carefully you read the news, you never know the whole story until he puts it in writing. The book is full of small details that you never heard about, but are huge in painting a portrait of the real mobsters in this world. If you don't already have one of Joe Bruno's books, get on the ball and get a copy!

5.0 out of 5 stars

Another great one!

By **lcook0825**

As I have said in the past Mr. Bruno is the best writer of books concerning the Mafia that I have read, and I read everything I can. This was a great read from beginning to end. It was accurate according to everything else I have read regarding the Mafia. Thanks again for a great book, Joe, and keep me posted on your next release.

5.0 out of 5 stars

Fascinating!

By **koalaman35**

Joe Bruno's books are a wonderful trip through the history of mobsters, thugs, and other ne'er-do-wells in the mob. I love Joe's writing style.

*****

Bibliography

The research done for *Julius and Ethel Rosenberg – Spies or Scapegoats? You Make the Call*
came from the more than 75 crime/history books that I personally own (some I stole from the library, but don't tell the library police).

Almost all of these books were purchased from Amazon.com. I have Amazon Prime ($79 a year), so I always receive free two-day shipping on all my purchases. This comes in handy, when I realize I need a certain book to complete a chapter, and presto, in two days, that book arrives miraculously at my front door. I also have my new Amazon Kindle, which, with its Amazon Whispernet, magically sends me a book I need for research over the Internet almost instantaneously. But all things being equal, I'd rather have the actual print book in my hands.

I guess I'm just funny that way.

I've also used several Internet websites including *Wikipedia, Six For Five, Tru TV Crime Library, Newspaperarchives.com*, and the online archives of the *New York Times*.

The books and videos that I used for my research include the following:

Cohen, Rich. *Tough Jews*. New York: Vintage Books, 1998.

Feklisov, Alexander. *The Man Behind the Rosenbergs*. New York. Enigma Books, 2001.

Fried, Albert, *The Rise and Fall of the Jewish Gangster.* New York: Columbia University Press, 1980, 1993.

Newton, Michael. *The Encyclopedia of Gangsters*. New York: Thunder's Mouth Press, 2007.

Roberts, Sam. *The Brother*. New York Random House, 2001

Rudolph, Robert. *Mafia Wiseguys*. New York: S.P.I. Books, 1992-1993.

Sifakis, Carl. *The Encyclopedia of Crime.* New York: Smithmark, 1992.

Von Hoffman, Nicholas. *Citizen Cohn*. New York: Doubleday, 1988.